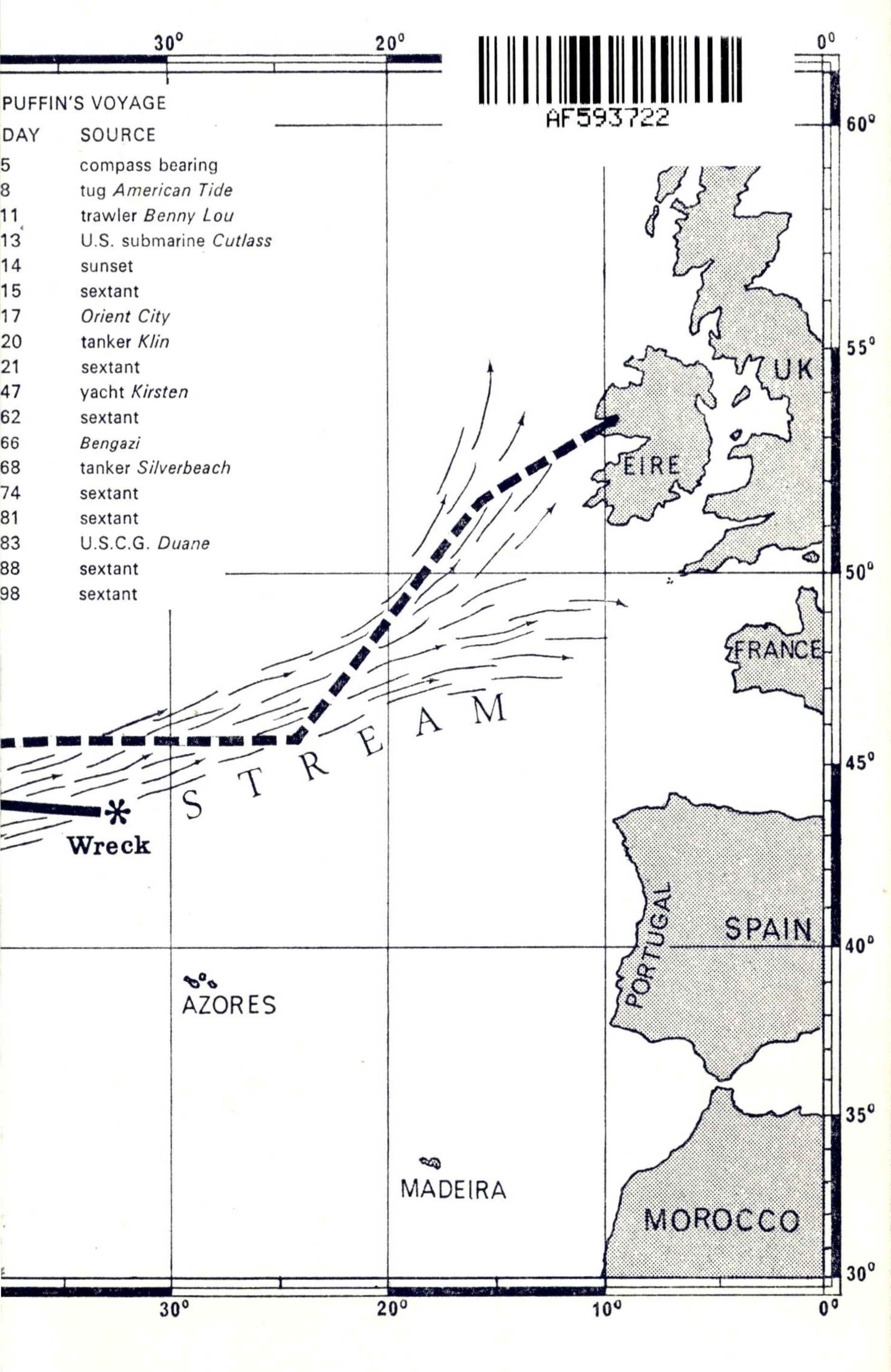

PUFFIN'S VOYAGE
DAY SOURCE
5 compass bearing
8 tug American Tide
11 trawler Benny Lou
13 U.S. submarine Cutlass
14 sunset
15 sextant
17 Orient City
20 tanker Klin
21 sextant
47 yacht Kirsten
62 sextant
66 Bengazi
68 tanker Silverbeach
74 sextant
81 sextant
83 U.S.C.G. Duane
88 sextant
98 sextant
AF593722
30°
20°
0°
60°
55°
50°
45°
40°
35°
30°
10°
UK
EIRE
FRANCE
SPAIN
PORTUGAL
MOROCCO
AZORES
MADEIRA
STREAM
Wreck

Merton Naydler

THE PENANCE WAY

The mystery of *Puffin*'s Atlantic voyage

HUTCHINSON OF LONDON

HUTCHINSON & CO (*Publishers*) LTD
178–202 Great Portland Street, London W1

London Melbourne Sydney
Auckland Bombay Toronto
Johannesburg New York

First published 1968

This book has been set in Baskerville, printed in Great Britain on Antique Wove paper by Anchor Press, and bound by Wm. Brendon, both of Tiptree, Essex

09 088840 5

To the memory of David Johnstone and
John Hoare, brave men abundantly endowed with
the eternal spirit of adventure.

'I began to think of a two-man trip as a desirable purity of idea: Go the penance way.'

David Johnstone

ACKNOWLEDGMENT is gladly made to

MRS. MICHEL JOHNSTONE
for her unfailing interest and wise advice, and for giving me the opportunity to write this book.

MR. AND MRS. R. HOARES
for details about John Hoare.

ANDREW JOHNSTONE
who contributed the characterisation of David.

COLIN MUDIE
for permission to reproduce his drawings and for general technical assistance.

DR. DAVID LEWIS AND CAPTAIN H. N. TAYLOR
for giving me the benefit of their encyclopaedic sea knowledge.

U.S. DEPARTMENT OF COMMERCE (*Coast and Geodetic Survey*) AND U.S. NAVY OCEANOGRAPHIC OFFICE
for local marine information.

BRADFORD BOAT SERVICES LTD.
for permission to reproduce details of the Yorkshire Dory.

COMMANDER J. I. MANORE, R.C.N.
for a detailed account of *Puffin*'s discovery and salvage.

BOB TAYLOR
for information on navigational decisions taken aboard s.s. *United States*.

MY WIFE
who endured endless 'Listen to this'es' and truthfully answered 'What d'you think of that?'s'.

CONTENTS

ILLUSTRATIONS

FIGURES IN THE TEXT

AUTHOR'S INTRODUCTION

During the five years I had known him David Johnstone had appeared, disappeared from and reappeared on the Farnham scene with disarming inconsistency. Fired by his irresistible enthusiasm, I had variously found myself taking up the cudgels against the local planning authorities, trailing round muddy factory sites where a new kind of tool was being used for the first time, and preparing for a thoroughly undesirable parachute drop just for the hell of it. That was during the period when he was a reporter on one of the newspapers of our small Surrey town.

When he made one of his reappearances in the summer of 1965, after an uncharacteristic two-and-a-half-year absence, to suggest that I might join him in an attempt to row across the Atlantic, little heart-searching was needed on my part to resist the temptation, even though he assured me it had been done before. His proposals had already achieved wide publicity. He contended that the attempt would be no more dangerous than a sailing expedition to the Arctic in which I had participated two years earlier, and which I had provisioned for a crew of five: that was in fact the maiden voyage of Dr. David Lewis's catamaran *Rehu Moana,* in which he subsequently sailed singlehanded across the Atlantic and later circumnavigated the globe.

Typically, David Johnstone disappeared once again, though the world's newspapers kept me informed of his serious intent to row the Atlantic, and within a few weeks there was a series of meetings at my home during which I told him what I knew about provisioning a long voyage, and the many preparations necessary for life at sea in a small boat. At that time I had no idea of how small a boat he was going to end up with; nor, I suspect, had he.

The passage of the weeks eclipsed the matter from my mind, until in mid-December 1965 he telephoned my office in the Temple, asking to see me urgently. He sounded worried. I could not, however, meet him before the ensuing weekend, when we drove together to the Hamble River where I had to visit a client who lived aboard a large yacht moored there. The client happened to be a former Oxford rowing Blue who I felt sure might have some advice for David after we had concluded our business. On the journey down from Farnham the problems emerged. By now David had decided to limit his crew to two, had commissioned Colin Mudie (incidentally, *Rehu Moana*'s architect) to design a boat for him, had visited victualling and sea-safety experts, but had no money to build the boat and finance the expedition and no idea how to raise it.

'Frankly,' he told me, 'I have what I'm standing up in plus my old car, worth perhaps a hundred and fifty quid.'

Knowing that newspapers paid substantial sums for exclusivity on his kind of story I suggested that he try to sell it.

'How much should I ask?' he demanded.

I had very little idea, but I did know that that kind of story could be serialised, and syndicated world-wide, and that there was obviously a book in it. David told me he had been keeping detailed notes. I advised him to employ an agent who would handle the whole business for him, and recommended Nicholas Thompson, who was David Lewis's literary agent. In the meantime I would guarantee the first £200 to enable work to start on his boat. Aboard his yacht, my client was suitably startled by David's story.

David must have gone to see Thompson first thing next Monday morning, for later that day the agent was on the 'phone to ask if my friend was okay. I assured him that if Johnstone said he was going to do something he'd do it. Within a couple of weeks David came to tell me that he'd turned the corner, a deal had been fixed up with one of the national newspapers, and everything was swinging ahead.

Our meetings thereafter were few and of no significance; he was immersed in the vast preparations he was undertaking to make the voyage a success. But on one of them he was extremely agitated that a competitor, an officer in the Parachute Regiment named Ridgway, was trying to mount a rival expedition, disappointed (he thought) at not having been accepted by Johnstone as his crew, having offered himself. Apart from an occasional 'phone-call and a gaudy postcard from America, my only news for some time was what was publicly available from the Press and radio; Johnstone and his crew, John Hoare, were by now very famous. During the period I had become close to David's brother, Andrew, and the latter's wife, Diane, and during the early summer of 1966, when Johnstone and Hoare were rowing *Puffin*, having left Virginia Beach in May, I got to know them better than I had ever known the introverted David. Just as I was later to become obsessed with the *Puffin* saga, Andrew was at that time painting picture after picture of her in mountainous seas, and asked me to describe what it was really like to be in a mid-ocean gale in a small boat. I could not accurately tell him, for although *Rehu Moana* is only forty feet long, that is more than double the length of the tiny *Puffin*, and, of course, *Rehu Moana*, being twin-hulled, is enormously stable compared with a small rowing-boat. I did, however, know that even in a full gale it was unusual to encounter waves more than twenty-five feet high measured from crest to trough.

As the summer progressed and anxiety heightened at the lack of news of *Puffin*, the Johnstone family became the focus of world-wide attention. My own view was that there was no cause for concern until the end of August, but that by mid-September a search should be mounted if there was still no sign. My calculation was based on the last information about *Puffin*'s re-victualling, related to the necessary calorific intake to maintain life, and on the belief that the boat was strong and seaworthy, and therefore reliable. But with the news, early in September, of Hurricane FAITH in close proximity to the boat's estimated position there was a universal sense of foreboding. The report a fortnight later of a wrecked boat in the same vicinity finally dispelled any lingering doubt concerning *Puffin*'s fate. When Andrew asked whether the crew could possibly have survived by taking to their inflatable dinghy I felt he was clutching at straws. Yet the Johnstones refused to give up hope. Nor, secretly, did I.

Some months later, early in 1967, long after *Puffin*'s wreck had been picked up in mid-Atlantic, and with it, miraculously, Johnstone's journal of the voyage, Andrew suggested that I might write a book about the adventure; much as I would have liked to, the pressure of my work put it out of the question. Then in late summer of the same year, by when I had been able to relax my efforts a little, the suggestion was made again, this time by Mrs. Johnstone, David's and Andrew's mother, for whose courage and dignity I had an enormous respect and admiration. Her reasons were simple : I had known and liked David, I had some knowledge of the sea and small boats, and I had published a book about my Arctic trip called *Cook on a Cool Cat*.

Having an inkling of the amount of work involved in writing a book, I was hesitant, but agreed to read the 45,000 words typed by David before he left England for New York in April 1966, the transcript of six tapes he had dictated up to the time of *Puffin*'s departure from America, and a typescript of the Journal. It was the last which dispelled my hesitancy. I found myself profoundly moved by its superb quality and became convinced that here was something the world ought to see. I had seldom before read of courage of so epic a nature, or of determination so heroic. It was now my turn to become obsessed with the *Puffin* saga; rather, with the fantastic courage of her crew.

My plan was to rearrange and edit David's pre-Journal material, supplemented where necessary by facts culled from contemporary newspaper cuttings and interviews with the people involved, in order to provide a simple setting for the jewel of the Journal, without comment or embellishment. The Journal itself would be edited only in order to make sense of some confused phrases, largely the result of the typist's inability to decipher some of the smudged handwriting, and I would number each day of the voyage for reference purposes. That is in fact what I did, but by now my mind was gripped by the recurring question : Why was *Puffin* where she was, when she was? For by all accounts she should have been home and dry weeks before Hurricane FAITH struck mid-Atlantic.

Bit by bit the clues unwillingly emerged. It was like a gigantic puzzle, and I was the fascinated investigator. It was an enormous mystery, and I had to track down those reluctant clues by sleuthing as painful and slow as it became exciting when one startling fact after another was dragged into daylight. For weeks I ate, slept and drank *Puffin*, which occupied every spare moment of my time. I decided that the Journal had to be taken apart, analysed under a dozen different heads of investigation : meteorological, psychological, navigational and various technical components. I received prodigious assistance almost whereever I asked for it, and considerable research put me on the track which finally led to the mystery's solution. The result is the first and third sections of the additional part of the book entitled 'Commentary', and four of the appendices.

One job, however, remained to be done : to test *Puffin* in an open seaway : and she was accordingly put into the necessary condition to enable tests to be carried out which would relate fairly to the boat's performance as it is described in the Journal. Those tests, and their results, are included in a further appendix.

Finally, I wish to make clear that John Ridgway has told me that he does not accept as accurate the remarks ascribed to him by the newspapers to which I make reference, nor Johnstone's interpretation of the reasons for the interview which he sought between them. And, for my own part, I am sure he had no inkling of the effect his challenge would have on Johnstone.

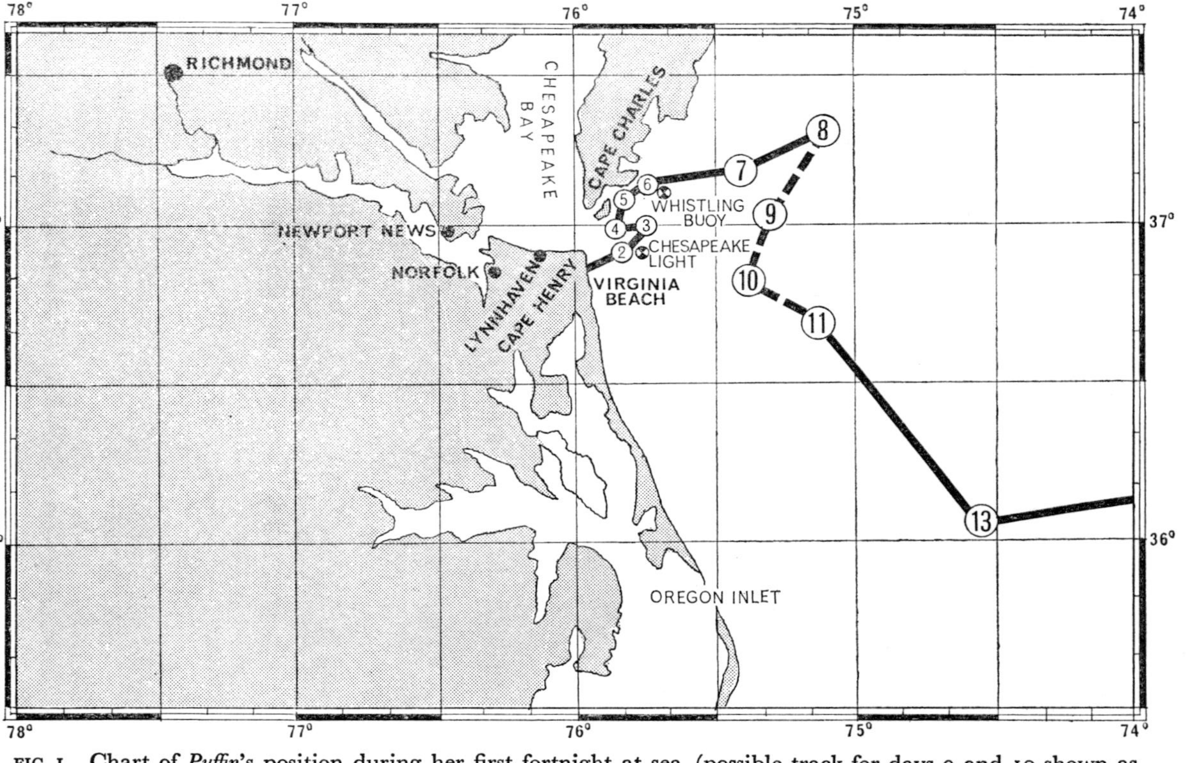

FIG I Chart of *Puffin*'s position during her first fortnight at sea (possible track for days 9 and 10 shown as dotted line)

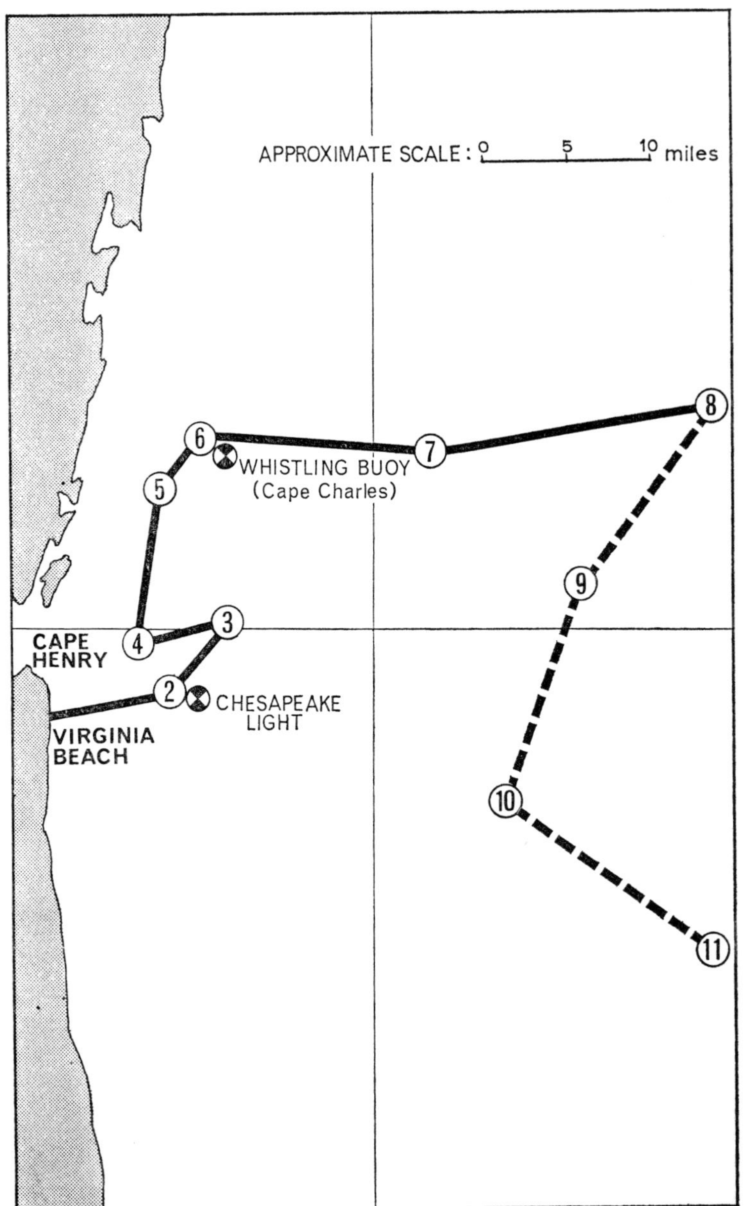

FIG 2 Chart showing the effect on *Puffin* of the Chesapeake Bay currents (possible track for days 9 and 10 shown as dotted line). Compare with page 8 from Journal

PART ONE

Birth of an Adventure

I

Late in the afternoon of 14th October 1966 the port look-out of Her Majesty's Canadian ship *Chaudière, on* the Great Circle route from Nova Scotia to the Mediterranean, reported an unidentified object three miles off the war-ship's port bow. *Chaudière* was 800 miles south-east of St. John's, Newfoundland, swinging along at an easy sixteen knots. A mile off the unidentified object, Commander Manore, the warship's captain, signalled to the engine-room to slow ship, and *Chaudière* steamed gently within fifty yards of the white upturned hull of a small plywood rowing-boat; bobbing in the idle swell, its bows were completely submerged, its stern where it showed above the surface was encrusted thickly with barnacles. *Chaudière* circled cautiously to come alongside, until it was abreast the wreck. Craning from the upper decks of their ship the crew watched as, at Manore's command, black-suited frogmen strapped on oxygen bottles, flippers and masks, then splashed off to investigate. Surfacing from their dive, they confirmed that there were no bodies aboard and that no name was visible on the derelict.

The wreck was drawn alongside *Chaudière*'s port side, level with the after gun. Inside the capsized hull, weighed down by a heavy growth of marine vegetation, the divers found sea-ruined food, cameras, charts, clothing, water bags, oars and sophisticated radio equipment. One by one the remains were hoisted tenderly aboard the warship. While the frogmen passed strops round the tiny boat, the crew rigged tackles and took up the strain, but the strops immediately began to part under the weight of the water-filled hull. Tilted to empty her as she inched out of the water, the wreck was slowly raised, under the glare of floodlights now illumining the dusk scene and, suspended clear of the water, was drained. A lifeline, its end frayed by the sharp barnacles, provided mute evidence of tragedy. A pile of salvage, lifted in buckets, mounted on *Chaudière*'s deck, joined finally by the wrecked vessel itself. A sodden notebook was handed to Manore, written on waterproof paper and barely decipherable, its blue ink pale and smeared by the sea. A few minutes in the light of his cabin with the soaking notebook enabled him to identify it as the log of the rowing-boat *Puffin*. He gave orders to resume the journey.

Next morning the inventory which his crew prepared included the item: 'one journal consisting of 149 handwritten pages'. It was the account of a voyage from Norfolk, Virginia, embarked upon 145 days earlier: *Puffin*'s participation in a fantastic 3,000-mile race across the Atlantic between two rowing-boats, a race which had already been over for forty days. A race its crew had not only not sought, but one which they had sought hard to avoid.

Chaudière had recovered the boat some 300 miles nearer England than a wreck reported four weeks earlier by the liner *Ocean Monarch*, which had not stopped to examine it. At that time, after several anxious weeks when there had been no news of the rowing-boat, it had been established beyond reasonable doubt that she must have been in menacingly close proximity to an area of the Atlantic which had been struck by Hurricane FAITH in early September. World-wide apprehension led eventually to Lloyd's of London transmitting a request to Atlantic shipping to look out for the missing coracle, at the behest of the family of the man whose writing filled the sea-smeared pages: David Johnstone. Together with John Hoare, a twenty-nine-year-old press officer from Leicester, Johnstone had spent nine months planning to row the Atlantic in a small boat specially designed and constructed for the purpose, finally leaving dry land for the last time on 21st May 1966. Earlier that year, a few months before leaving England, he set out his ideas in a Press handout, headlined AN OUTLINE OF A TRANSATLANTIC ROWING VOYAGE TO TAKE PLACE IN THE SUMMER OF 1966:

'In 1896 two men rowed from New York to a landfall in the Scilly Isles, a distance of about 3,100 miles, in 55 days. They used an 18 ft. long clincher built boat with a beam of 5 ft. On at least two occasions they boarded passing steamers for supplies.

'In September last year I asked Colin Mudie to design a boat for a two-man Atlantic rowing voyage. He has prepared a design for a 15′ 6″ surf-boat which is, he thinks, probably the smallest boat that could carry out this crossing. She has been named *Puffin*. The beam is 5′ 6″, and the weight of the craft herself will be about 700 lbs. She is of cold-moulded plywood, in three skins with a combined thickness of 7 mm. She will put to sea at about a ton and a quarter.

'Covered accommodation aft will allow one man to sleep in comfort; a second berth is available should it be necessary to lie-to during adverse weather. A small area of decking forward will cover buoyancy bags and some stores; water and the rest of the stores will stow beneath the cockpit floor. Mudie calculates that the boat has 100% self-rightability when fully loaded. *Puffin* will carry full safety equipment, including an emergency radio transmitter receiver, a radar reflector, lifejackets with lifeline harness, an inflatable raft and emergency flares. She is being built by W. A. Souter and Son (Cowes) Limited.

'Rowing accommodation is central, and allows a variety of rowing positions and methods to be used, including standing up facing forward in ferryman style. We will take at least six pairs of oars, in various lengths to suit prevailing conditions. One pair will be experimentally collapsible into two sections for easier stowage, enabling us to take longer oars than would otherwise have been possible. All the oars are being made for us by a firm of international repute in the racing world.

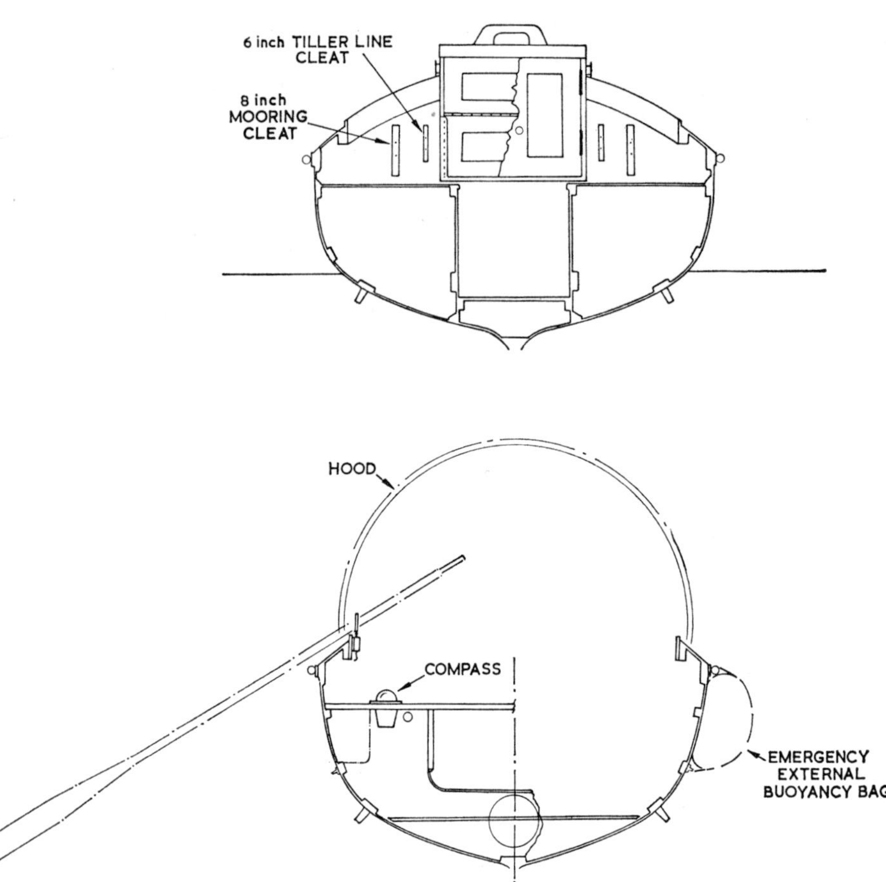

FIG 3 Working drawing of *Puffin* showing sections through the cabin bulkhead and the fore cockpit well

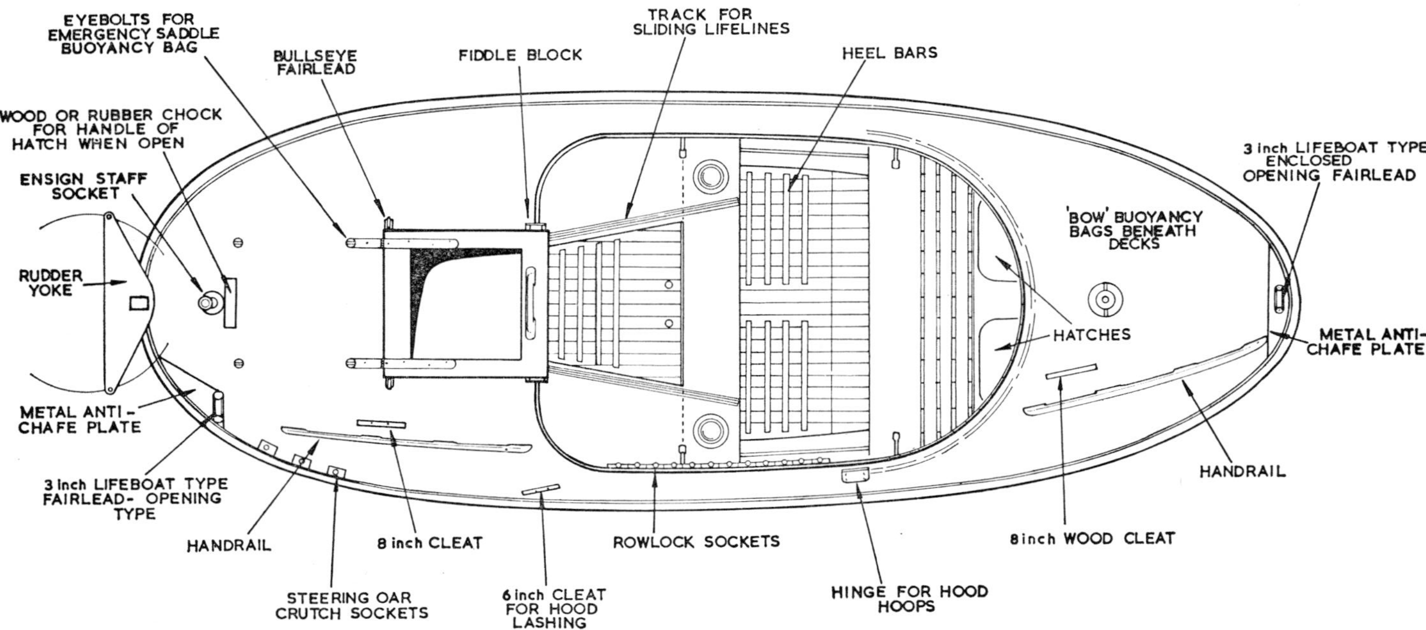

FIG 4 Plan view of *Puffin*

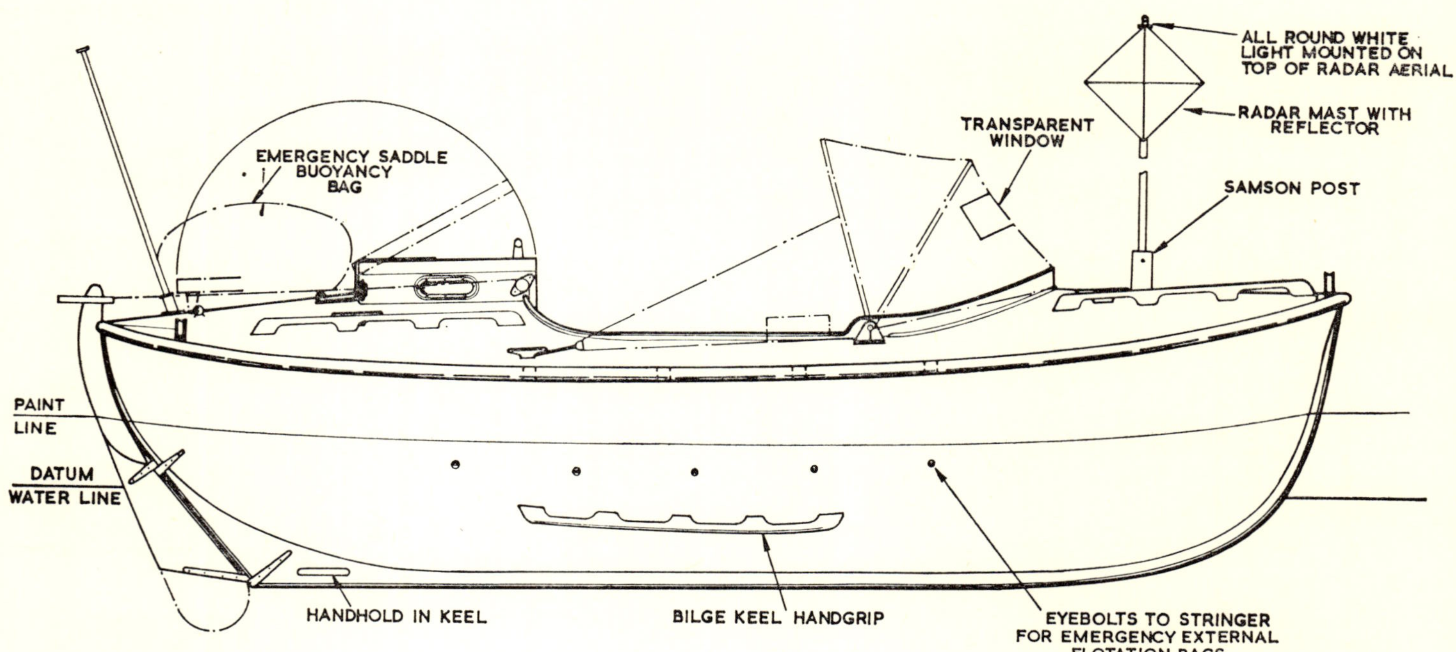

FIG 5 Side view of *Puffin*

'Food is being provided by a firm well known for more than half a century for the victualling of all forms of expedition. It will be largely in dehydrated unsalted form, and will furnish around 4,500 calories per day in chosen proportions of fat, protein and carbohydrate. We will take a supplementary vitamin diet.

'*Puffin* will carry 1,000 lb of water and supplies will be augmented by sea water desalinisation tablets. Further emergency water supplies will be provided by a rainwater catchment canopy and a solar still.

'*Puffin* will be ready by March 31st, and there will be three weeks of trials and tests before we leave for Boston in the last week in April. On arrival in America we will carry out a concentrated training programme until mid June, when the rowing voyage to the south-western tip of England will start.

'The favourable prevailing winds and currents in the North Atlantic will give us considerable help in the crossing, and I have set fifty days as our target journey time, giving us an arrival date in early August. We will not know our precise course until much nearer the starting date.

'The designer of the boat, Colin Mudie, is well known for his crossing of the Atlantic in the balloon *The Small World* (they landed in mid ocean and sailed on in the balloon's gondola) and for his part in the year-long voyage of *Sopranino*, a twenty-one-foot sloop, from the United Kingdom to North America. More important to us, however, his reputation as a marine architect is unsurpassed.

'The builders, W. A. Souter and Son (Cowes) Limited, were awarded the 'Boat of the Show, 1966' trophy at this year's Boat Show for a cold-moulded yacht which they built and displayed. Souter's were world pioneers of cold-moulding, and apart from over 3,000 dinghies they have made some of the world's fastest racing power boats; Souter-built yachts with cold-moulded hulls have featured strongly at the top of results list in ocean races in recent years.

'CREW :

'David Johnstone :	34, unmarried, 6′ 3″, 17 stone; journalist.
'John Hoare :	29, unmarried, 6′ 0″, 15 stone; press officer'

According to their plans, the voyage to England should have taken fifty days. Totally inexperienced oarsmen, they had gone to great pains to ensure that they had the right boat, properly equipped in every respect, and that they had invoked an adequate knowledge of meteorology and navigation to achieve the crossing safely. They were tough and fit and, aware in a complete way of the hazardous nature of the enterprise, had prepared themselves to face what they well knew could be a strenuous ordeal : a trial not only of their boat and equipment, but of themselves, their stamina, physique, moral fibre and seaman's skills. The trial was of their own seeking, a mystical necessity which becomes clearer as the characters of the two men take shape.

But why did *Puffin,* an essentially strong and seaworthy boat, the creation of a renowned naval architect, capsize? Why, after over a hundred days at sea, had she only accomplished half of her journey? What had gone so drastically wrong? Although strong and seaworthy, was *Puffin* the right boat for the job? Were the men themselves inadequate and if so in what ways? Had they experienced freak weather conditions which had frustrated their progress? To what extent had matters been affected by their finding themselves, reluctantly, involved in that fantastic 3,000-mile race which they had desperately striven to avoid?

The handwritten pages of Johnstone's Journal reveal the answers to these puzzling questions, and at the same time disclose heroism of an epic order. How, after ninety days at sea in their tiny cramped vessel, Johnstone and Hoare viewed with equanimity the prospect of another sixty cooped days in the minute boat. How, given opportunity after opportunity to surrender without shame, the thought of surrender at no time entered their heads. How they endured with uncomplaining fortitude the agonies of seasickness, the wrack of gale after Atlantic gale battering their tiny craft, the suffering of hunger and the almost certainty of the extinction which finally overcame them.

The answers which emerge to these questions lead to the ultimate question put to every man of action, a question never satisfactorily answered: Why do it? Why indeed? The superficial cliché answers are of the ilk: Because nobody has done it before. Because it is there. Because it is a challenge. Because it is irresistible. The real answer is probably in every case, because man is endowed with a spirit of adventure which is part of his natural instinct of survival.

Johnstone, who did not live to see his thirty-fifth birthday, was the eldest of three children of an intellectual journalist and an Australian opera singer who had met romantically in 1927 in Berlin and promptly fell in love. From his donnish father, an eminent Fleet Street economist, he inherited a deep understanding of human nature and a tolerance of its frailties, but his mother was descended from adventurous stock: her paternal grandparents had emigrated from Alsace to Australia, journeying three months in a sailing ship with their brood of thirteen children; and a botanist cousin had visited Antarctica.

His secure and prosperous background notwithstanding, Johnstone was a rebel from the outset, a strong individualist whose boyish delights included making precise model planes and engines and taking motor-bikes to pieces before remaking them. As a small child he suffered severe physical illness. At sixteen he sought permission to use his parents' music-room to build a novel helicopter which he had designed, to which they not surprisingly suggested that he first take a university course in mathematics. By the time he left school, well over six feet tall, he started travelling, with various short stays in Denmark, Sweden, Belgium, France and Italy on holiday, and a trip to Port Said, Aden, Karachi and Bombay as unpaid assistant purser on a British India Steam Navigation Company vessel. Back home again, he took temporary jobs, as postman and general factotum at an Oxford hotel, then spent three months in Austria learning German.

After the first year of a three-year course on hotel management in London his parents sent him to Australia, a Grade IV health rating ruling out National Service. He sold travel goods in a Sydney department store, then worked as a boundary rider on a remote sheep station before being fired after a month. He lasted only a short time as a lubritorium assistant in Melbourne where the management disapproved of Johnstone's squirting grease over the foreman's back. His next job as a gravedigger, which according to the foreman was pensionable at sixty-five and for which he found Johnstone eminently suitable, required one grave per day to be dug seven feet deep and measured by a standard rod for length and another for width across the shoulders. It was hard work, but after a week there was a day of respite for the annual holiday of the Melbourne Gravediggers' and Undertakers' Union's annual visit to the seaside. Johnstone was the only member not in a black suit and wide black braces.

In the second week heavy rain, which would otherwise have waterlogged the graves and impeded operations, was countered by rigging tarpaulins over the grave-sites. At about five feet down under his tarpaulin Johnstone was digging away when a funeral party arrived at the adjoining grave which he had dug the previous day a foot or two away. It was raining cats and dogs. Instructions were that during burials gravediggers should cease work and stand by respectfully until the ceremony was over. Faced with a sousing out in the open, or the shelter of his grave, he stayed where he was, lit a cigarette and waited for the funeral party to move off. Five minutes later the Chief Undertaker lifted up the corner of his tarpaulin and hauled him out. Smoke had been seen rising from his grave during the burial, and the funeral party was waiting assembled in the vestry while the distressing phenomenon was being investigated. Given a week's notice, Johnstone left on the spot. Then followed jobs in a fruit cannery, as a State-wide furniture-remover, part-time unpaid theatre carpenter, lorry driver and timber yard foreman, insecticide packer, gents' shirts and Holland blinds salesman, and sheep station jackeroo.

In between jobs he lived in digs on milk and paper-backs until his money ran out. He then read offers of employment in the evening papers and applied for each job in the order in which they appeared in the paper, unconcerned with which was the most suitable or attractive.

Returning to England, he took his father's advice and entered a great-uncle's lawyer firm in Bristol. His father's early death a few months later affected him deeply, unsettling him once again. After studying at an Oxford art school he was found unsuitable to hold the job of driver of a mobile snack bar at a nearby American air base. He lost his next job as a nightwatchman and showroom attendant in a small Surrey sports-car factory after having forfeited his driving licence for a year. Promoted twice during nine months in the offices of a London television insurance firm, he bought, managed and sold a South Coast coffee bar: at a loss. A brief spell as photographic assistant at an Acton soap factory was followed by casual employment in a number of London bars owned by an hotel group.

Among the bars were two in Fleet Street, England's newspaper heart, where he met and became enthused by a number of journalists. Now a gigantic six feet three inches and weighing eighteen stone, the bearded bespectacled Johnstone moved to his mother's house in Farnham, Surrey, and found a £3-a-week job on a local newspaper chain. For the next few years he enjoyed the comfort and solidity of the background provided by an understanding mother, who concealed the deep concern she felt for his welfare. By now there could be no lingering doubt that her eldest child was a rolling stone of massive dimensions, in every sense, and she could see no hope for him unless he could settle down to conventional domesticity with some reasonable girl; but although his attitude towards women was physically healthy, he had no inclination at any time towards accepting the burden and responsibility of a wife.

Living principally at his mother's home, he spent the ensuing two years writing humdrum wedding reports, theatre criticisms and local motoring notes, and sold advertising space. He moved to another local newspaper as senior reporter and profile writer, for which his new-found interest in photography proved a boon; he specialised in property-deal stories and motoring, and fighting the battles of the underdog. Close contact through two jobs with Army public relations staff at nearby Aldershot, home of the British Army, yielded a number of interesting working holidays. He flew to Singapore with the Parachute Brigade on exercise during a fortnight's holiday in 1961, taking part in heat-exhaustion trials and jungle training. And in 1962 a trip to Bahrain to write up a regimental changeover included a four-day tour of the Trucial States. Later the same year he bivouacked in the Libyan desert to cover a Marines *v.* Parachute Brigade mock battle, and accompanied the Sandhurst cadets on their annual exercise against the French military academicians at St. Cyr.

At weekends he sailed his seven-ton Bermudan cutter on the Solent from a Hamble River mooring, enlarging a working knowledge of seamanship and sailing learnt during boyhood when he had regularly sailed in his father's yacht. He never entertained the idea of a career, and as writing was his only consistent enthusiasm over the years, when the need for change stirred him again after an unprecedented four years' stint in local journalism he accepted a contract from a Nairobi publisher, flying to East Africa early in 1963 with a four-day working stopover in Copenhagen. Within a fortnight he was in Mogadishu working on an official Somali government handbook, and in the next eighteen months wrote hundreds of thousands of words for books and pamphlets in the Middle East and East Africa, plus magazine articles during brief visits to the publisher's Kenya head office.

Writing and illustrating books for the Kuwait and Tanzanian governments on such varied subjects as trade, education, health, finance, oil companies and oil processing, water distillation, agriculture, traditions, history, tourism: any subject, in fact, having any significance in the countries he visited: he also found opportunity in Aden and Bahrain to write commercially sponsored books, interviewing senior governmental officials and ministers, often against the background of a tricky political climate.

Three-quarters the way through the contract Johnstone terminated it for what he considered a number of good reasons, and holidayed for two months in the Seychelles Islands, spearfishing and sunbathing. With a companion he voyaged through the islands to Portuguese East Africa in a small sailing boat, a not unskilled piece of marine navigation, before taking the train to Nairobi, travelling through Rhodesia, Zambia and Tanzania by bus and Land Rover, and then home to England where once again he made his headquarters in his mother's Farnham house, between times flat sharing with his London friends and sleeping in his brother Andrew's studio, also in Farnham.

It was unextraordinary for him to appear in one or the other abode without warning and not infrequently accompanied by a band of friends. He seemed to move in three circles; his family, that is his mother, Andrew and the latter's lovely wife, Diane; a circle of what might be considered friends acceptable to his family largely in or near Farnham; and a third, a London circle of people unkown to his family but which they suspected to be demimondaine: a wild undisciplined lot into whose bosom David from time to time sank without trace, to emerge, seemingly none the worse for his experience, at his mother's home. Knowing his giant appetite and the likelihood of his reappearance at any unlikely moment, the refrigerator was kept well stocked with pounds of steak. At two o'clock, morning or afternoon on days when he turned up at his mother's house, he ate the meat voraciously. While a couple of pounds or so was cooking, he sustained his vast frame with several tins of anchovies. An inventive cook, his steak recipe was simplicity itself: the meat, on a raised perforated grid inside a large fryingpan, oozed its juices into the pan's bottom as unadulterated gravy.

His rich palate also inspired a unique chicken dish. After removing the parson's noses from forty-six chickens they were thrown away. That is, the chickens were discarded. The parson's noses were stewed all day in an earthenware casserole lined with one-quarter-inch thick ham with a sauce of liqueur brandy and apricots, then after adding mushrooms and a rich brown sauce were placed in a silver dish and served up hot to the cook. He found the dish rich beyond the dreams of Croesus.

He engendered for cooking the same enthusiasm as for whatever might be his latest inspiration. At the rear of thick lenses his eyes glinted excitingly, while the corners of his mouth twitched into the betrayal of a smile. Although laughter was never far away, it was somehow confined to his belly, which frequently heaved in silent inward mirth.

Andrew saw in him a combination of extreme nonconformism and an absence of ambition for the things in life which provide the driving force for most people; career, family, money and similar materialistic attributes. He fitted into no pattern, at school, at home or outside, and strenuously resisted any effort to make him conform. It was quite impossible to *make* him do something, and he would often reject good advice along with bad rather than compromise his freedom of choice and decision. Recognising that this was a dangerous absurdity he explained that he was unable to help himself. If someone tried to interfere, or offered help or advice when he had not specifically asked for it, his reaction was to do the exact opposite, regardless of what that happened to be. He would chew the cud for hours with friends, or with Andrew, but any decision had to be his own. He was a 'loner'. His non-participation in games or in any other form of group activity was another facet of the same characteristic, and may also explain why he tended to prefer the companionship of friends rather than family, to whom he was nevertheless devoted. He had his own key to Andrew's house where an outsize bed was fitted up for him in the studio, yet he frequently stayed elsewhere in Farnham, sleeping on someone's sofa or someone else's floor. He felt freer there.

This side of his character was further illustrated by the impossibility of pinning him down for meals or any sort of activity that needed a decision in advance. He very rarely accepted an invitation to a meal, or any other form of meeting needing a time and place to be fixed, without saying that his coming depended on what he happened to be doing at the time. If pressed for a definite answer it was always no. He would only accept a relationship in which he retained complete control of his own movements and decisions, reacting compulsively to any effort to pin him down, by either rejecting what was offered or by just failing to turn up. In the end his friends just had to accept this, as did his family. It seemed the only way he could manage his affairs. He had to have absolute liberty of action without emotional fetters of any kind.

His total rejection or non-acceptance of the things in life which drive most people on meant that he completely lacked these in any normal sense. Certainly he liked having money, but it was strictly for spending, or giving away, as quickly as possible. A few extravagant gestures and back on the bread-line. When he was broke he expected friends and relatives to provide him with money when he needed it and not to expect to be repaid. At the same time, if he was unexpectedly flush his generosity was lavish; and equally he did not expect to be repaid. For him money was a side issue, really a nuisance, most of all when he did not have any. He seemed devoid of motives, for he had long since accepted that he would never accept the restrictions of marriage, and had almost no regard for personal belongings; and certainly no desire to accumulate more than could be carried in a couple of suitcases.

The only driving force behind his writing was either earning his bread and butter: and compared with most people with houses and families he did not need much: or his own feeling that he had something to contribute. His attitude to material possessions was quixotic. His shoes were never mended, just allowed to wear out and discarded. His clothes, emanating from exclusive Hanover Square, were worn until they fell apart. He did not send a suit to the cleaners until all his clothes were so unpleasant that he had nothing to put on. Nothing was ever mended until full of holes and by then unmendable. Clothes, like money, were a nuisance; but, like money, one had to have them. His wardrobe, strewn over various houses in southern England where he might have stayed in the preceding six months, resembled a poor man's jumble stall. There were quantities in left-luggage offices, boarding-houses, friends' garages, or just left in hotels.

His other possessions amounted to a collection of Seychelles shells, two old wooden chests picked up in Zanzibar, an expensive gold and topaz necklace-and-earrings set he designed and had made up in Dar-es-Salaam, an assorted lot of photographic kit, a few worthless odds and ends, sundry papers and photos which uncharacteristically he kept in good order, and crates of paperbacks which he read avidly.

From time to time he toyed with the idea of buying a small house of his own in Farnham as a base, or perhaps Italy or the French coast, but any money he might accumulate would go on his mother, whom he adored, a fast car, a boat of some kind or other, and the rest spent on just living and perhaps a trip to some exotic part of the world until it ran out. He liked company and people and got on well with them. He was a good listener and somehow attracted confidences; he never gossiped and was meticulously honest. But he found himself a difficult person to live with and found the going tough. He accepted that the restrictions and responsibilities of marriage were not for him. He liked women, but usually as 'incidents', not affaires. He also liked children, but would have been driven mad by his own.

Over the years he did a great deal of self-examination

from which he learnt what made him tick, and the limitations imposed by the odd quirks of his character. He saw clearly that he did not fit properly into our organised society and knew from experience that he could not adapt to fit. So he made his own life as best he could and tried to soften its impact by devices such as his refusal to accept invitations or to become stuck in any one clique or group of friends. He moved around in his three circles, each deliberately isolated from the others, and only went where he could be reasonably sure of acceptance on his own terms. Yet, as he grew older he increasingly came to terms with himself, the result of a continuous self-analysis and the realisation and steady acceptance of his limitations.

He once said that for him life consisted of a search for worthwhile challenges. It was the acceptance of the challenge which mattered, not its fulfilment, and thus he only found things worth while attempting if he was not sure that they could be done. If he knew they could be done, or had done them once, then that was the end of his interest and he looked for a new challenge. The challenges he sought were impersonal, as he tested his ability to overcome a physical or intellectual problem, or a set of circumstances. He was not interested in competition, which to him proved only that men are different, not that one is better than the other. This may have been a rationalisation of a characteristic trait.

For example, at the age of ten or eleven he made a series of beautiful clay models but never repeated the endeavour; he only ever concluded one painting : a brilliant cartoon of his father, lampooning the latter's immersion in the unwordly; he designed the décor for a R.A.D.A. showpiece of the late 'forties, repeated only by his designing a single set for the Melbourne Little Theatre a few years later, in an interval between labouring jobs. Although his talents were not great they were extraordinarily varied, yet his personality never gave him the chance of exploiting them to the full. It was just the way he was made. His better achievements were one-off efforts, never a sustained attempt at something he knew he was good at: because he knew he could do it. On returning from Africa in 1964 he had ideas about everything under the sun except journalism, the one job he knew he could do but which, typically, he only started doing after his father had died.

Cars played a big part in his life, perhaps because they provided an escape and a relaxation; for the same reason he avoided working with them, unwilling to commit himself to them any more than to anyone or anything else. He found them a great safety valve and burnt up the night roads at high speed to work off his frustrations. His cars were driven flat out until they needed major and expensive repair or were crashed, when they were discarded like a pair of old boots. He never sold a car or claimed insurance. At the Cooper school he got down to the last dozen out of thousands of would-be racing drivers tested at Brands Hatch. Other interests, by contrast, were butterflies and seashells.

Johnstone had a dread of growing old. He could see no future for himself as an old man, and consistently maintained that he had no intention of ever being one. His plan was to press on and find some way out in his fifties or whenever he found life becoming intolerable. Probably he did not value his own life particularly highly at any time. He refused to pay National Health Insurance contributions on the ground that he would be gone before he could possibly benefit from them.

He was an attractive and endearing person. Whenever there was a knock at the door of Andrew's Farnham home he and Diane both hoped it would be David rather than anyone else, and were as delighted to see him as they were frustrated by his refusal to base himself more permanently with them. At the same time, a visit by him probably meant the larder being drained of milk and whatever food was in it, with a good chance that Diane would also be lumbered with a stack of washing, and the house inevitably a shambles when he left. But they still hoped it would be him at the door; and sometimes, completely unexpected, he appeared with armfuls of food and a bottle of wine from the nearby Wheatsheaf, to take over the kitchen for hours on end and produce a monster, lavish and beautifully cooked meal for whoever happened to be there; he then disappeared with a 'See you some time'. At birthdays and Christmas his presents were either non-existent or lavish.

He knew he was not an ordinary run-of-the-mill man, limited by near horizons of domestic contentment and familiar bliss, yet to the world he had demonstrably failed to show what he was made of. As he poured away the years of his young manhood, Johnstone felt an increasing need to prove to himself and to the world the stuff of which he was really made, an implicit acknowledgment of the extraordinary qualities he had long sensed but had not yet translated into comprehensible or recognisable reality. He needed to make a mighty effort, heaving himself by his own bootstraps out of the succession of shallow ruts in which he had so far allowed himself to stifle. He needed also to undergo suffering and fear, necessary ingredients to lead to a catharsis which would exorcise the ghosts of failures past, and clear the way for a more positive and purposive existence at a generally unavailable level. He was unable to make do with a second or third best, another manifestation of his non-conformity. There was no real niche for him in the conventional world, but in the days of piracy or empire-snatching he would have been great.

The *Puffin* adventure was the challenge he had been seeking.

2

Perched on stools in the saloon bar of The Bush, a favourite local pub, Johnstone and a band of cronies were discussing the arrival at Falmouth of Robert Manry, a middle-aged American journalist who had just sailed the Atlantic single-handed, in a small boat. When the others went off to watch a boxing match on television, Johnstone sat musing at one end of the bar, his back against the wall, increasingly oblivious of the barmaid's small talk as the germ of an idea swiftly took root, sprouted and blossomed.

As he sat muttering inwardly the only two remaining customers departed. The Atlantic *had* been rowed, he mused. In 1896 two Norwegian oyster fishermen, Harbo and Samuelson, had rowed across to the English Channel then down the Seine to Paris, wearing bowler hats, in a boat called the *Richard K. Fox* . . . Seventy years ago. They had taken some sixty days. He had read a story about the odd exploit. The tale was told that on their return trip in a cargo boat which broke down, they were lowered over the side to row the remaining 200 miles to New York to bring help. The whole story was dubious but it was a good tale. The twinned lines of thought, Manry and the Norwegians, were rapidly interfused with Johnstone's own restless, adventurous spirit, constantly questing the satisfaction of excitement and novelty, preferably combined.

By the time his friends returned an hour or so later, he had made the decision to row the Atlantic, 'downhill' from west to east (the approximate direction of the prevailing winds and currents) and was promptly bet ten cigarettes by the incredulous that he would not even get as far as his first step, advertising in *The Times* for oarsmen. Next morning he wrote out the advertisement and posted it, with a cheque: 'Will five fortitudinous oarsmen over 28 join me and engage in second-ever transatlantic rowing voyage?'

Almost immediately he received a slightly disheartening shoal of replies: a telegram from an unlikely adventurer of fifty, another from a German youth, a letter from a Frenchman, dozens of others from a mixed bag of enthusiastic youngsters, too inexperienced to merit serious consideration. Replies from Belgium and Canada, France, Portugal and Germany, altogether well over a hundred but including one which he liked so much that he wired the writer asking him to make immediate telephone contact. Within ten days of the pub daydream, Johnstone and John Hoare had met and instantly accepted each other, though still four men short of the contemplated crew.

Hoare, a tall and good-looking twenty-nine, was a fit, muscular, outdoor man. Outwardly conventional and perhaps less imaginative than Johnstone, he was a romantic with an inbred sense of adventure. As a schoolboy he was extremely popular, physically and mentally strong, and although gentle and easy-going his anger was quickly roused at injustice. He excelled at rugby football, an activity he carried into manhood, and by contrast also enjoyed caricature drawing, at which he was adept. He loved adventure and adventure books, and became infatuated with the heroism he dug out of World War I books, which he read avidly, studying military techniques and tactics until he became authoritative about the War's battles and the generals who conducted them. He had gathered material about Captain Ball, V.C., one of the great flying idols of 1914–18, and was engaged in writing a book about him. He was a great admirer of courage and of writers about courage, and thus a Hemingway fan.

During military service he became a parachutist, and while stationed in Germany learnt to speak the language fluently. After his discharge from the Army he joined the Territorial reserve, continuing his parachuting activities. He also enjoyed shooting, and was a first-class swimmer. It was important to him to maintain a high standard of physical fitness, but equally he enjoyed good restaurants and good conversation. He owned fast cars which he drove in rallies, and was as comfortable in rough outdoor tweeds and corduroys as in the dark suits his work demanded. During his military service he had studied free-lance journalism and taught himself to type, and became feature-writer and motoring correspondent on a Lincolnshire newspaper. In conversation he was laconic and very much to the point; he could not tolerate hypocrisy, a characteristic which was totally lacking in him. He loved dogs, and was accompanied everywhere by his own boxer. His thinking was straight, and his expression correspondingly direct. His sense of humour was such that he derived maximum pleasure from the innate folly of the human situation; he laughed at himself rather than at his fellow men, for whom he felt profound compassion. Tallying at so many points with Johnstone's own personality, he was at the same time a perfect foil for the man whose advertisement had evoked the instant response of a parallel adventurous spirit.

Another likely reply to the advertisement, if only by virtue of its persistence, was from a Captain Ridgway, telephone calls from whom cropped up at Johnstone's various Farnham haunts, and not long after meeting Hoare he accepted Ridgway's invitation to the little house opposite the Farnham parish church where the latter lived. In no time Johnstone was convinced that they could not possibly get along together in a small boat. Ridgway, a lean, tough parachutist, seemed exactly the right man physically for the adventure, but the sensitive Johnstone was instinctively aware of an assertiveness which he feared would bring about a clash of personalities he was unwilling to risk, and therefore studiously avoided making any commitment.

Friends in the street, having heard about the adventure on radio or read it in the papers, stopped to ask: 'You're not really going to do it, are you?' and receiving an affirmative reply commented, 'Well, I hope you can swim!'

With Hoare he promptly embarked upon investigating the initial problems of oars, food, place and time of departure, type of boat, charts and meteorological information, matters of which both men were almost wholly ignorant until visiting various experts in those fields. Having realised that they should be ready to start as early as possible in the new year, once the unsettled conditions of winter had passed, they busied themselves with listing equipment and clothing, and the design, costing and building of the boat they intended to row.

Among facts discovered from the experts was that a man

can live for ten days without food, provided he has a quart of water a day, or on only a pint a day if he has four ounces of sugar; that fat provides nine calories to a gramme, protein four and sugar four; that for avoiding hunger pains, protein and fat are best because the body takes longer to assimilate them, although fat alone can poison the system and must have sugar with it; that for long-term survival, a hundred grammes of protein a day is the minimum for survival, but that if there is less than a quart of water a day available then protein should not be taken, because it absorbs water. Seawater should never be drunk, as it draws water from the body cells for dilution. Salt tablets should not be eaten, but dissolved first in water. Maintenance of a steady work level required half a gallon of water a day, and food producing 4,000 calories; about thirty-three and a quarter ounces of dehydrated food, measuring 10 in. x 4 in. x 4 in. Water should be carried in several small containers rather than a single large one, so that if one failed all would not be lost. Plastic water containers float in the sea, which is heavier than fresh water. A four-man fifty-day voyage would require nine cubic feet of dehydrated food and thirty-two cubic feet of water, a total weight of four-fifths of a ton.

But acquaintances by the dozen were telling the men it couldn't be done, and only a few enthusiasts showed any confidence in them. They explained their venture next to Colin Mudie who promptly agreed to design a boat for them. They sat in his Victoria office, an exciting place with walls covered in plans of speedboats, sailing craft, maps and charts, and shelves filled with books about boats, odd lengths of line and nylon sheet and bits of canvas lying about haphazardly, and models, particularly two of *Small World*. Mudie also had extensive experience of the Atlantic from his long cruise in *Sopranino*, which encouraged him to the view that a small boat was perfectly safe in the Atlantic. Johnstone enthused handsomely at the rough sketch which the designer there and then produced, though he thought the vessel looked a bit too comfortable, perhaps more suitable for a Mediterranean cruise. He wanted something that looked more spartan. Particularly he was worried about a little mast which Mudie had drawn in, until reassured that it was intended not for a sail but for a reflector which would help large ships see the rowing boat on their radar screens. To Johnstone, Mudie was a man who obviously had a tremendous feeling for boats, as he explained about 'crispness' which, after a boat had been distorted due to wave action, snapped it back into shape immediately, in contrast with a soggy type of craft which being less whippy and well braced did not reform so crisply. Animatedly they debated the technical advantages of a clinker-built against a cold-moulded-ply boat, discussed possible ship builders, where the compass should be positioned, and a host of structural details. Mudie promised that by the end of the week he would have prepared a sufficient drawing to allow a builder to cost the boat, and the two men departed in a happy frame of mind. They had got speedily under way.

Slowly over the ensuing days, struggling to accept that he was acting out his dream, Johnstone attuned to the realities of the adventure, screwing down his mind to further and yet further degrees of discomfort and privation which he knew he would suffer, anticipating that when the time came he would be prepared and able to lie on the bed which he was beginning to prepare for himself. Serious from the outset, despite the scepticism of many of his friends, he was with accelerating intensity placing himself in a position of non-return. The wild idea was rapidly becoming practical and was beginning to carry him along with it.

Simultaneously, he began to think that a crew of six would be a crowd for the voyage, and that four was a more suitable number. Hoare and he even began to consider going it alone, but at that stage dismissed the notion as unpracticable. They were now concentrating their minds on the basic idea of the adventure, trying to accept it as a reality, distinct from what had been merely an exciting prospect. What had initially made the mind boggle was already becoming steadily less indigestible. The idea of four men instead of six became increasingly firm, until Andrew told his brother bluntly that if he were doing the trip he would have as few as possible, in fact that if he could not go alone he would not go at all. At the most, he'd have one other man with him. Although David automatically rejected the suggestion, he found it filtering into his conscious thoughts with increasing strength, until within a few days he was unable any longer to consider the venture other than as a two-man show. It was suddenly obvious.

> *The thinking reduced the idea as if it were a soup or a stew simmering slowly to boil away the water and taste the essence. I began to think of a two-man trip as a desirable purity of idea: Go the penance way.*

When consulted Hoare agreed with alacrity, influenced especially by the fact that the Norwegians had been only two. Suddenly it seemed all too obvious, and David telephoned to tell Colin Mudie to hold his horses, as they might very well be wanting a smaller boat. He still had to clear three main doubts : First, if there were only two men then there must obviously be times when only one was rowing, and could one man row in a seaway with two oars? Secondly, what was medical opinion from a physiological point of view? And thirdly, on a direct aspect of design he had to discover the most suitable length of oar, height of rowlock, and width of boat to suit the chosen oars. Only then, it seemed to him, could Mudie calculate how deep in the water the boat should sit, allowing for the estimated weight of provisions and water, and thus complete his design.

At the Royal Naval School for Safety Equipment and Survival Training, Johnstone sought and received valuable advice on suitable clothing, electronic devices, also desalination and physiology.

'Are you a married man, Mr. Johnstone?' he was asked first.

'No, why?'

'Well, the last man seeking our help turned out to be running away from his wife and family. We didn't know at the time. We're not anxious to act as divorce brokers.'

His bona fides established, he was variously told and noted the position of the Atlantic weather ships and lectured on appendicitis and seasickness, learning that anyone can be made seasick under certain conditions. Long term seasickness, being incurable, must be discovered before crew were enlisted, for drugs which were of temporary utility could not make permanently better a man who did not recover within the first couple of days at sea. No additional safety hazard arose from the fact that the crew consisted of two, rather than four or six. Appendicitis was an unlikely result from a change of diet.

In the far corner of a room full of Civil Service desks he was lectured on seamanship and particularly sea rowing. He found the atmosphere redolent of the period of Samuel Pepys, with jack tars, cannon-balls, bolts of sail cloth, salted pork and telescopes just round the corner, and Nelson keeping an untypically genial eye overall. He was fed volumes of statistics on oar lengths, shown vast tomes of drawings of different kinds and sizes of oars, and was loaned books on *Survival at Sea, Seamanship* and *The Propulsive Efficiency of Rowing.*

'Use the biggest oar you can get,' pronounced the expert. 'Let's see; we have here a seventeen-foot oar. You'll definitely want to use those in the calmer weather. Larger than your boat? Well, in any case don't use anything less than fourteen feet long.'

After further discussion, fourteen became ten, reluctantly admitted to be the largest-sized oars of which one man could handle a pair.

By Christmas, Johnstone was overwhelmed with the enormity of the preparations he had undertaken and felt like calling the whole thing off. He found himself hoping he would become too ill to go on with the project and thus have an honourable excuse to unburden his oppressed mind. Hoare being only available at the end of a telephone, Johnstone found himself increasingly isolated, and badly in need of moral support. Matters were not helped by the too frequent suggestions still coming from acquaintances that by now he'd dropped the idiotic idea of rowing the Atlantic. Even among his closest friends he sensed a sort of heaviness, an expectation of failure, an exaggerated feeling that vultures were sitting on a tall tree nearby waiting to peck the remains of the miserable fellow's idea which had fired their imagination only a few weeks previous: perhaps, he felt bitterly, because he had leapt out of line and was somehow showing up their own inertia. His response was the physical toughening of his massive frame, and he sought the hardest labour available.

One or two mornings later, at 6.45 a.m. he was on the job at a nearby breeze block factory. 'They say it's hard work,' the woman at the Labour Exchange had pronounced, 'but it doesn't seem very popular.' The factory seemed the most depressing place he had ever clapped eyes on.

An individual breeze block runs it a close second, but for sheer horror there are few sights to beat the slag and dust of years of breeze block making, with unthinkable breeze blocks standing everywhere in stacks. In the middle of the grey open factory building there is a machine for making them, a process starting with Stan shovelling the dry breeze, made of ashes and like substances, into a tray to which a tiny quantity of cement is added. Stan then pulls a lever and the tray lifts up and tips the whole lot into the waiting mouth of a vast mixer. With a lot of banging of hammers on the outside of the tray, Stan gets the last bit down into the mixer's maw, then adds a quantity of water. Down comes the tray to be filled again and so the process is repeated, each load comprising fifty-seven deep wide shovelfuls of damp ash, before Stan is ready to lob in the cement and pull the lever and send the whole lot flopping into the mouth of the mixer.

But there is worse to come. After allowing the mixer to rotate for long enough to achieve the right consistency, Stan pulls another lever, whereupon the mixture runs out lumpily on to a rubber conveyor belt up into a machine of ultimate torture, the actual shaper of breeze blocks. Presumably there are no better methods of shaping breeze blocks or someone would have bought one. The dreaded grey-brown mixture drops into the top from the belt, to fall into a sort of scoop. A tremendous heave on a five-foot lever sends the scoop along over the moulds into which the breeze mixture falls. Another heave on the lever brings down five tamping shoes into the moulds, vibrating to work the breeze down to size and press out the bubbles. Finally the tampers and the mould are lifted, leaving five new wet blocks sitting neatly side by side on a wooden palette.

It is my job to help Derek to lift the palette and carry it across the yard where the blocks will dry out in the open. We pick up opposite sides, a hand at each corner, then walk with a kind of twisted sideways gait to place it down some twenty yards away, the paletteful weighing at least a hundredweight. After carrying the first load I am gasping, my muscles at the absolute end of their capability to go on holding up the palette, my fingers beginning to tremble as if they are going to come off. My eyes bulge and my temples pump as the palette is lowered. We put it down, I straighten up with relief and we walk quickly back to where the next palette of blocks is already being vibrated. As we reach the machine Stan pulls the lever, up go the tamps and the mould, and there is the next paletteful ready to be carried. Derek jumps across the lever lying on the ground in repose after its labour, and I spring wearily to my side of the palette, lift, twist, and then walk with the load in increasing agony to start with, finally with torture cast across my moist brow. As we bend to put the second palette on top of the first my back trembles, the palette wobbles and the corner of a block falls off dryly. Derek says nothing. I straighten up and stretch my back to ease the trembly feeling, hurrying back to the machine at least twenty paces behind Derek who is already bending down holding his side of the next palette by the time I arrive.

After two or three more loads I am prostrated with breathless agony. Sweat pours down my face and my arms are shaking. I can feel my heart going at least twice as fast as seems right. I sag against the machine and croak to Derek: 'Just a quick spell, eh? I'll be all right when I get used to it.'

Derek turns to Stan. 'Always the same; too heavy for 'em. Remember that bloke said he was a weight-lifter? Started at seven, gone by ten. They come and go.'

I say, 'I'll be all right. Give me time to get used to them and I'll be O.K.' I bend down and lift the next palette.

Even the management recognises the work as harder than average, for after the first hour and a half there is a long break for tea. I see everybody going into the back of the gloomy shed. 'Tea up,' says Derek. I shamble after them and find a place on a narrow wooden bench. I have brought nothing to drink or eat but the management provides pint pots of tea. I sip some of mine, then stretch and yawn.

My left arm gets stuck in the air. I find I can't control the muscles to bring it down again. I reach across with my right hand and pull the arm back into place, my right thumb starts to curl around into the palm of my hand. I press it against my knee to straighten it. Immediately the whole hand begins to twist inwards to the wrist, like a huge bird's claw trying to grip a branch. I have been working in the factory for less than two hours.

At lunch time I begin to wonder whether I should go back in the afternoon. I sit down and am instantly asleep. I awake in time to open a tin of sardines, gobble them and race back to the factory. That evening I almost make up my mind not to go back next morning. I reckon I have lifted more than thirty-five tons of breeze blocks in a day.

Next morning I go to work in gum-boots without socks on, being completely fixed in a standing-up position and unable to put on socks or tie laces. I sleep during the coffee break and lunch break, doze through the tea break, then go to bed at six o'clock for the first time in twenty years. By Wednesday evening I know I will have to last the week out to keep any pride together, and by Friday an almost unique industrial dispute happily closes the factory there and then and I leave. It has been a week of horror, with only a few relief moments when the lorries have to be loaded. In the end it was always back to the palettes.

The following week he transferred to a door factory, down on the timber tracks putting hemlock into stacks for the kiln to dry, sometimes as many as eighteen or twenty tons of wood in a day; simple, sympathetic work, compared with the breeze blocks, and unsupervised into the bargain, so that as much or as little work was done as took the fancy of the individual. Although it was sometimes difficult to find enough to do to keep warm, Johnstone at least toughened up his hands, never wearing gloves, and as time went on there was a steady diminution in the number of chilblains and cracks he had previously suffered.

His literary agent swiftly sold his story to both publishers and a national newspaper at a price sufficient to finance the building of the boat, a problem which had caused great worry.

Johnstone now gave Colin Mudie the go-ahead, the two-man boat to be designed to take ten-foot oars, to have a freeboard of not less than sixteen inches and a beam of five and a half feet. It must be less than sixteen feet long, so as to be smaller than the *Richard K. Fox*. While he lay on his side under Mudie's desk, the latter darted around him with a tape measure to calculate the height and width of bunks and galley, while chairs pushed hither and thither indicated the galley's position.

Drinking coffee under the desk, with Mudie peering at him through the kneehole, they talked excitedly about the tiny cabin, Johnstone leaning on one elbow and puzzling where Hoare would lie if they were both resting, or sheltering during a storm.

'That's the area you'll be living in,' Mudie stated to the reclining giant.

'Fine. Can I get up now?'

'Isn't it a bit soon? You realise you're there for three months!'

Mudie made it abundantly clear that the boat he would design would not cater for novices, and that experience would be needed to row it.

In other words he has not pulled any design punches in making it easy to row just for the sake of helping us. We must learn quickly!

The preliminary specification which was drawn up postulated a boat intended for a passage under oars only with a crew of two in the North Atlantic from west to east during the summer months; weight would be saved everywhere as far as consistent with the intended voyage. The boat, fifteen feet six inches overall, thirteen feet six inches at the water-line, five feet six inches across and two feet six inches deep, would be shaped along traditional surf-boat lines but with a fuller deck-line at the ends to increase their buoyancy and also the dryness of the boat in a head sea. So as to be extremely light and thus increase the power/weight ratio, it would be constructed of moulded mahogany plywood some three-eighths of an inch thick on oak and spruce structural members; the decks would be of laminated plywood of the same thickness, with beams only as required to stiffen the structure.

The layout would provide a small cabin at the after end with two full-length berths extending in tunnels into the cockpit below the level of the thwarts. One berth would normally be used as a galley and for storage, but its contents would be capable of being folded away to allow the second berth to be used. A lifting hatch with flaps would augment the available headroom in the cabin. In the cockpit a single rowing position would be provided on the after thwart between the two berth feet boxes, with a double rowing position on the forward thwart, the position from which the boat would normally be rowed and which would be protected by a canvas hood fitted around the forward coamings. The depth at thwart-level would continue forward to the bows, with hatches allowing access to storage space beneath. The space between the main foredeck and the thwart-level deck would also provide storage space for two buoyancy air bags, heavy warps and sea anchor. Handrails would be fitted not only to the decks but also to the hull, to facilitate righting the boat in the event of capsize. A flagstaff would be fitted to the aftdeck, at its peak a white, battery-operated light visible through 360 degrees. There would be three alternative positions for the rowlocks, and a trimming rudder connected by metal rods to a hinged tiller on the forward cabin bulkhead. Altogether, a comprehensive and formidably professional specification.

Designers will say, and sailors acknowledge, that no boat has ever been perfect for the job and that every boat is a compromise. The emphasis in the design of Johnstone's boat was on strength and safety : strength to withstand the storms and consequent seas which could be expected on the Atlantic in summertime, and safety in rowing from America to England, carrying two men and a ton of stores. The result was therefore, a strong, seaworthy, but tubby boat, with lines familiarly like those of a lifeboat : a mini-whaler. An integral aspect of the design was the position of the stores, which would be placed not only in the bilge but also in net lockers as high up as possible, to increase the metacentric height of the boat. The more weight that can be put aloft, the more sea-kindly the vessel's behaviour as the centre of gravity is lifted.

It was not long before the crew was immersed in visits to the builder at Cowes, in between long sessions with Mudie over such problems as buoyancy and stability. The tiny cabin would be a sealed unit and Johnstone asked what would happen if the boat went over with one man inside, and the other unable to help him through injury.

'No trouble,' advised Mudie, 'just push the hatch open.'

Johnstone found himself hoping that in the event the designer proved to be right.

'Also,' added Mudie, 'I think we must do this in trials: capsize her in a dock or somewhere and see what happens. But in practice in a seaway when you do get turned over, the boat will roll right over and come up again. This is tiresome for everyone concerned, of course.'

But better than stopping half-way in the upside down position, thought Johnstone.

New Year's Day and a party at Merton Naydler's house. Oliver Moxon was talking about the trip in terms which led me to think he reckoned it couldn't be done. He had only two minutes previously mentioned to me that he owns a casino in Farnham. I asked him for odds against my succeeding. We shook hands on my ten to his thousand in pounds that I would not row the Atlantic in 1966.

Johnstone's next introduction was to Archie de Jong, a mine of ideas and observations as well as a dietary expert.

Plucking volumes from a shelf in his office he thumbed through them and threw across useful bits of information for Johnstone to note down. Hole-stopping: take fibre-glass patches. Waterproof paper for notes. Balers with malleable wire rims are best. Take ten fags: even ardent anti-smokers swear to their value. Plastic vomit bags are better than paper. A fixed stiff ladder is better than a flexible one for getting back on board. Motor-bike or racing visor for rainy weather. Take woollen wristlets. Food should be of four categories. 1. Extreme emergency pack. 2. Working emergency pack. 3. Daily diet in three different varieties. 4. Luxury pack for one day a week, to provide something to look forward to.

There should be two cooked meals a day with snacks in between. Better, advised de Jong, take things which need only boiling water added, then if they spill you have lost no food and only have to clear up hot water.

As far as exercise was concerned, Surgeon Commander Baskerville, to whom he introduced the pair, counselled that all they would be able to do was lie on their backs, hold their legs in the air and wiggle their feet, but as their feet would in any event get very little exercise they'd probably find their ankles swelling. He demonstrated with an outstretched arm and a hand wiggling at the end of it. After duly collecting rainwater, distilling seawater, and turning seawater into fresh water by chemicals, they turned their attention to medicines for cracked lips, sunburn, headaches, toothaches and constipation, the last no serious problem because of the low residual quality of the dehydrated food they would be eating. Also they decided on clothing: bathing suits, long woolly underwear, quilted suits, waterproofs; and augmented their list of the Atlantic weatherships, their positions and nationalities.

A few days later, racing through the fog in Johnstone's battered Volkswagen to catch the Isle of Wight ferry on their way to the first view of the embryo rowing-boat, a further wager was struck, as the two oarsmen discussed the trip.

'I think we ought to have a bet as to who's first across a bird after we get back,' Hoare challenged.

'You'll have to be bloody quick off the mark, man,' Johnstone retorted. 'I'll be right there on the job in full view of the cameras, television or otherwise!!'

He drove furiously, his foot flat down on the accelerator, determined that the fog would not prevent their arriving in Southampton in time to embark. Mud spattered up on to their windscreen as they pulled fiercely into the quay and rushed aboard the ferry a moment before its departure. As the *Carisbrooke Castle* rolled into Cowes an hour late, Hoare said out of the blue, 'You know, it's not going to be at all like we think.'

Johnstone, attired in his favourite garb of jeans, several sweaters, and shabby blue donkey-jacket, paused between his last forkful of bacon and eggs, expecting the pronouncement of an easy passage with no trouble whatever.

'Maybe I've got too much imagination,' Hoare continued, 'but I think it's going to be a lot different from our ideas. It's going to be much harder than we think.'

Johnstone was silent. He had thought a great deal about being at sea, and wondered if it would indeed be worse than he had imagined. But he had been preparing himself for the worst.

They were met outside Souter's yard by the foreman. 'You'll be horrified at the size,' he greeted them cheerfully. 'It looks terribly small. Come in then, let's scare you properly.'

They entered the main building shed and there she was, in a gangway between the other boats with wood shavings and the smell of wood resin everywhere. The bows of a large ocean cruiser stretched out over her from the back of the shed, dwarfing the tiny coracle. Alongside sat a large polythene boat in course of being covered with plywood layers. The bows of a clinker-built day fishing-boat hung over her stem. Even though she stood in the gangway the tiny vessel was hardly in anyone's way. Johnstone and Hoare walked up to her in silence and Hoare smiled down. There was a pause.

'She's got great lines, hasn't she?' he said enthusiastically.

Johnstone said nothing. The boat was much smaller than he had expected, but her appearance pleased him. Although neither the flared bow nor the little rounded back end were finished, he found himself standing there, fascinated by the mould, imagining the vessel alone in the middle of a vast ocean, with no land for a thousand miles, and he was frightened. Unable to drag himself away, his thoughts kept turning the mould right way up to judge how it would feel sitting in her, sleeping in the rotund little stern, being confined in such a tiny craft for so long, unable to walk anywhere . . . their womb. He stood for a time engrossed in fascinated thought. Then they walked off down the road from the yard, feeling proud of their boat, for the first time enjoying a sense that they were really on their way. After months of words they had at last had their first glimpse of anything to do with the expedition that was made of more than paper.

On the return trip from the island Hoare irritated Johnstone by the suggestion that the voyage should be from New York to London, rather than Boston (200 miles nearer England) to whatever Cornish landfall they might make.

'Rowing the Atlantic is a feat. It doesn't have to be spelled out in seventy-two-point Bodoni,' snapped Johnstone.

'I'm willing to leave from anywhere, David, but I just thought it was worth considering.'

'Well, I've considered it, haven't I?' ended the discussion abruptly.

The pressure of the intensive preparations was beginning to tell on Johnstone, hundreds of letters, telephone conversations, scores of interviews, hours of intensive study related not only to the design and performance of the boat itself, but to its complex mechanical and electronic equipment, and necessary provisions, clothes, meteorological and navigational knowledge which would enable them to accomplish a safe voyage.

He was still worried by many of its technical aspects, despite his familiarity with boats and the sea. Rightly, he wanted the best opinion on positioning rowing-seats and rowlocks, and the size, quantity and style of oars. That problem had by now begun to resolve itself. While Mudie had thought eight-foot oars about right there had been the indeterminate duologue at the Royal Naval School some time earlier, and other intelligence had yielded the suggestion of six pairs of assorted eight-, nine- and ten-foot oars.

Johnstone decided to visit the country's leading oarmaker on the Thames embankment near Putney Bridge, a man taller than even Johnstone, the walls of his office lined with oars, each with a note of victory, the crew and the year lettered in gilt. Unfolding Mudie's drawings of the boat as his credentials, Johnstone explained his plans and predicament, and was relieved to be taken seriously as he was led ducking under the low door into the workshop, where great slivers of wood were being spokeshaven away from the backs of embryo oars. Several stands of unvarnished dinghy oars poked their blades in clusters near the rafters.

'These aren't hollowed out like racing oars are,' shouted the oarmaker above the woodworking din, and tapped the solid stems with a huge knuckle. 'Yours will have to be solid too or they'd never stand up to it.'

Johnstone nodded assent. 'There's an idea I had about the oars,' he ventured: 'We won't have much room for stowing them. I thought we might get our heads together on something which comes to bits in the middle. Then we could stow the short lengths easily, just screwing in the appropriate blade to suit the conditions we encountered. That would mean we could take up to twelve-foot oars, to use in smooth water.'

He had no idea what response to expect from the oarmaker, whose family had been making traditional oars for over a hundred years. His host seemed delighted, then stroked his chin thoughtfully.

'It's a question of flexibility. I am not certain you'd get it right with metal joints in the middle. We once made a pair of racing oars, which are hollow, putting in an aluminium tube for strength. But they broke more easily than ordinary racing oars, at the point where the strengthening tube stopped. We'd destroyed the controlled flexibility, you see,' he explained.

Johnstone understood the point, recalling Mudie's conversations about the necessary 'give' of the hull, so that it had life. So intrigued, however, was the oarmaker with Johnstone's idea that there and then he offered to provide free of charge all the oars which were needed for the trip. But as they shook hands Johnstone's mind was already directed to the long inventory of outstanding requirements sitting in his brief-case; the next big items to get hold of were an emergency radio and a radio direction finder.

He turned to yet another practical problem: the possible contamination of freshwater supplies by the intrusive action of the sea. An experiment quickly satisfied him that the osmotic action would be one way: seawater wanting to be fresh, so to speak, attracts fresh water to dilute itself. He was relieved to discover that fresh water did not want to be salty.

Towards the end of January, in his mother's house at Farnham, there was what was to be a final brain-racking session to decide on a name for the new boat. For months the question had been thrown about without any sign of a decision.

'You'll know it the moment you hear it,' Mudie had counselled. *Plankton*, the smallest form of sea life, was offered by Hoare. Diane's natural classicism produced *Deianeira*, a suitable deity, but sounding pretentious and certainly suffering from a syllable surfeit; *Sabrina*, for good mythological reasons; as well as *Undine, Scylla, Circe* and *Danae*.

'*Cockleshell*,' Hoare ventured, 'because that's what it damn nearly is.'

'What about *Come-in-Number-Two*, as shouted in rowing-boat pools?' suggested Johnstone.

'Or *Skylark*, of Any-more-for-the fame?' Hoare countered.

Boomerang and *Pushbar* having been similarly rejected, a fresh silence fell on the assembly. An interval or so later Diane leapt to her feet.

'*Puffin*,' she yelled excitedly. 'Why not *Puffin*?'

Johnstone knew immediately that it was right; what more apposite than that short, tumpy and slightly clownish looking seabird. Diane beamed with delight.

On the next visit to Cowes to inspect the boat's progress he casually mentioned the name to Souter, who looked at him as if to say, 'But surely you've heard of So-and-So's well-known . . .' and his heart sank as he realised that some emperor or king must have called his magnificent yacht *Puffin*.

Surprisingly, Souter said, 'H'm. Well. *Puffin*, eh? Do you know, that was the name of a class of dinghy we used to make here. In fact, come to think of it, it was the name of the very first cold-moulded dinghy we ever made. There now?' He put his fingers up under the back of his cap and scratched his head, pushing his cap forward, and smiling thoughtfully at Johnstone.

They laughed, confident that the choice of name was an excellent omen. Affectionately Johnstone ran his hand over the boat's rotund stern and was covered with silver paint which he rubbed off with a handful of shavings. He found her shape perfect, all that he wished for in the way of a sea boat. He and Hoare stood admiringly for an hour, watching the first strips of plywood being laid on, before visiting Harry Spencer who Mudie said would give them a lot of tips about rowing.

Over a little triangle of pavement alongside the Vectis tavern they passed through a green gate into an untidy yard lumbered with a grey half-deflated rubber dinghy, some ancient anchors oars and rowlocks, old bits of boat everywhere. In an upstairs loft, where thick stiff stays were spliced and swaged into steel deck-screws, they told Spencer of their plans. His eyes sparkled and he grinned as he bent down to feel Johnstone's hamstrings.

'Don't be surprised if you meet me going the other way,' he joked approvingly. Short, with a jutting chin and huge beam, a beret firmly fixed on his head, he disclosed that for six years he had regularly rowed between Cowes and Southampton, taking as long as four hours or as little as forty-eight minutes, depending on tides. He had also rowed right round the island in eighteen hours.

'The two parts of your body which take the friction are

your hands and backside. You must work and get these hard. If you don't you'll get water blisters first on your hands, and then they'll burst and turn septic, and that's the end of your rowing. If your backside isn't used to the friction you'll get boils. I've had salt boils, and once you get those you just can't row. The action of rowing tries to pull the skin from the top of your palm towards the fingers, that's why you get blisters there.'

He turned to the subject of propulsion.

'The longer the oar the better leverage you have. You'll do no good at all with short oars. You want a good long oar, and only half the blade in the water, otherwise you're wasting effort. The length of oar depends on the freeboard; the more freeboard, the longer the oar. You will break oars. Think of the strain on the oar at the rowlock. The rowlock is the pivot and very important. You want a good thick stem on the top part of the rowlock, say three-quarters of an inch, otherwise it will bend and perhaps break; also the base of the rowlock must be secured by a nut and bolt. The action of the oar, back and forth all day long, can only force screws out, if you used those, and then where would you be?'

He continued. 'If your arms ache after you have been rowing then you're not rowing correctly. Your arms are like the connecting rods in an engine, and you ought to row with the whole of your body. Keep your arms as straight and long as you can, and only bend them when you have to.'

Johnstone was busy scribbling down the obviously sound advice. He was also thinking of three million oar strokes across the Atlantic.

'When you've a following wind you'll see the waves coming up towards you. Row like hell, and you can go with a big wave for quite a time. But they usually catch you. The problem is that as this kind of sea is pushing the stern of the boat, its remaining length tends to swing to right or left and then you can get broached and capsize.

'Don't train in skiffs. Anyone can make them shoot

along. You want a good heavy old boat with plenty of weight to pull. When you are out there and you are down, and you will be down sometimes, have a good laugh. However bad things seem, or however rough it may be, and even though you might feel done, remember what Harry told you and have a laugh. It's a great thing. I think you'll do it all right, but you're bound to have some rough times.'

He pointed down the quay to a blue rowing-boat hauled half up the slipway. 'Take her out this afternoon,' he said. Unfortunately they selected the wrong boat.

'Hey, quick, go back,' yelled Hoare. 'She's filling with water.'

'Nonsense,' retorted Johnstone, 'she's a splendid old tub, she'll last us out the afternoon.'

At the same moment, looking under Hoare's seat, he saw water spouting into the boat. 'Christ, there's a bloody great hole in her, it's pouring in.'

Hastily they returned to the slipway, to discover that they had taken out an old wreck awaiting scrapping. In good heart they took turns exuberantly at lifting a huge anchor lying in the weeds, before making for the ferry and home.

They decided to invest in certain essential navigation equipment, whether they could afford it or not, notably an electronic Harrier log which would indicate speed and distance run with great accuracy, an important morale booster as they would know exactly how many miles a day they had achieved; it would avoid the vacuum of intense effort unrewarded by any knowledge of its result. However, a check each day on miles run would help avoid the serious situation resulting from either of them being idle, for whatever reason, while the other was sleeping; a horrible thought which had not previously crossed Johnstone's mind.

The other item to accompany the Harrier was a Homer-Heron direction finder, a radio set incorporating a hand-bearing compass which would enable them to tune in to and ascertain their position by reference to radio beacons on the American, English and continental coasts from as far away as several hundred miles, thus saving a great deal of position-finding using a sextant.

Towards the end of February their agent told Johnstone that the new editor of the national newspaper which was sponsoring them was wildly enthusiastic about the story and wanted to run it in his paper that week. Johnstone was dismayed. Not only did he want secrecy to complete his preparations, rather than invite competition by publicising the adventure, but Hoare had not yet even told his employers of his plans. Moreover, there were still a number of important decisions to be made about cooking arrangements and buoyancy bags for the boat's stability; diet and ship's routine remained to be worked out in detail: nothing imponderable or unanswerable, but as a result of premature publicity questions could be asked to which he would be unable to give a concise reply. Most important, he knew from experience how time-consuming publicity could be, when they were already on a tight schedule, necessitating strict timing.

Hoare too was reluctant that the story should break, but at an interview at the newspaper's London office Johnstone's objections were one by one knocked down. Hoare must write to his boss immediately. There was no time for competitors. 'When the others see the way we write the story they'll know that it won't be much good making a play for it,' so they would be spared by the other newspapers. And it didn't matter about the time not being ripe. Now what about money? Would £750 on account do?

'Take David off and give him a good meal,' ordered the man in the editorial office. 'Fill him up with a steak. I can't stand the sight of hungry men around the office. I think this is going to be the news story of the year. You two boys are going to make a lot of money.'

3

A week or two before the newspaper feature Ridgway announced to another national daily that he was to participate in a two-man attempt to row the Atlantic in a boat presently under construction, but that for professional reasons he could not say who began the venture. His wife was reported as stating that the other man involved lived in Farnham and had been round to discuss the project with her husband. Hoare read the news and was furious; friends telephoned to say they had thought that it was *he* who was accompanying Johnstone on the trip, and now . . . He wanted a correction published immediately and insisted that Johnstone should telephone Ridgway for an explanation. Alive to the danger of putting Ridgway into competition Johnstone decided to keep quiet. A week later when he 'phoned Mudie about one or two technical defects the latter told him that the Parachute Regiment had asked him to design a boat immediately but that he had gently brushed them aside.

This was definitely a grey shadow cast across the whole thing from my point of view. After all this work to get a hint of opposition, as if we hadn't got enough on our plates already without being hurried by the possibility of someone taking away all the fruits in one fell swoop.

He told Mudie of their unhappiness at the possibility of a challenge; after discussion, they decided that it was unlikely that Ridgway could build a boat in time.

We felt the idea was our own and we should have first go at it and we could challenge anybody next year . . . rowing teams in Russia, America, Germany, France, anywhere they like. And the Parachute Regiment and the S.A.S. and the Marines and anybody who wants to come along can have a whack then, but let's have our go first. We thought of the idea.

From then on, the possibility of an unwanted race weighed heavily on Johnstone's mind, and his desire to avoid it began to influence his major decisions. By 8th March Ridgway had publicly thrown down the gauntlet and Johnstone was overcome with deep gloom, unable to concentrate on what he was doing. He decided to face things squarely and see what was actually involved; he thought Ridgway, riled at not having been invited to join the expedition after having announced that he was participating, had to do something about it, and that meant mounting his own show.

We do know that Ridgway's a hard man, we know that he's terribly keen to do the trip, but I feel at the moment he can't possibly find the boat and he can't get the arrangements done in time to start off on anything like the same day as us.

That was the hope in Johnstone's mind of avoiding a race, as he and Hoare began to direct their energies towards finishing *Puffin* and getting under way at the earliest possible moment. Souters had promised the boat by 7th April, but Johnstone, explaining the seriousness of the situation promised extra money if the date could be advanced to 31st March, secrecy to be maintained at all costs. With Hoare he examined the possibility of moving all the proposed dates forward. If *Puffin* were ready early, the departure date for America could be advanced from 6th May to 22nd April. They had planned extensive trials in the English Channel as well as off the American coast, but now decided to cancel them: not a bad idea, anyway, they thought, as the Channel seaway was not representative of the Atlantic, being crammed with ships, the waves coming from a different angle, and their lengths different. They could carry out their trials after arriving in America, anyway. A couple of days would soon prove the rights and wrongs of various features of the boat and they would know before arriving there what they wanted to adjust;

if the worst came to the worst, the necessary work could even be done on the way over.

They decided to tell nobody of their plans, publicly confirming 6th May as their departure date, and then when the real day came they would tell a few people and just go. That way they would actually be in America during the first week of May, ready to row off in the second week if necessary, which would give them a distinct advantage over Ridgway, however he might be planning things. This was a very different programme from that outlined in the Press handout of a few weeks earlier, the concentrated nine weeks' rowing programme cut down to as many days.

Johnstone quickly overcame the worst of his despondency and decided that they could in fact beat Ridgway quite easily if they tried, though talking about it got his nerves on end again. Bob Taylor, allocated to the expedition by their sponsor, insisted on discussing ways of beating the possible challenge. Having worried for months about their plans and having made arrangements for the trip to be a success, Johnstone recognised that his basic fear was that unless they arrived in America before Ridgway they might as well not start at all, with the unthinkable consequence that he might then have to pay back the money he had received from newspaper and book contracts, already expended on building the boat and financing the expedition. He realised that his apprehensions would only be diminished by ensuring that they organised their expedition more quickly than the challenger, and achieved the crossing ahead of him.

He raced away with finalising provisioning arrangements, Archie de Jong providing a sixteen-day emergency pack for the life-raft and a ten-day walking emergency ration. De Jong would also provide rations for 1,037 of the 4,500 calorie requirement per day, the balance being made up by the rowers of their own choice, with particular emphasis on a Sunday treat.

The same afternoon the rest of their clothing was collected, and at the United States Line office in Pall Mall

Johnstone booked berths for himself, Hoare and *Puffin*, for 22nd April, to arrive at Boston on 1st May. In the evening Johnstone evolved a plan for their arrival at Boston. He wanted to avoid seaways for which they were not prepared —channel seaways, for example—and to practise from Boston would be a great nuisance because of the fact that it was a bay where there were bound to be difficult seas for a boat of *Puffin*'s size. It seemed to him that the best thing was to arrive in Boston, lower *Puffin* over the side into the water, and over to moorings immediately; or have her transported to moorings by road. They could stay a day in Boston to obtain charts, then row across to Cape Cod for a berth in a competent shipyard which Bob Taylor, who was to accompany them, could organise. All their practising could be done from Cape Cod, and they might even row off from its eastern side straight into the seaway, possibly from the beach or from a landing stage, thus getting straight away from land at the outset of the voyage and avoiding rowing through a bay and still being in sight of land after a day's rowing.

But thoughts of Ridgway kept welling into his mind. Perhaps if he went to see him and explained how far ahead they were with their preparations they could discourage him from competing. Even though they would have to disclose their plans to no inconsiderable extent they might thereby despatch the only fly in their ointment. It might even be a friendly gesture to make, though a day earlier he would have committed Ridgway to the devil. After all, it was a bit strong, he reflected moodily, that Ridgway should have gone, first to Colin Mudie, then to the same builder who was making *Puffin*, and finally to have decided on starting from Boston. For this is what he learnt Ridgway had variously done and decided, bent on competing on precisely identical terms.

Johnstone's prime objective was now no longer to row the Atlantic, but to row it before Ridgway; to avoid a race by rushing ahead and setting off from Boston so much earlier than Ridgway could possibly do, that no question of a race could arise, and into the bargain there was a chance that Ridgway might be discouraged sufficiently to drop his competitive plans altogether. Agitated, he called in on Colin Mudie to check whether Ridgway could in some way be prevented from using the design mould prepared for *Puffin*. Mudie put his mind at rest by explaining that while he could scarcely refuse to design a boat for Ridgway, which might lead to the latter hashing up some unseaworthy old vessel, he would not use the same plans as he had drawn for *Puffin*'s design.

'Would you just alter the drawings, then?' enquired Johnstone anxiously.

'No, it would be a completely fresh boat, starting from scratch.'

'What about the mould? Could he use that? Then he wouldn't need plans.'

'That would be an infringement of my copyright, whoever the mould belongs to. My permission would have to be obtained and I wouldn't give it without your approval.'

Relieved of that particular anxiety Johnstone concentrated once again on final preparations for the voyage: the possibility of a radio transmitter was ruled out on grounds of weight and space: a paraffin stove was selected which could be folded away in a small suitcase; lifejackets and an inflatable dinghy were decided on; sleeping bags, watches and vitamin pills arranged; underwater torches chosen; and decisions taken on food very much in the form originally planned. There would be sixteen days of rations in the dinghy, ten days of emergency rations stored in nets under the gunwhale, and the rations de Jong was providing would be made up to a total of 4,500 calories by the inclusion of items chosen by the crew to suit their specific tastes. There would be separate packs for the special Sunday diet which would break the weekend monotony.

A few days later came the startling good news from Bob Taylor that Ridgway had dropped out, unable to obtain the sponsorship he had banked on.

'It's all off,' he announced over the telephone.

'What's off?'

'The other people. The others. They're not going. I 'phoned Ridgway myself and he told me he couldn't find the money to build a boat so they weren't going.'

Yet within a few minutes Johnstone, suspicious and defensive, began to think this might be some kind of trick to cause him to relax the intensity of his own efforts. Mudie confirmed that he had heard nothing from the paratrooper. Yet Johnstone did not relent, fearing that Ridgway might find and convert an old rowing-boat, and each day saw an increasingly detailed intensification of his efforts, now directed particularly towards safety devices such as rockets, radar reflectors, flashing lights, detonators, and powerful torches, all intended to attract the attention of large vessels which might otherwise constitute a hazard to the virtually invisible coracle, or whose assistance they might wish to seek. From his sailing experience he was well aware that small boats frequently failed to show up on the radar screens of large vessels which, because of their size and strength and the noise of their engines, might be oblivious of a collision. Even a near miss could prove disastrous to a small boat, the bow wave of a fast-moving large vessel being sufficient to capsize a small boat in close proximity.

With Mudie and his small son beside him in the Volkswagen he raced from Victoria to Southampton in thick fog, missing the Cowes ferry they had aimed at but catching the previous one, delayed by the Solent fog. Johnstone's mind was filled with the business immediately ahead, but he dandled the small boy on his knee, and in between his dialogue with the designer found time to play with the child.

'That's a super tractor,' he observed.

At Souter's yard *Puffin*'s forepeak was already decked in, her cabin half built, handrails fitted, and stem and stern posts fixed and shaped off, so that she was beginning to look really like a boat. Side by side in the cabin Mudie and he measured the bunk space and found there was room enough to put knees up; but it was difficult for a man of Johnstone's great size to squeeze out of the bunk and back through the cabin top hatchway. He was delighted to find that it would be possible, after all, to row in tandem, two oarsmen side by side. At the same time, he decided that seven-foot buoyancy bags would be fitted along each side of the boat, with a special device to let the air out so that there would be no trouble in deflating them in an emergency if the boat was upside down. There would also be an external saddlebag strapped to the aftdeck so that, if capsized, the boat would be self-righting.

Now yet again Ridgway entered his life, for his continuing enquiries showed that the paratrooper was actively trying to find a ready-built boat and had been in touch with the life-saving authorities for advice and information. Johnstone believed also that he had approached the same people who were to provision *Puffin*'s venture, following in Johnstone's footsteps with almost uncanny accuracy, as if some strange agency was bent on facilitating his making a race of it.

Devoting his energies to finding out more about his rival, he learnt that Ridgway had acquired a twenty-foot dory, a type of flat-bottomed, pointed-ended seaboat used for open waters for centuries, and more recently for Grand Banks work by the fishermen of Newfoundland. On account of its length the dory would be faster than *Puffin*, but clinker-built : that is in overlapping planks : and therefore heavier than the ply boat, and accordingly less easy to row.

> *So we have got Ridgway with us again but I find he has less of an effect on me now. It's far better to take the worry off our minds and just get on with the problem rather than to sit thinking: 'Christ, here's Ridgway bearing down on us all the time.'*

For he was aware of the enormity as well as the nature of the task he had undertaken, chief among his concerns being the importance of independence, so that come what may nobody else would be involved or put to any risk because of the adventure. Constantly this was in the forefront of his mind. Not that he had any doubt of the success of the voyage. It would succeed, they would reach its end in good health and with no injuries or loss of life, but this necessitated the most careful and serious planning. Then, even if they were overdue, no one need have any concern for their welfare, because every contingency would have been catered for.

But a considerable amount of his effort remained to be directed finally at the means of the boat's propulsion, for all the safety devices in the world would not move them across the Atlantic ocean. He knew that there was more to the oar than just its size or the blade-shape. There were questions of whether the handle should be formed for one hand or two; whether it should be of large diameter sufficient to be held with the fingers only, or smaller so that the thumb could go underneath, near enough to meet the fingers to provide a solid grip; whether the leather binding should be sufficiently long to enable the oar to go into the rowlock so that the oar ends crossed each other, or missed each other, and if so by how much. Should the leather be ten or fourteen inches, or more or less, or in between? Which would provide the optimum leverage? Should a removable button be provided, capable of being screwed in at any of several points depending on the length of oar to be utilised outboard the rowlocks?

These and many other problems were discussed with expert oarsmen, one of whom introduced them also to the ultimate in rowlocks: of cast aluminium on nylon bearings round a steel shank, which Johnstone immediately converted mentally into an extra long shank to give extra spread and thus extra leverage. And would it not be better to avoid electrolytic action: the consumption of metal by the mere proximity of an unsympathetic metal, known well to sailors: by the use of stainless steel and bronze, rather than aluminium and steel? It is a fact that a copper-bottomed boat moored alongside a steel hull wreaks havoc in the latter within a few weeks, a hazard familiar to owners of steel-hulled boats who accordingly exercise care over the constitution of their neighbours. Johnstone ordered a dozen pairs of rowlocks for the voyage.

On 5th April he and Hoare collected the trial oars from Putney, and at breakneck speed drove the Volkswagen to Southampton to catch the Cowes ferry. On the way across Johnstone fell gloomy and morose. Throughout his life he had recognised the extent to which he differed from his fellow men, the almost oppressive sense of individualism which harried him, and the increasing need to prove to himself and to the world a justification for a natural nonconformity which somehow denied him a necessary companionship.

> *Although I have many friends and constantly have company of my own choosing, I seem to be alone, with John only, perhaps, to understand fully what is in our minds. In many ways I wish we could talk to Ridgway and compare notes. He is the only other man in the world, with Blyth, who is preparing anything like this. We are few and should be together, but I have been made nervous and unhappy at times by Ridgway and his behaviour has in some respects put him out of reach. All these people going across to Cowes for such normal reasons. I do not feel a part of them or of any section of society. And this is where the loneliness arises, although a strong sense of responsibility to the family and to close friends, and to people who have helped us in confidence. Only complete disaster must prevent us from completing the tasks, and I hope John and I are strong enough to permit ourselves to accept that if the occasion arises.*

This was perhaps the nearest he could come to prayer.

By the time they arrived, *Puffin* was in the water, tied alongside *Myth of Mallam* and looking gay in the colours Mudie had chosen for her: yellow deck, orange topsides, pale grey inside, and a white bottom of adequate anti-foul propensities: that is, resistant to the marine growth which clogs a vessel's under-surfaces. They would have to brush off all the weed before leaving Boston, and might have to repeat the process once more before reaching England. For three hours next morning they filled water bags to stow in the dancing boat, so light that she bounced like a ping-pong ball.

They told us she was very lively. You could almost tip her over.

By midday she was ballasted to within six or seven inches of her water-line, still far from completely. In pouring rain they bored out rowlock holes, mounted the oars, and were ready for the first trials. At last they felt they were doing something really practical, as they mounted the Harrier and, clad in nylon suits, light-weight waterproofs and short seaboots, rowed off.

There were two available positions for the rowlocks, inboard and outboard respectively, but only the inboard positions were available for the first trial. Superb though the spoonblades proved to be it was immediately apparent that the rowlocks ought to be outboard, as the men found themselves rowing with the oar handles almost at the level of their faces, which made rowing doubly hard. Additionally, the oars slid through the rowlocks with only the handle ends inboard at times, and they realised that although the test was unfair, the boat being so far out of the water, they must opt for a square racing rowlock, with a corresponding square-stemmed oar with button tops.

They found too that in a moderate wind the boat constantly swung by the stern up into wind and Johnstone, who was rowing, had to pull on a single oar for a minute or more at a time in order to keep the boat on a straight course, the arm holding the non-working oar tiring more rapidly than that doing the pulling. His immediate reaction was that they were going to be in for a tough time. With Hoare by his side, each pulling an oar, shoulders together, he looked over and grinned.

'I think it's going to be a bloody sight tougher than I'd ever expected,' he commented.

'We've done half a mile and I'm out of breath,' grunted Hoare. 'Think of another 3,000 miles to go. Hey, look at that tremendous current coming out of there,' nodding towards an effluent stream where it entered the river.

'It's the Gulf Stream,' quipped Johnstone.

The Gulf Stream, a swift, saline current of clear blue water with warm upper surfaces, starts in the Gulf of Mexico and flows north along the east coast of the United States with considerable velocity, at its greatest six knots, reducing to one knot or less by the time it has reached Cape Hatteras in North Carolina. From that point it turns increasingly eastward under the combined effects of the deflecting force of the earth's rotation and the easterly trending coastline, until it reaches the Grand Banks of Newfoundland. Eastward of the Grand Banks the whole surface is slowly driven generally eastward and north eastward by the prevailing westerly winds towards the coastal waters of north-western Europe. This broad and variable wind-driven surface movement known as the Gulf Stream Drift, or North Atlantic Drift, shifts with the seasons, and is considerably influenced by the winds, which cause fluctuations in its position, direction and velocity. The Drift, joined by the Labrador current in the vicinity of Cape Cod, makes the latter an ideal position for the start of a west to east Atlantic crossing.

It was therefore from Cape Cod that Johnstone planned to start the great adventure, using the Drift to carry them in a roughly north-easterly direction from America to England, at a speed of at least one knot over and above whatever they achieved by their own muscular propulsion, aided by the following westerly winds normal in the Atlantic a great deal of the year, particularly in summer. It is little known, and certainly was not known by Johnstone, that its major currents are far from uniform throughout the width of the Drift; or that adverse head currents of as much as six knots can be encountered, followed by beam currents, as well as the more familiar north-easterly set.

'Right, let's row with it, mate,' Hoare answered, and they did.

Caught by current and wind, they progressed slowly across the river, ate an enormous lunch at the Folly Inn, then rowed home with the wind mostly behind them at two and a quarter knots, the Harrier showing occasional bursts of three for up to a minute, a speed they found impossible to maintain for more than a dozen strokes. With the wind heading them, one and a quarter knots was about as much as they could reach, from which Johnstone concluded that an overall average of one and a half knots was a reasonable target. The crew of a pair of beer barges cheered as they raced past, their wash rocking the rowing-boat, but the two men rowed steadily ahead, pleased with the way she handled although so far out of the water.

Johnstone was glad to find that *Puffin* kept her way on; even when they were doing only two knots and then stopped rowing for ten seconds, the Harrier still recorded a knot and a half. Although tired at the end of the day there was no sign of blisters on either of them. They tied up to *Myth of Mallam* and brought themselves and their kit ashore, well satisfied with the first outing, leaving instructions for the outboard rowlock mountings to be installed immediately.

Back in London, Mudie questioned the need for a life-raft. Although they had settled for the small inflatable dinghy, the designer's argument was that if, in effect, one was going to try and cross the Atlantic in a small dinghy, what was the point of taking a second one to get into? Impressed, Johnstone concluded that perhaps there was no real need, especially as *Puffin* was to all intents and purposes a lifeboat which certainly wasn't going to break up, and which would be rightable if she capsized. Their emergency equipment should after all be for a situation where one of the crew was really ill or otherwise out of action; why bother taking any other form of life-saving equipment, apart from the radio device for signalling an emergency?

Increasingly concerned with the need to thicken the veil

of secrecy around their preparations, and aware that Cowes was not only a very public place but that the Medina River with its swift current was an unsatisfactory practice pitch for a one-and-a-half or two-knot boat, he planned to ship *Puffin* to Scotland for further trials during the last few days before the journey to America. At the same time a fresh passage for men and boat was booked on *American Veteran*, due to leave Glasgow the following Tuesday week, which would sail them to Boston. It was now Friday, 15th April.

After celebrating his nephew James's second birthday at his mother's home, by cooking a splendid *coq au vin*, Andrew and he had the family car converted to tow a trailer, then drove over to Mudie's home to borrow one he had offered.

'There are a number of serious things I want to tell you,' Mudie greeted him. 'I think we ought to discuss them now. I've got a list.'

It transpired that the builders had run into several problems which appeared insuperable in view of the new time factor introduced, first by Johnstone's advancement of the departure date, and most recently by the decision to move *Puffin* from Cowes to Scotland. There was nothing Johnstone could do about it. He was not cheered when, as Andrew drove away towing the trailer, the latter confided to his brother how anxious their mother had become now that the reality of the project had so suddenly come nearer home; but that night at dinner in a nearby hotel, they jointly set about reassuring her. Bob Taylor, who was also there, satisfied her that they were in good hands and that the right people were making sure the trip was viable. The meeting was a great success. Hoare arrived soon after midnight in preparation for the journey to Scotland and the two men sat up until nearly three in the morning discussing their adventure. An alarm call at quarter past five roused them for the last trip to Cowes, which they reached two hours later.

Johnstone could not fail to be aware that they were

hurrying things. The dodger, the protective canvas hood for the oarsmen, needed further supports; the tonneau cover was still unfitted, the shock-cords which would hold it in position not yet having been threaded; men were aswarm the tiny vessel, fitting the mast and rudder to ensure a good fit, then removing and packing them in the cabin; one steering oar rowlock seating was missing; the ventilators seemed inadequate; there was no hasp and lock for the cabin; the rudder arrangements seemed unsatisfactory.

The boat looked almost ready but not quite. Still if it hadn't been for Ridgway, there would have been another fortnight to tidy up all those details, which obviously take a lot more time than one imagines. Building the boat is only half the game.

At the last minute they pushed a nine-foot inflatable dinghy into *Puffin*, unhitched the trailer and manhandled the boat on to it.

At Southampton, with boat and trailer loaded on to a lorry, they were ready to drive through the night to Glasgow, only to discover to their dismay that the lorry was not scheduled to leave until the next morning; it would stay that night at Carlisle, and arrive in Glasgow the day following.

Two days later they were met in Carlisle by Taylor who announced that there was bad news. Johnstone's heart sank. Surely Ridgway had not departed ahead of them? But the bad news was that *American Veteran*'s departure had been postponed by a week.

A whole day's frantic telephoning led to a rearrangement of plans whereby they would now travel from Southampton on the liner *United States* on Wednesday 27th April, arriving at New York on 1st May, the U.S. shipping line accepting responsibility for transhipping *Puffin* from New York to Cape Cod, Boston. The news meant not only that they must immediately turn around and drive all the way back to Southampton, but that the sea trials they had planned must be abandoned. If only they had known, *Puffin* could have remained at the builders' yard several extra days and much of the outstanding work been carried out. The wild rush north and back would have been avoided, and the two men could have spent a few extra days quietly with their families.

Back at Southampton *Puffin* and its crew embarked hastily on the great liner, accompanied by tea chests stuffed with their accumulated equipment and stores. Final farewells, then Southampton receding into the distance. The wild rush, the almost panic decisions, the stampede induced by the course of events meant that up to that moment their only experience of rowing *Puffin* remained the single outing at Cowes; they had absolutely no inkling of how she would behave in an open seaway, a proposition entirely different from the sheltered waters of the River Medina. Spurred on by the necessity to keep faith with their sponsors, the pace was hotting up, and with it the pace and amount of Johnstone's concessions, compromises and resulting errors of judgment.

Regaled royally on the short transatlantic passage, and sinking into an understandable relaxation after the sustained efforts of the past months which had culminated in the frantic wild-goose chase to Carlisle and back, Johnstone momentarily turned his back on the analytically detailed preparations he had up to then pursued. But during the voyage one of the ship's navigational crew who was an acknowledged expert in the art of marine navigation particularly familiar with the Atlantic, produced charts to show that by starting from a point much further south than Cape Cod, *Puffin* would reach the favourable Gulf Stream current with less effort. Admittedly, the 3,000-mile voyage would be extended to 4,000 miles. He recommended the rowers to start from as far south as Cape Hatteras, where the current from the direction of Mexico ran as fast as four and a half knots close inshore.

'From Cape Cod you'll be lucky to reach the Gulf Stream in under a fortnight,' he advised. 'Cape Cod is out.'

He produced further charts to substantiate his contention but Johnstone, reluctant to add as much as a thousand miles to the journey, decided that it would be a reasonable compromise to start from Cape Henry at the South point of the Chesapeake Bay, especially as the Bay contained many suitable creeks and small harbours with chandleries, where their tiny craft could be finally fitted out and adjusted for the long voyage. Now influenced unreasonably by his obsession with Ridgway he felt he would achieve a double blow to his rival : a faster and therefore better start, and a further impediment to Ridgway's plans for a race, by secretly changing his starting point. Johnstone neither knew nor was warned of the treacherous Chesapeake Bay currents, which signified nothing to a powerful motor vessel but could cause havoc to a rowing-boat. Although its ebb and flow is toward or away from the Bay entrance when close to land, the current, once offshore and unconfined by a definite channel, changes direction continually, and in a tidal cycle of twelve and a half hours sets in every direction of the compass. This rotary current varies from hour to hour, and when the moon is at new, full or perigee the current's velocity can increase by as much as two-fifths above the average.

In no time they were off New York, Johnstone now feeling very nervous at the prospect of the reception he knew had been arranged by the publicity vendors.

At half past five there was a knock on our door with Duke saying 'Five thirty, five thirty, time to get up.' We'd packed most of our gear the night before; we went up and had breakfast and soon the Washington Bridge was in front of us and in a little while we could see the main buildings of down-town New York. It was all tremendously exciting and also very nerve-racking. I was terrified of the prospect somehow: this was going to be such an important and adult city to visit, and so fast and unknown that I was quite worried. I took a tranquillising tablet.

It had been arranged that the Press was there in force, and television cameras, with interviews, filming and photographs in a special cabin aboard the liner until both men were completely exhausted, repeating their story over and over again.

'Even Nelson was seasick,' answered Hoare in reply to a by now too familiar question.

'Who's this guy Nelson?' demanded the reporter.

By agreement the two men withheld the fact that they had indeed felt seasick during the giant liner's crossing, advised that the revelation would create a bad image. Although rushed through immigration formalities, it was three hours before *Puffin* and their baggage had been assembled and lied through Customs. They lost no time in resuming their preparations for the return voyage, and next day, 3rd May, collected charts and supervised the transportation of *Puffin* and her equipment from the pier where *United States* had berthed to an adjoining one where she was put aboard *American Charger* bound for Norfolk, Virginia.

Enquiries at the U.S. Coast Guards' office produced a calculation of a minimum of one hundred days for their voyage; optimistically Johnstone had planned on half that time, thus comfortably beating Harbo's and Samuelson's crossing. The Coast Guards also gave them a five per cent chance of success and a very severe warning against doing the trip, but the promise of full co-operation, should they decide to go ahead, on such matters as Notices to Mariners, information on radio frequencies and weather, and aerial surveillance for the first few days out. They also confirmed the advice received about starting from Cape Hatteras. Simultaneously news arrived from England that Ridgway's boat would be leaving on 6th May, and the man himself flying over with his crew on 20th May.

It's a dory and a very seaworthy boat for the trip and makes him even more of a risk than he is now to us—a threat.

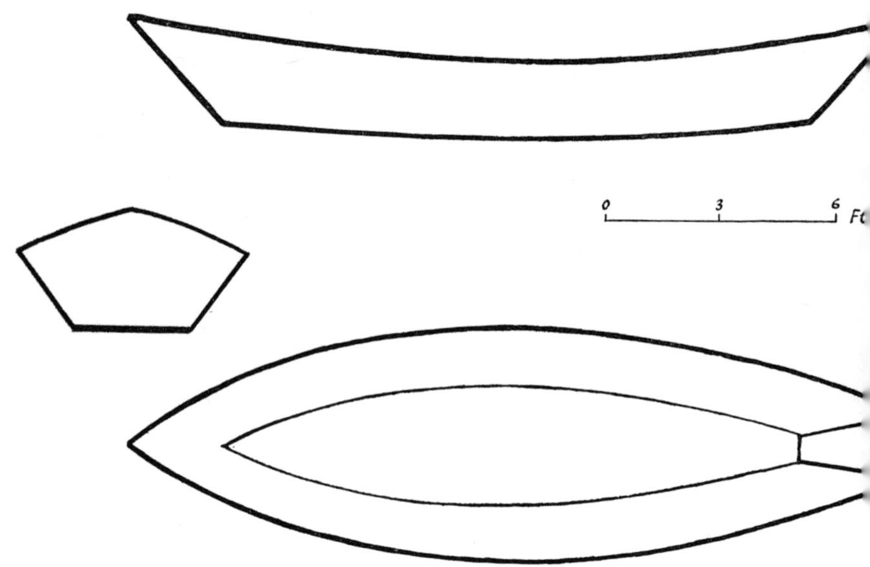

FIG 6 Lines of the Yorkshire Dory, of which *English Rose III* was a modified version

On Wednesday, 4th May, the day for their departure on *American Charger*, a further false trail was laid in case Ridgway should discover their Norfolk start-off and follow them; the story was therefore promulgated that they had been given a free trip to Newport, Rhode Island : a famous yachting centre : to spend a fortnight on repairs and maintenance and generally preparing the boat, during which time a final choice of departure place would be made.

Hoare disagreed. 'Why announce anything? Leave him to find out. He may never do so,' while Taylor counselled that it didn't matter if Ridgway did find out about Norfolk as people were bound to find out or guess anyway, but by now Johnstone, imbued with a deep distrust of his emulator, was in no mood for compromise or what he regarded as unnecessary risk of jeopardising their plans.

Jammed in traffic the whole way from the hotel to the

pier they came as near as makes no difference to missing *American Charger*, a typical Johnstone performance, with just enough time to ensure that *Puffin* was aboard and that their fifteen crates of stores were not.

We creamed off into a splendid evening, standing on the afterdeck looking back at New York through the binoculars.

The trip to Norfolk was fruitful, occupied with navigation and radio lessons from the crew: rough methods of ascertaining latitude and longitude by use of the sun and a chronometer but without a sextant: and the available radio frequencies for coastal, coastguard and aircraft communication (2182 kcs), for WT morse or emergency (500 kcs) and for actual inter-ship conversation (156·8 kcs). Early next morning they entered the Chesapeake Bay and tied up at Norfolk in time for a dawn breakfast, then rapidly ashore to chase up the crates which had been left behind in New York, eventually tracked down and destined to arrive in three days' time.

News reached them that instead of flying to America Ridgway now intended sailing on the same boat as his dory, *English Rose III*, thus advancing his arrival date. It now became urgent to get *Puffin* into the water with her stores aboard, so that she could be properly balanced and enable her crew to familiarise themselves for the first time with her behaviour as it would be during the long pull; the decision also required to be taken of the precise departure point in relation to Norfolk and the Chesapeake Bay. It had to be a point from which they could row straight off into the Atlantic and towards the Gulf Stream, without fear of becoming embayed by onshore currents which their tiny craft would be unable to counter: a very real apprehension in view of the current effects of which they were totally ignorant.

After examining the facilities at the Norfolk Yacht and Country Club, the Lafayette Club, the Tide Water Club and the Virginia Beach itself, they drove on to the coast road round Cape Henry before it occurred to Johnstone that the best take-off place really was precisely where *Puffin* presently was, the quay where *American Charger* was berthed. The boat was there, the crates would be deposited at the same spot from New York, *Puffin* could go straight into the water and be towed to a quiet corner, tied up, loaded and trimmed for balance. After further familiarisation the voyage could at last get under way.

That decision made, the two men felt able to accept some of the abundant hospitality showered on them by the friendly Virginians. In their host's Chevrolet they set off for Richmond and Williamsburg, the old town restored by the Rockefeller family to look exactly as it had done in colonial days. A carful of girls made them overlook the 65 m.p.h. speed limit, overtaking and waving, then being overtaken in turn, until in a tempest of speed they shot ahead and away zooming to ninety and straight into a police trap. A large black Ford leapt after them with lights flashing and siren hooting to gesture them into the side of the road. Their host left the car looking a little pale and, unable to produce his driving licence, was obliged to follow the police car to nearby Beeksville, under arrest. Fortunately the law permitted him to bail himself out for sixty-two dollars, amassed after a whip round, and the journey was resumed through superb wooded country, with delightful clapboard houses set off by the new spring green. Richmond disappointed them, but the Governor's palace and the old colonial White House at Williamsburg provided adequate compensation.

Despite the wave of intensive shopping for further domestic requirements, Johnstone felt a returning irritability at the obvious loss of momentum which had resulted from the changed course their plans had taken. He felt that had they adhered to their *American Veteran* arrangements they would have been able to keep up the speed of their previous efforts and done some intensive navigation studies on the way over. They would have arrived at Cape Cod, have put *Puffin* in the water and by now actually be on their way. As it was, they had hit the easy life on *United States* and were now hanging around awaiting the missing crates. He began to feel as though the whole adventure was slipping between his fingers, that Hoare and he were both losing the attitude of mind which had made it possible : certainly he himself was : and how precious a thing was that frame of mind called morale which is built up over a period and by no means painlessly. But his spirits quickly rose when he rationalised over the extent of their past efforts, and its physical manifestation in the shape of the boat itself, complete with its massive inventory of equipment and adjuncts. After all, it was now only a matter of clearing up a few details.

The crates arrived from New York, and preparatory to launching *Puffin* the two men spent Wednesday 11th May working on the fairleads, the tonneau cover and the dodger which would give them some small protection from the Atlantic waves. That night Andrew telephoned from London to announce that Ridgway had not yet left, but that *English Rose III* would leave on Friday the 13th, Ridgway and Blyth following by air two days later. On Thursday morning *Puffin* was slung ashore from *American Charger,* fork-lifted from the pier down on to the quay, where they strapped her round with warps before she was lowered into the water before a dozen newspaper cameras, to float once again like a ping-pong ball. The same day came the bad news that their request for the loan of a radio transmitter had finally been turned down. While their radio equipment included a suitable receiver, they were still without the ability to send even an SOS, unless by rocket or torch to a vessel within sight.

They encountered absurd difficulty in filling their water bags, the pierhead supplies being suitable only for large vessels with large tanks, and ended up in the kitchen of their hotel, the Monticello, boiling seven gallons at a time in massive receptacles which were trolleyed to the service lift and hoisted to their room to be tipped into the bath to cool, fourteen gallons in all. By the time the water had been transferred to the plastic bags the men were exhausted and decided to fill the rest of the bags with ordinary tap water, placed the lot in a laundry basket, and wheeled them to the waiting cars, then down to the boat where they were stowed aboard. The food when unpacked out of its crates would lodge in the net lockers slung under cover round the sides of the cabin and in the forepeak: constructed out of fishnet threaded by nylon cords and fastened to the boat's sides. Efforts to obtain adaptors which would enable the rubber dinghy to be inflated by compressed air bottles were unavailing, and they were faced with the contingency of having to rely on a foot pump should an emergency demand the use of their escape equipment. The adaptors were obtainable, but had to come from Pennsylvania and nobody knew how long that would take.

They made elaborate and new arrangements for their start. Directly they had finished loading, *Puffin* would be towed out to Lynnhaven, a three-hour tow, where they would moor and wait for favourable weather, for that purpose keeping in constant contact with the Coast Guards from whom Taylor was, on their behalf, obtaining unstinted help. The first morning that brought a favourable weather report they would be towed round to Virginia Beach between seven-thirty and nine o'clock, anchor out there, then return ashore in the towboat for breakfast, back out to *Puffin* by motor boat, then off and away. They knew that their initial rowing would be in the company of television boats and one from the Coast Guards.

Saturday, 14th May, was designated for filming, but the pouring rain and a weather report of unsettled conditions for the succeeding four days drove them to the relief of the available female society of Portsmouth and Norfolk, with visits to houses, clubs and bars where they sought temporary distraction from their labours. They accepted the offer of a vintage Gibson transmitter, an archaic radio device which in case of emergency could be persuaded to emit a distress signal provided a balloon-hoisted aerial were first deployed.

Johnstone was becoming increasingly agitated at the way in which time seemed to be slipping away. He had hoped that they would leave as soon as the crates from New York had been sorted and their contents stowed, yet somehow the days were flitting past and he felt himself surrounded by an attitude of social jollification, the blame for which he laid at the door of his various American sponsors. There were so many people they were required to meet, so much time to be given to publicity outlets, so many parties at which their attendance was desirable. He was perhaps too close to the situation to be able to recognise the extent to which the initiative had passed out of his hands the moment he entered into the financial arrangements necessary to enable the initial vision to become a practical reality.

It was however his function as leader of the expedition and skipper of *Puffin* to maintain whatever degree of control might be necessary to enable its precise functioning, however much the idea was tending to become master of the man. Perhaps, having stolen a sizable head march on Ridgway, he was influenced by circumstances he would otherwise have been able and anxious to control, but it was almost as if he had become seized by a lethargy of diversion penetrated only from time to time by the real pressure of events. Every sailor is familiar with that lethargy when in harbour and knows that a departure time and date must be set and firmly adhered to, come hell or high water, and the natural reluctance to wave farewell to cosseted living overcome with an iron will. It is well said that harbours rot ships and men.

Sunday, 15th May, the mountains of equipment trailed from their storage shed to the quay were lifted out of their crates and containers, shrinking rapidly to manageable proportions. Clothing and other bulky items were segregated from the small and expensive items of equipment there on the quay. The net racks on each side of the boat between the thwarts were ripped out and a plywood barrier provided, behind which those stored items which were impervious to the weather would be prevented from falling out into the oarsmen's leg hole. Thereby they departed from an essential factor of *Puffin*'s design, the placing of weight as high up as possible to increase her sea-kindliness. Shock cord was fixed to the cabin roof to provide a dry lodgment for the crew's clothing, accessible yet out of the way. Warren Henderson, representative of one of the American sponsoring agencies, provided a pair of sea-anchors, canvas drogues to hold their boat steady in storm conditions. As they toiled, the camera crews whirred spiritedly at the men passing the kit down into the boat, then storing it, until finally with a movie camera mounted on the stern the two rowed up and down while an interviewer fired the by now familiar questions at them. By Wednesday, 18th May, the Gibson transmitter had been checked by the Coast Guards and pronounced satisfactory but it was now a week later than their estimated departure date and still they were not ready.

Ridgway is hard on our heels, noted Johnstone after a further telephone call from England to confirm that the paratroopers would be leaving there on Saturday, 21st May. Rattled, he rebuked Taylor for his newspaper's failure to notify him that the other team was getting so close to taking off, and even found himself hoping they would encounter the same difficulties in getting started as the *Puffin* crew had already experienced. The trigger mechanism of their departure from the Norfolk quay proved to be the distracting chatter of the dock workers sitting on the rail above *Puffin*, calling down and chucking empty cans into the water all around them.

Their towboat, *Richie*, attached a rope, and at what seemed like eight or nine knots tore them across the bay to Lynnhaven in four and a half hours. *Puffin* was reluctant to respond to the tow, her tiny trimming rudder refusing to hold them on course as the water foamed up level with the foredeck and creamed over on to the crew, distinctly unhappy despite the application of successive layers of warm dry clothing. They became wetter and wetter as *Puffin* half filled with water because of the speed of the tow, the sea pouring in through the open cabin hatch. The last three-quarters of an hour were accomplished in complete darkness, with only *Richie*'s small rear lights to indicate their course, but when eventually they pulled up at Long Creek Marina there was a crowd of friends at the quayside to greet them, all anxious to help them tie up, and plying them with sandwiches and drinks. Johnstone's faith in *Puffin*'s seaworthiness was reaffirmed and his confidence was high.

> *It seems as though she is the sort of boat which will never turn over and never let us down.*

He was perhaps clutching at straws of comfort, for *Puffin* had still had no sea trials whatever. Worse, the two men had still not rowed her apart from the cloistered outing on the Medina just after the launching. Everything had been done in a mad rush in his determination to frustrate Ridgway's challenge. Most seriously, none of the external buoyancy bags, important to her self-rightability, had been fitted.

Next day a final telephone call from England confirming that Ridgway would be leaving there the following day, Saturday, 21st May, led to Johnstone openly assailing Taylor for faulty intelligence. Probably he was reproaching himself for having slackened his efforts: possibly the real explanation lay in his overlooking the seductive effect of harbours on sailing men. Certainly he was momentarily losing sight of the prodigious help he had been receiving from Taylor over the past months, acting voluntarily as the expedition's manager.

In scorching heat they sweated bathfuls of their personal equipment down to *Puffin*, observed by great crowds of onlookers. As they made their final preparations, they were helped by strangers who ran errands, carried the oars down to them, brought a bunch of red roses. As they walked to the store to slake their thirst, people waved to them from passing cars. In the store their beer was purchased by total strangers who insisted on pumping their arms, and the storekeeper gave them sunhats. Poses for photographs, autograph books to sign: they were as popular to the crowd as any gladiators, and as curiously mysterious. Publicity-wise, this was the right image. Johnstone's normally unresponsive mien served him in good stead. It would not do for his adulators to realise that he was worrying about how they could escape from *Puffin* should she founder: that his mind was agitated by the problem of survival in an emergency sufficiently long to be able to pump up the rubber dinghy for which he had been unable to obtain any other inflation device than the original foot pump: suitable at a quayside but hardly appropriate in the middle of an ocean. A strange worry, for what useful purpose would a nine-foot rubber dinghy serve in the Atlantic wastes to men whose bodies, already immersed in the sea, would be chilled down to a temperature at which survival was unlikely for more than an hour or two, even at midsummer?

On Saturday, 21st May, one day after new moon and with an outgoing current of double usual strength, *Puffin* cast off for England.

In fact Ridgway had arrived with Blyth at Boston on 18th May, three days before her departure, and *English Rose III*, their twenty-foot dory, had already been offloaded. Sixteen days later, and twelve days after *Puffin*'s departure, aware of her position at that date and publicly confident that they would catch her, the paratroopers left Cape Cod, 500 miles north of Virginia Beach, and nearer to England by about the same distance. That was the point from which Johnstone had originally planned to depart, forsaken on uncorroborated local advice about ocean currents and in an effort to fox Ridgway. He did not know that the latter was fully aware of the departure switch or that, on his own admission, he would have followed Johnstone to Norfolk but for shortage of funds. The race was on.

PART TWO

Johnstone's Journal

I

Departure, 21st May 1966 [1]
05.45 rise and out to Long Creek Marina. Remembered list of last minute items, films for still, radio, length of wire my goodies—John bought his the previous day in Bagshore Stores. Ray Richardson was waiting with *Richie* and crew waiting to fish. Small crowd watched departure. Two hour tow to Virginia Beach accompanied by various vessels, viz the *Wtar II*, radio station boat. Ashore in rowing boat towed by sloop motor-boat. Mayor of Virginia Beach gave us a parcel each at stand of Union Jacks and Stars and Stripes. Autographs. Sharing Clark bars, Anne and Jean Monte, Mike Lawless, Bob Taylor, Warren Henderson, Ed Watson, Mary. Breakfast—too nervous to eat. Up for interviews with radio and press, out to Beach again where Mayor of Norfolk gave inscribed book of Norfolk gifts to Mayors of towns we land at, and lucky charm for *Puffin*, all in front of a dozen cameras. Kids with 'God Speed *Puffin*'. Members of British community said they were all there (12) to wish us well.

At last off, sharing and handing out Clark bars, kissing girls, shaking strangers' hands, through the surf with cameraman in bows, tow by sloop to *Puffin*.

Cast off 11.11 a.m. (15.11 G.M.T.). Nearby motor vessels hooted. John took first spell of an hour, making super progress, and soon Virginia Beach out of sight, with only occasional sightseeing boat anywhere near. By mid-afternoon alone on E. course. Albatross of Coast Guards flew over with cameraman, also light plane. Short, choppy sea made us both feel not too good. Started sleeping immediately on 'off' periods being sick simultaneously, late afternoon. Suddenly very depressing the thought of the trip—wished we could be rammed, unable to go on, anything. The night awful, difficult to row because of chop. Lights off Virginia Beach still in view. Tired, sick, unfed, drifted on N. setting tide and S. wind. *Puffin* in terrible mess. Everything thrown in cabin at last minute. I was apprehensive about emergency catching us unawares, doubtless all due to nervy tummy about ceremonies etc.

Sunday, 22nd May [2]

By now I felt so low I thought I had a touch of heat stroke like in Melbourne in '53. Just stared, no appetite, no strength. Not like sea sickness. The stove was difficult to get going this morning—John spent 3 hours on it, while I listened to cussing and blinding half asleep in the slot. Finally he said, 'Now I've got you, you bastard', and we had tea and ham and eggs from the dehydrated pack. Ham and eggs awful, as they were the next morning when I cooked them. Tea weak. However, we soon learned, but I was very worried about the stove, and the whole expedition seemed to fall about my ears.

On the trip to Virginia Beach tried out Harrier—not working. Today changed batteries, still not working, so must take it to bits. It must have got banged in transit. This is a big disappointment from our morale point of view. It is so important to see a result from one's work. Masthead light not working either. Discovered this the night before we left. Got kicked or knocked in transit I expect. And now stove giving trouble. It really looked to me then as if—1. Cold food all the way chewing Archie's curry bars! 2. Row back and get gaz. 3. Ask Coast Guard to drop us gaz. But I was overall depressed too, with sickness, whatever it was, and the other two items not working. This evening John got the stove going again at first try, and we had curry and rice—tasty but I couldn't finish mine. I also felt I began to smell horrid and determined to wash tomorrow morning properly.

As dusk fell 22.5.66 we saw flashing light we recognised from previous night. For the last half of the day we had had N. by N.E. sometimes quite strong with a little rain. Light turned out to be Chesapeake Light at entrance to the dreaded Bay—and on an ingoing tide. John was rowing and when I had slept he said, 'That light—I can't tell whether it's nearer or not'. One look told me it was nearer, bearing WNW. Still we were being taken in on tide. My stint came and I had to try and row away from it. But no luck, and soon it was about obvious no amount of rowing would keep us off it. It got to ¼ mile away, flashing so brilliantly I couldn't keep my eyes open. Then tide turned, and it swilled us back to sea again.

23rd May [3]
By the end of John's row early in the morning, the light had disappeared altogether. There was fog about and lots of fog horns. One small tanker brayed about 200 yards away as she slid silently past. All morning there were naval ships from Norfolk direction. Two subs came past blowing fog horns, and the *Requin* altered course as she heard me blow ours in reply. Her Captain shouted down from the conning tower our position. Five miles away from that wretched light only.

I noticed in the distance what looked like a huge ship aiming straight at us. Two cruisers and a battle ship motored out to sea after the subs, and still this huge ship remained. In fact it got closer and closer then further again, then closer, and by the time dark fell it started to flash. It was the Chesapeake Light seen in daylight.

We were horrified and dis-spirited, and furious with the forecasters. All day the wind had been east. We wondered how anyone could have made such a huge mistake. Bob could have erred too. I would certainly never have considered leaving if I'd known that adverse weather. 'It's bloody rotten whoever sent us off, that's what I think,' said John. 'I hope they can lie in bed straight.' And so we both lazily rejected rowing in the face of this absurd situation.

I took my spell at the oars, drifted almost to the light. John rowed part of his not to much avail.

Tuesday 24th May [4]

By a.m. it was cold and miserable, both tired and hungry. By mistake had opened same food packet as yesterday, so ham and eggs again. (This is 23.5.66 still). In evening we cooked two fresh eggs and tinned ham with lumpy Horlicks and coffee.

The Chesapeake Light. Dispirited, dismayed, dejected, disgusted, and just drifting. We breakfasted off dried ham and eggs again, with tea, and drifted on. A motor boat stopped and gave us the wavelength of *Wtar* and the forecast and the time of high tide. Wind in the east still, cold, a bit of a sea. We decided to drift to Warren's sea anchor. To try again to go out later? To ask for tow to Gulf Stream? To tie up at Chesapeake Light? or back in Bay until five day forecast O.K.? Still drifting and sleeping in turns; late afternoon a ship aimed for us. We flashed light and it turned off, then back on again. I started a mad scramble for the white Mars flares stacked under the oars, fumbling and pulling at things to get to the flares.

'Not run down now for Christ's sake—that would be too bloody stupid,' I said to John. By the time we had the flares the Greek ship was upon us, going 100 yards across our bow. Two officers staring down from bridge. A cruiser came and had a look, and when we took turns to row against 20 mph wind and ingoing tide a rubber necking aircraft drove John barmy. Too strong wind to row in, always blowing us shorewards.

By late evening racing into Cape Henry with both sea anchors out and doing the one dangerous yachtsman's trick, of drifting on to a lee shore. Kept careful watch, and at one time mistook an unmarked buoy for the charted buoy, thereby placing ourselves on the Cape itself. In spite of predicament, a sort of contentedness reigned in the face of a real danger. Eventually all the various lights came to a standstill and there was no sight of Cape Henry or beaches about to be run into, so both crashed our swedes till daylight. Archie's curry was good, double portions. David cooking.

Wednesday, 25th May [5]

Awoke to calm swell, ensign limp, hazy and pleasant. John asleep in cockpit, me in cabin. Today radio reported us as having been again on U.S. shore to give up. Breakfasted on porridge, tea and a little pot of jam, then we decided: 'Let's row a bit North of East until tide turns to fill at about 6, then row North while there's no wind and get away from the dreaded light.' I took first stint, and after half an hour was pulling on my cape leather windproofs and stripping to the waist. Having a glance round saw a lump on horizon. Out with the binoc's but even without could confirm it was the Chesapeake Light bearing 172 or so S. and at least 12 miles away. Jubilation. We gladly took our stints and rowed hard towards a moaning old cow of a whistling buoy way out, and to the ENE. As I approached it on N4SE on my watch I saw a little ship behind it. Gradually she became a U.S. Coast Guard vessel. She stopped next to us with the whole crew lining the deck. John came up out of our cabin. All I could think of to say was 'Could you tell Donald Moore of the *Ledger Post* where we are, as he has been looking for us on the radio'. (Which he had. John picked him up talking to Chesapeake Light earlier this a.m.)

We rowed off a bit embarrassed at the crowd, but they came after us. 'Anything you want?' There were lots of things but all that came to mind was a spare consol chart of Hatteras to Sable, as ours got wet last night in the entrance to the bay. They lowered a line which I caught and pulled us in and they kindly passed down a spare chart. John asked, 'How far is the Gulf Stream?' '30 miles about.' That meant we could be there in 15 hours or so and really on our way. The Coast Guards motored off slowly and I went up to the whistler buoy to check for drift. Perhaps something slight to the South but nothing much.

We set off again N75E and within minutes had pouring rain. Heard Coast Guards were searching but finished at midnight.

Even after four or five days we are still not used to the food. Not eating everything though we should for proper health. Tonight I will eat my stew on biscuits, as biscuits are important but not eatable alone. The submarine pinging noise is something worth mentioning. When we were nearer to Norfolk there was this strange high pitched 'sonic' type of noise like a little song by a bird.

'It's the asdic or radar morse from a submarine; you listen; it's quite regular.'

I timed a few songs—all the same—and they didn't come at regular intervals. I said, 'It's a bird somewhere, one of those little martens or terns that are always swooping about.' 'No, it's too metallic for a bird.' I quoted a few birds from imagination. 'What about the anvil bird, the striped Brass band bird from N.Z., the . . .' But he wasn't convinced. Neither was I when a destroyer came past singing a similar song. Later another little song was played when nothing was around us.

'It must be a submarine bird,' I said.

We rowed hard in spells until ten into an easterly that increased in strength every minute. Finally I was spending more time keeping course than going forward so hung out both little sea anchors and tucked myself under the tonneau with half a bottle of cognac. Two hours later John came on, the wind rose, the waves steepened and we had a bit of a howler round our ears. John had nearly slipped overboard with his lifeline *off* at the change over. Now I worried whether he was going to be swept clean overboard by a sea. Every now and then *Puffin* went $\frac{3}{4}$ of the way on to her side but always came back up dry. In fact the only water shipped was stair rod rainwater by the gallon, and about half a pint of sea which came through a cabin ventilator and into my ear. I had got very wet since the tonneau seams didn't keep out water.

Thursday 26th May [6]
At six John woke me, I dressed for my stint, and drifted innocently SE without anchors. After an hour the Whistler was there ESE of us about ¼ mile away, Cape Henry and the Chesapeake Light visible. Back where we were. So an E course was chosen and for a while we actually had a W wind. Very light. Lots of sun and dried all our clothes from last night.

We were on 2 broadcasts today. N.Y. Times station mentioned us, and WTAR said today was good day for our attempt at final escape, on 3.30 news. Tide and wind fair for us. But WTAR then spoke of N.E.lys which not so good. Spotted by Navy fighters buzzing and waving fast and slow. Buoyed up by the weather and the fact that the horrible Chesapeake Light was already bearing W of South by about 4 p.m. was encouraging. It started at about N170E and by 19.30 we had rowed the bastard round to S225W. The pooper moaned incredibly distantly. We rowed 2 on, 2 off with a break of ten at the 55 minutes.

For the whole voyage so far, no routine established, weather is a factor. Can't row in certain seas because of difficulty either keeping oars in water or keeping boat on course. Odd how she lies beam on to the sea at sea anchor. But now I understand remarks of Colin's about making no concessions to our inexperience in the designing of *Puffin*. She is exceptionally tender but safe as houses.

For tonight 26.5.66 we ate our F.M.C. rations to avoid 1½ hours of cooking. By 7.30 there was a light SSE brightening and we were worried for its eventual strength and direction.

Thursday evening, and the wind did not materialise against us. We rowed in two or three hour spells all night, shortening the changeover, stopping for ten every spell. Gradually the Chesapeake Light went well down in daylight, and at dark there was the 5 sec. light on Cape Charles. Gradually the pair went down and away until both could be sighted only by their looms on the low cloud. Fishing boats seen. Both very tired and sleeping like instant logs the moment we get our swedes crashed.

Friday, 27th May [7]
Early a.m. No sign of anything. Fog down to 200 yards. I hooted several times, made Horlicks and woke John up. John : 'What annoys me is our lack of concern for it. Here we are hundreds of miles from the nearest other bloke, and we don't seem to mind at all.'

'I suppose it's because we've been thinking about it for ages.'

'It's one of those things which are O.K. when you do them but seem simply frightful when you think about them in front of the fire at home.'

Clothes. Our 'oranges' were completely waterproof. We both remembered there being a fly on the ones we saw at Pat Mullay's, yet none on ours.

David : 'I expect old Harry stitched up the flies out of spite when you brought the suits back for the sleeves to be gussetted.'

Then our blue showerproofs which we didn't like because they condensed moisture on their insides. Our batman suits, white and blue. My Virginia Beach jersey. Our longjohns. Our thick woolly jerseys. And of course the inevitable had crossed and re-crossed our minds, as it had the minds of everyone connected with the expedition. 'Surely you're going to take a sail with you?'

Now we asked jokingly, 'When does the joiner and rigger arrive for work?'

'What work?'

'Well, getting that square-rigged sail made up out of our bit of canvas which we said we brought for putting over holes which flotsam railway sleepers are going to make in the bows?'

'The joiner and rigger is on holiday till August he told me, but he'll work for a few hours before then if necessary.'

'You mean if Ridgway's beating us?'

Friday still. We succumbed to the temptation of hot

food, and got out meat bars, peas, potato and Oxo cubes. Pulled up the dodger, put out the sea anchors. It was drizzling with rain, the rowing had been across seas all day with a fair to strong S. wind (said to be coming round SW.) At last we were really away from land, and since there were no landmarks, I decided to get a consol fix on Nantucket with the B & G. After finding the chart I hung out the aerial and the earth, tuned to 194 and got immediate results. The count was clear and I got it first time. Just as I'd finished John announced that the little blue earth plug and line were in the water. I yelled to scoop the water with an oar and pick them up but too late. The first count gave me 45 and 15. Looking it up on the consol chart at first didn't register. 'It can't be *that* 45 because it's too close to land and the other's too far away,' I thought. But a DF check proved it was the close one, only 20 or so miles from the coast after all that rowing, and the Gulf Stream as far away as ever.

Although it was calm, still an E or ESE wind, I had no heart for rowing after such news :—we were now both talking to ourselves, and I have heard dogs barking and lots of women talking! Also exotic dreams of driving flash birds about in Alfa's and Rolls's.

Saturday, 28th May [8]

We have pulled out our fingers on the rowing again since very early morning. I confirmed the consol position was a little moved E after the effort, which was some reward. The whole morning passed without seeing or hearing any other man-made object, and in fact all we saw all day was a jetsam packing case which we approached with caution.

I woke up early today with the feeling that we were unprepared for an emergency. The useful old forepeak had become a junk shop of dirty pants, punctured buoyancy bags, used but unstowed sea anchors, old packets of oats, rancid butter, and a number of other things given up as lost. But worst of all was the fact that it was not, as designed, a proper buoyancy chamber. Colin's advice not to pack the space with expanded polystyrene had the inevitable result—the junk shop—and I was surprised at Colin for saying, 'You'll find it useful for all sorts of odds and ends.' Ded rite mate!

The sharp copper tips Ayling had put on the oars pierced the 100 lbs. bow bag in 5 places, and I found it a shrivelled shape. Patched it up with the repair kit then started a big clear out lasting 6 hours. Chopped up two pairs of oars—the 8's and 8′ 6s and sent them over the side. The lavatory seat made out of Warren's old lifejacket. More old rowlocks, a canvas zipbag. One of our two spoons (accidentally dropped). We seem to be using so little water, about six gallons altogether since we departed, that we decided to pour some over the side; ten gallons. But I think it is a safe move since consumption at present rate gives us enough for 135 days, by which time food and the weather are long since gone. A final change today was to substitute the 9 foots for the 9′ 6s we started with: they are superbly balanced, light as a feather and just as fast. Got the wrong pair and had to change buttons. Also changed port rowlock which had never seemed quite the same, for no reason we could discern.

Another odd dream this afternoon, Chinese and Indians at some ceremony; very clear and lifelike, talking sense, some erotica, then I was woken, slept again and found myself interviewing ICI directors as a journalist.

As eve wore on, water calmer and smoother, like the Berkshire downs rolling quickly past underneath, lifting us smoothly to the tops and lowering us smoothly again. The moon was up over the starboard quarter, I was steering by it, and its path wriggled across the huge swell, scattering occasionally with the lightest gust.

As John turned in and my spell started, I heard engines. They took 1½ hours to arrive. I flashed the torch, and a tug, the *American Tide*, drew up 150 yards off, lopping gently in the swell. She turned a huge light on to us, blinding us.

'Do you need assistance?' someone shouted.

'No thanks, but can you give us our position.'

'Come alongside.'

(23.30) The bridge gave our position as 37° 19N and 74° 58W.

'You are about 40 miles ENE of the Chesapeake Light. Where are you from?'

'Norfolk. Virginia Beach.'

'Where are the sails?'

'We don't have any, we're rowing.'

'Where are you bound for?'

'England.'

'Rowing? Oh God. Have you got enough water?'

'Water?'

'You want water! We can let you have some.'

'We've got enough to go there and back on.'

'Food?'

'Plenty, thanks.'

'Well, good luck, and I hope the weather holds.'

Then in the fog, the rumbling of engines. Closer and closer, finally one white light, then the green, me blowing the fog horn, flashing, getting out a white Mars all at the same time. She missed us by 150 yards.

Sunday, 29th May [9]

And as I handed back to John at 02.00 we heard huge fish jumping and slapping back into the water all around us; eerie in the otherwise complete silence. Not a sound or noise from anywhere. Just my penknife rocking back and forth.

We rowed on smoothly, making good time until 09.45 when the smoothness and silence disappeared. Wind about 10 mph from the south crumpled the Berkshire downs, making rowing heavier and introducing an unpleasant movement. But by then we had had porridge and coffee; I spent much of my stint thinking of ways of cooking oysters and steak together. With a light oyster sauce in carpet bag style, on a stick together in hot pan of oil at the table, then masked with rich oyster sauce etc. Tried out big sea anchor.

Like being tied to the quay. John had his first pony. I felt utterly tired in spite of having done nothing all day.

At night incredibly smooth again, not a ripple, like the village pond, with a cupola of impenetrable fog over us of complete sameness, no moon or other guiding feature so that while the surface was ideal, with no wind we were unable to row because we couldn't see the compass. The little blue masthead lantern contrives to throw only a sideways light and not strong enough to be reflected downwards by a panlid. So we just sat.

Monday, 30th May [10]

John's watch from 1–4, but at 2.30 he came in—too rough, and he had the sea anchor out, wind against us from the NE.

Today for the first time with the nine foot oars I really noticed the power of the wind. Yesterday, one minute I was rowing well, say 2¼ kts., the next a gust from ahead made pulling trebly hard. It felt as if we still had a forgotten stern line to the pier. Monday, we cleared out the second berth and both got our heads down at the same time. Very cramped but at least there was no need for a useless 'deck' watch all day for one while the other slept. I started the Mayor's *History of Norfolk* and ate 5 Clark bars to keep going. In the evening cooked curry in the most extreme pitching and rolling. We shipped a couple of seas and one caught the radio, which now grumbles all the time, 'on' or 'off'. The Homer and Heron continue to perform, giving a signal coming down to 20 dashes late tonight from 45: I took the Harrier to bits again and it seems as if the mileage might work, but when connected up it didn't.

Tuesday, 31st May [11]

When we awoke in the morning the sea had abated, so we had the big anchor in and started to row. But with the wind about 5 degrees W of N it was best to go S with it. So I set a course of E170S and we really blew along; John fishing and getting the line tangled in the rudder gear. Two trawlers, the *Benny Lou* and *Aultry Ann*, came past, the former giving our position as 42m ESE of Cape Henry. So we are back at the old joke of last week. 'Johnstone & Hoare's tours of Chesapeake Bay, entrance £6,000, and row yourself.'

We are in fact at the mercy of the wind the whole time. Today's decision to row E170S is to get the maximum eastings out of a wind that by lunchtime was already a point to the E of N True.

As John said, 'Supposing there's a S wind tomorrow, are we going to row NNE?' and the answer must be 'Yes'. But I'd like to have that navigator bloke here to answer for the wind, in view of the fact that it was his suggestion to come to Norfolk.

The wind even from a few degrees N of NE, got under one corner of the dodger on a 160° course, and with oars we flew. But eventually the wind was so strong it was difficult to maintain course. All one's energy went into hanging on to 100°. So we rigged up the steering oar rowlock and from there on for seven hours did about 3 kts., even after dark, flying up the moonpath.

Life on board is settling down, but there are the various irritations of routine which are boring us both. Now that we can both sleep simultaneously, the second berth has sometimes to be cleared out, all the stuff going into the second rowing position, and being wrapped under the remains of Warren Henderson's Gentex covers—tiresome to do. Then the sea anchor got so tedious that we are going back to using Warren's two little ones. The big one is a man-hour in being retrieved and coiled and folded and stowed, and still goes out in a muddle next time. Food : we can still not seem to get a meal in less than an hour including washing-up time, and it's very boring getting it. I think probably the best time for me is rowing, two hours with my ten minutes break at 55 to 65 minutes, and sometimes three hours.

Being on the steering oar was an experience today. Sitting on the open hatch roof, pulling to bring her S of E, pushing when she went past S to SSW, sometimes high in the air with a terrific wave folding and sloping under the boat, sometimes with foam almost round one's backside as a following wave ruffled at the crest.

Wednesday, 1st June [12]
We saw ships on their Cape Hatteras to New York course, and one, the Seatram Co. vessel, asked, 'Are you alright?' We: 'Yes, thank you,' and on they went without slowing down. A huge school of porpoises cavorted round us, swooping underneath on their sides in pairs and staring up at the oars and the boat's bottom, folding their blow holes neatly out of the water in pairs. Brilliant sun all day. Not a breath of wind. We rowed two on, two off, due SE, and I reckon on consol we have 50 miles to go to Gulf Stream axis.

'What a ramshackle affair we are,' said John when I remarked, 'Let's see, my watch was 2½ seconds slow on Friday, what day is it today?' and then he said, 'You can put the batteries back in the radio, it should be dried out now then we can tune in to that Canada time station. You'll find the place to tune into on the back of the Mayor's book.' Taking our first approximate longitude sighting by sunset today. It came out at 74°, very approximate, but useful in mid-Atlantic.

Thursday, 2nd June [13]
At midnight a USCG vessel found us and said we were 40m off Oregon Inlet in North Carolina. Still smooth and calm, moonlit and windless, 3 hrs. on, 3 hrs. off at night. I awoke with bronchitis—and the rowing had become a nightmare.

This morning I was making porridge and tea before waking John, saw a sub in distance making a heavy diesel noise, going NW. It saw us from 5 or 6 miles away and specially came over. US Sub *Cutlass* E478 gave our position as 36° 06N and 74° 36W, which I have now transferred to the chart. All day hot and windless, and now 35 to go by above position. By 4 p.m. was down to 25m and we were taking water temp. This a.m. 59°, yesterday 52°, 53°, 70°. And lots of weeds and muck floating in the water. The oars floated off while John was rowing.

'Hey Dave, one oar's gone. Two.'

The oars slipped out of their rowlocks somehow. The port oar lay near the boat, hard alongside, the other immediately set off towards Cape Cod/New York.

I yelled to John, 'Get that one quick and pass it here.' I was standing in the hatch. He passed it, and I just managed to hook the last inch of blade over the button, and drag it back. Having just cut up 2 sets and despatched them to destinations unknown, we didn't want to lose one of our 3 remaining sets especially the nine foots.

I elaborated on my recipe for turkeys' 'parsons noses'. Just four big ones done like Open Country did them in a hotel room for two.

The dainty dancer birds are around all day and night, and have started to get familiar with us. Dropping their legs to gauge where the sea is, pecking weed etc., and our biscuit and ham. In evening the dodger up again and a little wind caught by it.

Friday, 3rd June [14]

When we had breakfasted it was obviously too rough to row, i.e. our course was across the valleys, short and steep, and not with them. But we began to feel we were near the axis of the Gulf Stream. Temperatures of the water in 76°–78° range all the time. Deep blue and clear; a different sort of weed. Wind N to NNE, meant we couldn't row upstream; so sat in the sun. I re-arranged forepeak, blew up some water bags; and found our consumption to be 1¼ gallons per day all told. So we have enough for over 80 days (including the tablets) barring mishaps. The squeaker doesn't seem to be working right, unless we are drifting at a fantastic rate. I make us out to be on the 25 line of dashes. Impossible, unless we have drifted 70 miles in 30 hours!

Either that or we rowed 60, and passed through the Gulf Stream axis altogether.

An odd situation has now arisen with regard to our position. The wind has been NE–NNE. We have rowed hard to the SE True. If the sub's position yesterday is the accurate last known position then we should have crossed the Gulf Stream axis tomorrow a.m. But all day I have been taking consol lines from Nantucket, allied to RDF bearings on Nantucket. First we got a reading of 35 dots agreeing with the sub at that time. Today however, suddenly 47 dashes, meaning either that we have hit the Gulf Stream and have been carried NE or the S wind has blown us down off Cape Hatteras. The former is the likely theory. I checked DF, we are not in the wrong sector. 2½ hours later we were on 39 dashes, and I was so flabbergasted I forgot to take a noon meridian altitude of the sun. We will have to wait until tomorrow. Every few hours I take readings and we are certainly moving at a fantastic rate.

John went swimming, and 2 hours later he was fishing and his bait was torn off twice together with hook. It was a baby shark. Later there were 2. He was looking over the side as we drifted, saying how lovely and clear and blue the sea was.

Suddenly he said, 'Hey, what's that about 30 ft. down there, Dave?'

I went to inspect it and it looked just like he said—a huge piece of excreta. Later he was asleep and we drifted along, I noticed this thing was still there, 30 ft. down in the gloom with the sun shining through to it. How could it still be there, keeping such accurate station, when we were being blown across the surface? Suddenly the answer dawned on me. I went to the stern decking. The fishing line was hanging over the port quarter, something was tugging at it under the sea. I pulled it in. It was John's jeans; drying on hatch cover, had fallen in, collecting hook and sinker on the way.

In the evening I took a fairly accurate sunset time and got 72° 54W.

Saturday, 4th June [15]
Late last night got the Harrier going on miles only. But most inaccurate. We rowed like hell all night with following wind and only did 13m. This a.m. the incredible positions go on; we're 230m from Cape Henry and have averaged 90m a day since the submarine! (4 days ago the ham. Marvellous to chew again. But the gristle wouldn't float for the delicate dancers to pick at).

We got out chart and took noon sighting of the sun. This time we tried at 12.00EST. I worked it all out, and was about to put down 73° and odd minutes when John said, 'I make it 74°.'

'How can you when it should be going down.' Then we remembered. We are 23° east of EST and should have got the reading at 11.40. Then further remembered eastern summer time, 12.40, and got the right altitude, just over 75°. (1440 GMT 4666, lat. 37° 06′ 9″ Nantucket N10°E 58 dashes).

Saw nothing, no ships, aircraft, but heard a plane very high. We tried a new night routine. One man does 2 on, one off, 2 on, then sleeps while other does same.

But there is a strange angle to this effort of rowing, which we both seem to notice. When things are very discouraging it is hard to find the energy—say when it is important to row against a wind in the first week of the voyage : and when we are swinging along—100 miles a day—why bother to add on one's puny 15 or 20 miles? We both hate rowing but not to a serious extent. It is bearable as the day's penance of boredom, but less inviting than doing nothing! The temptation is to do nothing because we are whipping along.

Sunday, 5th June [16]
First thing this a.m. the temp. was 74°. By 08.00 it was 72° by 10.00 it was 70° and by 11.30, 68°. I was on NE course though of course being taken EENE by the current. I turned due S across the sea and the wind to get back to the warmer water again. Several Portuguese men-o'-war and in

10 minutes we had regained 70°. But slow and heartbreaking rowing. As John says, why don't we leave ourselves to the current?

'It's being greedy trying to get those extra few miles when we're being taken along so well.'

In the evening I was rowing alone when a vast fin, brown and white, broke the surface off the stbd. quarter. I was pretty far away at the time and came to shouting, 'Hey John, a huge shark, quick.' It turned out to be a playful baby shark of brownish-green with big side fins tipped with white. John had the steering oar in near it very quickly, and it nudged it and swirled slowly round it on its side, scratching its tummy. Even after it had been given a sharp rap on the nose it came back for more, always approaching from port quarter. It left after we started rowing again.

John : 'I'd like to smack the axe clean between its eyes.' Later in the evening a really vast frightening scimitar fin knifed up at great speed from the direction of the sun, then raced off again without stopping. No more bathing now, but it is odd that no one has mentioned sharks to us.

(TIME CHECK. B.B.C. AND CANADIAN TIME SIGNAL 6 P.M. THIS EVENING SUN. 5 JUNE MY WATCH EXACTLY *10 SECONDS SLOW* OF EASTERN SUMMER TIME).

The radio has gradually recovered and we have had the first world news for 10 days. Refreshing. Gemini Nine and the space walk and the Canadian election. We almost had the prospect of going the rest of the voyage without news and not knowing the time. Yesterday we got half a time check—I was adjusting my watch when the set went on the blink.

We sighted a Constellation or DC7 miles up going NNW, but otherwise no sign of the existence of the rest of mankind but the radio. During the evening Consol proved we were still haring along, but today's reading may be the last for a while as an 'unreliable sector' comes up in tomorrow's run. During the night neither of us rowed, being worried about leaving the escalator. But a SSW wind blew us out at about 05.00 to a temperature of 62°. We were taking temps. every half hour. During John's spell earlier he rowed due True E. Which should have been all right. But gradually lost the temp. from 77° to 72°. My 62° was a big local emergency and I rowed cross seas into wind due SSE to find it again, and in 1½ hours found 68° and then 70° by 07.00 next day.

Monday, 6th June [17]

A Consol reading at 09.00 put us 107 miles ahead of yesterday's 12.45 reading. We then rowed SE True to re-establish course on escalator, as temp. only 69°. Burning sun.

At 10 o'clock I was half asleep and John was rowing. Suddenly he shouted, 'Hey Dave, there's a liner or an iceberg or something coming up. Pass the binoculars.' I used the sextant telescope but could make nothing of it. Gradually a cargo ship appeared on an almost due E course. It passed about ¼m S of us. John waved and it came round slowly, finally completing almost ¾ of a circle round us; someone shouted from the bridge and we shouted back for our position. All the time it was coming I got increasingly nervous. I said to John, 'When we stop you do the talking: I feel too nervy,' my hands were shaking. I suppose it was the idea of speaking to other people again. 'When we get back to U.K. I won't be able to speak to anyone for weeks for nerves. Ask him for our position first, then for some snouts, after that a few cans of grub.' I threw out my wallet with the dollars in it, 'We can pay for the stuff out of that.' I rowed like hell to catch up, having swapped places with John. He asked for the position and saw someone already taking a sight.

'Do you want anything?'

'Well, if you've got any cigarettes, and we'd be very glad of some cans of meat or something.'

We heard the steward being shouted for. We were only five yards off. She was deep in the water, and the whole crew lined the deck. *Orient City* Bideford on the stern. Funnel yellow red stripe, yellow star. The swell carried us up and down the side and we worried about hitting our mast tip against her plates. The Captain (Capt. Bayze?) shouted down 37 52N. I repeated it, then '66 40W' and I repeated that and thanked him. Someone from the after-deck called, 'Come alongside here.' An odd biscuit loaded with pork slice, corned beef and baked beans and 400 cigarettes. Then the Captain said would we like some beer. Soon they were throwing down bottles of beer like hand grenades.

'Course to the middle of the Gulf Stream? 85° True.'

'Magnetic variation 14°, not 16° yet.'

'Fine winds. S and SW. A very good forecast'—in answer to some of our questions. We pulled away slowly, waving and thanking them again.

'What a hell of a nice crowd of blokes,' said John. 'I expect we could lollop around here for years just collecting goodies from passing ships, don't you think?' While they were still near we opened beers, lit snouts, and shouted 'Cheers'. They waved and waved, taking course for Gib. and Karachi. Pork and beans for lunch with another beer, and a shade of disappointment as 66 40W put us back 30 miles or so. Still. And they had asked, 'Shall we report you?'

'Yes please.'

'We'll do that now.'

After the beer, a stupefied sleep, because we weren't used to it. I lay in the cabin, John weakly rigged a tent for himself out of one of the sleeping bags and the dodger. The little brass handle on the front of the compass box creaked annoyingly backwards and forwards with the swell near my head, but after a few moments I ceased to notice it.

Being a tender sailor *Puffin* is hell to do anything in in a lively seaway. I should say that in a second she can roll with a whipping motion from one side to the other and back, traversing as much as seventy degrees each way, in the process. This can make cooking the sort of scene the vicar shouldn't hear. Our stove has no gimbels, it lights fairly easily now. Put a pot on it to boil and it has actually to be held in a well gloved hand the whole time, with spoonfuls of curry being slopped out of it into one's lap and all over the stove from time to time. You can't eat one dish while another cooks because you can't hold both, so the one you've cooked gets cold. When you're holding *and* stirring you can't support yourself, and your waist becomes terribly tired of keeping you upright. The water for tea dowses the flame for the second time, and the third time it goes out, when the paraffin runs out. The home-made funnel and can-pouring effort starts another shouting match between the cook versus the weather, the boat, and all things else in sight. To be cook is unthinkable. Until recently on a placid evening we started preparations at 7.30. but now experience shows that 5 minutes later a dusk roll of exceptional severity started every evening, so dinner is being brought forward half an hour.

The delicate dancing birds have almost disappeared. A few still flit by, but not to stop and circle us as they used. There is still always a bird in sight somewhere, but it is usually a large fast-flying gull on a determined errand, swooping along the troughs with one sensitive wing tip stroking the side of a wave, occasionally sparing us the trouble of a detour but lazily just cruising swiftly past without a glance in our direction.

Tuesday, 7th June [18]

Last night, 6.6.66, there were mares' tails high to the NW, which reminded John of instructions to shipwrecked mariners he had read on the back of the waterproof lifeboat N. Atlantic chart. I read the instructions myself. (q.v.) The wind immediately came round to the SE, light in strength, black clouds gathered as instructed, and the rest of the whole ominous process seemed all set to follow.

But by late afternoon today there was nothing worse than a slow rolling swell, a blotchy mackerel cloud formation and no wind at all. The sun was intense and I had to wet my jeans with cupfuls of sea water to stop my thighs being burned. We each had our first really extensive bathing, using half a gallon each in the big porridge dixie. Boat festooned with washing, pants on the mast, towels and jerseys on dodger and oars. At local (ship's) noon it was too hot out, and breathless and heavy in the cabin. I took trouble over our reading of the Meridian Altitude— 75.15° corrected. It put us S of yesterday's position, in spite of having rowed N85°E True all night. An approx. longitude (time to arc) from the same sight gave us a disappointing 25½ hours run of only 45 miles all told, and we wonder if it is accurate. So we are rowing NE with no change from 72° temperature, in the hope of regaining the hot water escalator. No ships, no planes. We are in lovely blue water. Beer bottles can be seen going slowly down. We estimated 3 hours for one to sink in 2,500 fathoms.

John threw out some rancid butter, and 6 cheeping dancing birds found it within 2 minutes, heading upwind. So we sprinkled some rice pudding for them. Portuguese men-of-war frequently sighted now. John caught another in the bucket. 'They sting, don't they? What a grotty looking thing.' He stuck an oar blade through the next one that floated past. Blue tinged glass ornaments floating on the surface. When you throw them back their sails lie down but soon set again. We sat and contemplated the sea and the sky over a couple of beers in our respective plastic mugs.

'Funny little gurgles, yet you try and see where one's coming from.' John looked at the sea. We lobbed bottles over the side and smoked, me the Bensons and John the Lucky's. A little bit of a SW'ly built up. The sun shot smoky rays through tiers of cloud, heavy going at the bottom, cotton wool next, filaments of dark and light above through the holes, and the sky tinged with pale orange or cinnamon tablets. In the distance, toppling tufts with hot air pillars hung over the horizon. The standard picked itself up in the breeze and the gurglings spread around us. John : 'What'll we have for dinner? How about a nice bit of curry?' I oiled the Swiss Army penknife John gave me, put glassier cream on my nose and forehead and got out the stove, while John lay back in the cabin with Doris Stenton's *English Society in the Early Middle Ages.*

Dreams last night, John Dudley and I and Pam in a really massive hotel he owned, full of empty rooms, and was selling. Then the glove stall at some show with Ma and someone swapping the fingers to make the display look more interesting. Then one of each pair being sold to a well wisher by mistake by a temporary stallholder, leaving the others useless on the stall. I apparently began laughing in the dream, to my embarrassment, and woke in hysterics. But another dream, which ended when I woke and asked, 'John, is there anyone else on the boat besides us?' John said this evening. Such a strange thing to say. I cannot remember why I should think there was anyone else but us on board.

D : 'I reckon that just at the moment we are out of range of human help.'

J : 'That's a morbid remark; what brought that on?'

D : 'I was just thinking. If a shark came swerving up and took my hand and this thermometer just then, it would have been very tricky. We couldn't have called anybody to patch me up.'

J : 'You could have taken his temperature.'

D : 'What I mean is, I think this must be one of the very little used tracks of ocean. There probably really is no one for hundreds of miles. The old Gibson Girl hasn't got any range to speak of, and I don't suppose there's anyone using 2182 within range. Just a thought.' A seagull sat on the sea nearby this evening, pruning his feathers and then suddenly took off and swooped away.

Wednesday, 8th June [19]

The goodies from *Orient City* soon disappeared. We began having a can of beans with corned beef for lunch instead of an Archie snack, and sometimes again in the evening—unable to face the horror of cooking. The cook sat under the dodger in the rowing position with the stove beside him. He got out all the pots and pans, chose the items for the meal, assembled after a stream of furious invective, the cutlery by now down to the big wooden salad spoon, the sole remaining alloy spoon, 2 knives and 2 forks, one with only 3 prongs—I snapped one off opening a packet of something—and the penknife John da Silva gave me with all its various blades and openers. Get meths container and find it empty. Find (more invective) the ship-made funnel and the meths, spill more than goes in, and we're short of it. Open tank of stove and find that it is also empty. Fill from big can and funnel, but a major lurch puts paraffin all over the throat and the dirty old towel. Screw down pressure valve, put all tins away, find lighter, wick for transferring light to meths tray (swearing all the time at evening lurch), light meths. Fill dixie with water for stew, crumble meat block into water. Turn up paraffin. Huge inferno is lashed by wind into naked light, coinciding with further unprecedented lurchings. Water spilling already. Finally the vapour lights. Start to cook, stirring constantly to prevent burning. Tremendous wave slops stew over flame and into well of stove. Unlit paraffin vapour. Can't find lighter. Start again with meths as vaporising tubes gone cold. Can't let go of dixie while cooking or spills on to light. Then tea or Horlicks, wash up. Whole thing up to 1½ hours. This is why corned beef and beans has been so popular!

In the morning I took an accurate sunrise time, and corrected it. Got Long 62°W, meaning a fantastic leap forward in 2 days (WATCH ON GMT EXACT 1800 p.m. TODAY) an almost unbelievable result and one we dare not enter on the chart.

I decided to make it easier to adjust the rudder, putting eyes in sides of hatch coaming and lengths of shock cord in rudder lines. It was an immediate success. In the afternoon a five foot baby blue shark with yellow fins and tail had a close look and went away. During my watch the breeze began to stiffen from SW. A long ominous waft of grey cloud fringed with mares' tails reached overhead from the NW horizon, and mares' tails appeared all round us. The ensign stuck out boldly for the first time for days. The signs were all there, so I gave the sea anchor a check to make certain it would go over easily. The sun looked wet-eyed and the sky got the ground glass look. I decided to renew the shock cord in part of the tonneau as another precaution against swampings by a heavy sea.

Thursday, 9th June [20]

I came up for a breather to find John smiling. There was a tanker off the stbd ¼, about a mile away. We badly needed our position but he raced on past. Five minutes later he was back. A Russian tanker, the *Klin*, probably from Cuba, we thought. She circled us closely with all hands on deck and stopped. We attempted to row up but seas were far too heavy together with the wind. Finally he backed astern of us and we made an approach. I shouted up to a man with a megaphone in khaki shorts and shirt for our position. We were moving to his foredeck involuntarily and the man raced along after us. Finally he shouted 37° 56′N, 65° 37′ W. The longitude position seemed suspect and I asked him for a repeat. But John yelled at the same time, 'Hey, Dave, we're going to smash against the side.' A critical situation had quickly developed. I grabbed the steering oar and stuck it in the after rowing position, backing furiously and alternately pushing against the side of the *Klin* with the handle. But the wind was holding us against her and we were being swept aft, where the propeller, half out of the water, was still slowly rotating. It was a terrifying moment, with the Russians yelling for us to grab a line as a distraction. Inch by inch we rowed away backwards, 2 yards in 2 minutes, until we were away, by which time the propeller had been stopped. She waited 2 or 3 minutes and then sailed on, everyone waving from the poop deck.

Once on our way there was a big but fruitless discussion about our position. Had he really said 65° 37′? If so then we were here, only 45 miles in three days from *Orient City*'s position. Or had he said 55° 37 which put us hundreds of

H

miles E, impossibly far away and far too far South for our liking? Or had he said 60° *by* 37′ inadvertently, which would not have been bad at all? It was all very perplexing. Had he given us his yesterday noon position by mistake? I worked out all possibilities on the chart to no decision. John said, 'Give it up, Dave, if we don't know for sure then it's no good is it.' But I teased it over in my mind the whole day, unwilling to accept what I thought he said as being true.

The possibility of that was heartbreaking. Eventually I decided to keep a dead reckoning position every day—so much to the E on the Gulf Stream, so much to the NE rowing, so much NE from wind, and surface movement through the wind. That gave us NE 120m and E 188m of where we were in the *Orient City*'s position on Monday. Later today the wind rose, and it rained incredibly heavily. The choppiness between waves was completely flattened in 3 seconds, and the rain hitting the sea bounced off and left a haze above the water. Visibility came down to 50 yards. Sitting under the dodger like a well-dressed-for-the-weather Royal baby (in my oranges) in a vast nautical pram, it began to seem as we drifted as though the waves were still, and I were being pushed over little hills into exciting little misty valleys. The noise of rain speckering the boat and rattling on the dodger was tremendous.

Later when it had subsided a little I caught 4 gallons of rain water in 38 minutes from the tonneau. It was very welcome, as the 4 weeks old Monticello water had begun to taste stale and chemical. Rowing was difficult because of the almost impossibility of keeping tail on to the sea, and eventually we gave up, taking watch turns out of doors and eating FMC rations for dinner.

Friday, 10th June [21]

The sea still tempestuous. Took a moonsight by sighting every 2 minutes for 45 minutes, obtaining 39° 37′N, which could be true. During the sun sights I noticed a giant ring round the sun, greyish with a lighted edge. The whole thing about in proportion to a small record with the sun as the hole. I pointed it out to John.

J : 'Well, that's it then, isn't it.'

D : 'The last omen, certainly looks like it.'

We motored on at speed before a hardy SW wind until she couldn't be held on course. I took over the oars and John the steering oar and for two hours we whistled along, a line hanging over the stern leaving a trail of bubbles. It was so stuffy in the cabin with the hatch down and the front covered that I decided to sleep out all night. The waves had been bigger than ever during the steering oar business, with John higher than me by 2 or 3 feet sometimes.

'There go the front row forwards,' he said, looking at a vast pile of water rolling off to the NE.

'Hang on, here comes the Houses of Parliament,' I shouted into the wind.

J : 'What I'd like now would be to go to a nice restaurant in the West End with some good company and have . . .'

'Give her a dab with the oar. Sorry, carry on.'

'. . . and have a real nosh, right across the card. I think I'd start with . . .'

'Dabs, dabs,' I yelled as she slewed to port again.

'. . . with minestrone and slices of bread and butter, following a sherry, of course, and after that a little bit of . . .'

'Dabs, big dabs.'

'. . . bit of fish fried in butter, and then a huge steak, a red monster with about a pound of mushrooms over, then . . .'

'Huge dabs, big, big dabs . . .'

'. . . and a couple of bottles of wine with the whole thing, probably . . .'

D : 'Here comes an interesting one.'

John's backside, perched on the open hatch cover, was almost encircled with a crescent of foam as a larger-'n-usual comber went through.

The wind began to hum in the radar reflector and the occasional sea slopped on to the full tonneau. I scarcely slept and at dawn the whole thing had sharpened into the best part of a gale. By our previous standards the seas were enormous, towering slopes of water occasionally crested with breaking foam, vast canyons between them. The tops seemed to flop uncertainly about. Sometimes a peak would be about to engulf one, then at the last minute wobble off to one side. And at others we would catch the lot. By 6 we were lying beam on as usual with a dumper breaking and foaming right over every five minutes. The ensign stood like a sheet of red steel from the little teak staff, only its very end proving it was made of cloth. The first few to swamp us foamed across without much harm, and I pulled up the front of the tonneau and tied it over the dodger to keep myself dry. By this time I was pretty scared, and lit a wet cigarette and stared over the 'bib' at the oncoming sea. Without warning a colossal wave reared unexpectedly and slammed us. *Puffin* went over to a full 90° and the whole top 5 feet of the wave thundered across the tonneau and downwards, swirling round in the dodger on its way. I was terrified.

'Are you all right, Dave?' John shouted from the cabin, 'Christ that was a terror.' The retreating back of the wave seen from the crest of the next, was 30ft. from top to toe.

'I think it's time for the sea anchor,' I shouted back. (We had left it off in the hope of blowing a few miles). John let the dodger down in five seconds flat, and was back inside before another wave could catch him with the flap open. I noticed that we had been spun round and were facing the seas with the other beam. I started letting the anchor go. After 50 feet of the line was out it tangled hopelessly. Another colossal wave caught the whole boat and me unprotected, and spun us round again. I got the dodger up again and my protection tied up in place, and the anchor held us at a slight angle off the beam, which reduced the danger of a capsizing. But I still couldn't sleep. I was absolutely exhausted, yet was woken every five minutes with a bucket of water thrown in my face. Oddly the temperature had stayed at 75ish all night, but now, as we swapped places at 08.00, it dropped to the high 50°s, and later in the day to 52°.

I reckoned Force 9 was the maximum that gale reached.

John was lucky. Another half dozen big ones sluiced over us harmlessly, and then the rain came down torrentially. The savage movement ceased and the sea gradually quietened. The wind came round to a brisk NEly, preventing rowing.

D.R. at 10.6.66 from noon 6.6.66. NE 188M. E 120M.

Saturday, 11th June [22]

I had 8 hours below, dead to the world, and in the evening we were not hungry enough to bother with cooking. We cleared up the mess of the storm, cleaned out the cabin, put the bags under the tonneau and went to sleep, both in the cabin.

Sunday, 12th June [23]

Dawn. About 5 days ago I should have mentioned that after mastering, albeit rather roughly, the sextant, and the Reeds', I decided to go in for something a bit more abstruse in the way of navigation. I decided to rout out the *Little Ships Navigation.* I looked in the suitcase for it. Nowhere. Eventually we ransacked the boat. Nowhere. All the net-racks. Nowhere! 'If only we knew where we were,' we chorused. The only alternative was *Little Ships Astronavigation.* Today I got it out, and it is a perfect little gem, with the whole lot in it, Solar, Astro, and all the little tips. And I spent 3 hours reading it this a.m. and then went out in the afternoon (still on NE and a little sea running) and started to put it into practice. Working on an assumed position, I took 2 sunshots 2 hours apart and they gave us a fix of sorts. I then read back on what I'd learned and found I'd been making an error, though only small. I got all the books out from under the cover, and a wave came over and hit them all in the face, the first today, and soaked all the clothes I'd had drying. Still, the nav is a ring of hope in that direction. And it confounds all the folk who said there was no list of steps, one by one, by which navigation could be carried out.

A tanker came into sight, 4 miles away, on a SW course, and a Coast Guard or USN Neptune flew low over it and only a mile from us. All today the boat had been festooned with clothing. A sleeping bag zipped half up and hooked over the masthead light, towels and trousers on the dodger strings—a pair of my jeans went o/b never to be seen again —pants, sox and jerseys all over the tonneau. During the storm nothing was rainproof and even the cabin with the lid down. The sea squeezed through in a little waterfall of foam every time a wave hit. Not just a trickle, for everything was damp or soaked through.

I told John about the nav fix while he was fixing a goody dinner—Sunday—and he was disappointed in progress.

'By the time we get back people will be saying, "Who the bloody hell are you two? This is 1968 you know." '

The fix put us back from our D.R. position of 10.6.66.

'I think we ought to be further ahead than that. 880 miles in 3 weeks.'

D: 'Don't forget, John, we swilled about near Chesapeake Light for 10 days. That was only 40 miles progress, and you can't count that. I've almost forgotten how terrible that period was.'

J: 'I haven't forgotten, I'll tell you. I reckon we did well to get past it, don't you? No, it's just that we don't seem to have come very far for all that effort, that's all.'

The dinner was excellent. Mince, beans, spuds with cheese, pears from a tin, and tea.

Monday, 13th June [24]

The wind continued adversely, though from the SE. Our barometer is still playing silly buggers. With great rings round the sun and Force 9 winds, it said 'Fair' throughout. Today it managed to indicate fairer still by almost bending the needle against the stop.

I took 5 sights today and 4 gave us a position ahead of yesterday's on a likely course, and all within a few miles of one another. We still couldn't row for the 3rd day running, and John took the radio to bits without bringing it to life. A whale with a tail 6 ft across came within 100 yds, blowing twice a minute. It had a blunt head and square forehead. Then it dived and we didn't see it again.

Tuesday, 14th June [25]
We awoke to fine mild weather with a Force 4 southerly, and started to row NE. The *Saguaray* failed to sight us from 2 miles away. 3 sights gave us a 62m day's run.

Wednesday, 15th June [26]
By last night late the wind had veered in our favour, to SW and we sped along NE all day, though 3 sights gave us a northerly result with 62 miles run. Force 6 and a very boisterous and difficult sea to keep course in.

Thursday, 16th June [27]
For several days very bad tummy nerves, and a tranquilliser sorted it out finally yesterday. I am using the bucket 3 or 4 times a day, which is uncomfy and irritating, especially in the middle of the night. I think now that the full enormity of the task, the possible shortage of food, paraffin for the stove, meths, toilet paper, are beginning to dawn on us, and there is a certain depression in the air. Although we are only rowing 12 hours a day all told, the wind is keeping up our speed, and so is the good old Gulf Stream.

Two things are getting us down: the continuous round-the-clock activity, either rowing or eating, sighting, washing, means no sleep for more'n 4 hours, and the movement is boisterous, giving no peace while doing anything. For me, too, the night rowing is appallingly boring, though I don't mind the daytime stints at all. Concentrating on a tiny star for course, or on the flag, is very tiring, and the 3rd hour is almost insupportably tedious and tiring. Sometimes the passing waves make one seem to go backward, and the only positive forward motion are the phosphorescent whorls from the oars receding behind the boat. I would love to go for a walk or even to be able to stand up for a couple of minutes. But just standing is impossible.

The sunsights improve greatly, yesterday's and today's 3 sights having given 10 mile accuracy in a bad sight seaway! I took $\frac{1}{4}$ hr to get a good sight this a.m.

Last night there was a panic. A ship aimed at us and the torch is nearly dead. We got out flares and lit the hurricane lamp, and she passed 300 yards away, blinking unreadable morse at us. We did not reply—anything we said could have been misconstrued depending on whether they were saying 'Are you O.K.?' or 'Do you want assistance?'

Another ship today. And also a jaunt with a vast whale which we guessed at 30 ft long. He had a look from 100 yds, then came snorting back ahead of us 50 yds away. Finally 2 direct approaches, one to within 10 yds. The second and last appearance I was in the cabin when John shouted, 'Hold on tight, he's coming for us.' He passed 5 yds or less under our stern. We tapped a knife against a tin under water as a scarer and the whale didn't come back.

Friday, 17th June [28]

John attempted to fish today, but without success. For ages he swore at a black fish about 8 ins long under the boat. First a swoop with the net to see how crafty it was. He never got near it, nor near any of the others hiding in the early morning shadow of the boat. So a small hook with a piece of Uncle Josh's Pork Strip bait was lowered with no better result. We rowed for $12\frac{1}{2}$ hours between sights; saw no ship or fish other than the little companions. After a dinner of beef'n-pork bar, peas, spuds with cheese and butter, we had a few tunes on the mouth organ as the sun was going down. Tonight we will probably pass the 1,000 mile line, and now reckon on just after July 31st as a likely arrival date taking into account those 10 abortive days at the beginning. But we will need wind—today's windless mileage was down to $5\frac{1}{2}$ or thereabouts.

Saturday, 18th June [29]

We continued to row in sunny weather with light airs from the S. I had reckoned the boat's cargo to be too light in weight for about a week, and now we decided to replenish the water bags with sea water. All the fresh was taken from the main hold, and empty bags collected for replenishing. At least ½ a doz. of the fresh bags had holes, and it looks as though the paraffin in the bilges has been nibbling at them and at the stoppers. So we are down by 6 days water. Then for some reason we decided to look at the food in the fore-peak store, and found bad news. Many of the bags had been split by Bob Taylor and me to get the air out for closer packing, and we now found the store full of putrid water, black, stinking and paraffin-smelling, with water in some of the bags. Out came everything, all food bags were opened and a small amount of rotten food thrown away. Then we emptied our emergency four gall. drum of Monti-cello water into water bags, tasted it and found it very good. This meant that the plastic bags were tainting the water, too, and possibly with something poisonous. My cup was used to clean out the store, and half a bottle of Dettol did the disinfecting.

A lot of time wasted, and in the evening my sight showed us to have made puny progress, 18m to the SE.

D: 'What day is it? I thought it was Saturday.'

J: 'I don't know. Two or three days ago you said it was Thursday.'

D: 'Well, when I woke this morning I remember thinking—a month at sea, only two more to go—but now I'm not so certain. Don't say we don't know what day it is?'

J: 'Why do you want to know?'

D: 'Oh, it's nice to think the boys are in the Bush now embarking on an evening's drinking, and things like that.'

J: 'I thought perhaps you were thinking of taking a bird to the Saturday night pictures!'

Sunday, 19th June [30]
I spent most of my waking hours last night thinking of ways of increasing our efficiency. We are rowing only, at the most, a ½ of the available time. For 1½ hours a day we drift. I am asleep in the cabin for my 2 hour spell, John wakes me 10 minutes before time.

'10 minutes, David.' Then at 5 minutes.

At time he says, 'Come on out, time's up.' By ten past time we have swapped places. I have had a scratch, opened my eyes, got my gear together, cigarettes, lighter, clothing, and am out in the open. Ten minutes later I might just have started to row. At the end of an hour I will have a cigarette or even two, and waste more time. We linger over meals talking, we fish unsuccessfully occasionally, and sometimes we say, 'The current is taking us well, and if we row we might row ourselves out of a good thing. Let's just sit!'

John came up with the best idea. Three on, 3 off, and two hours rowing sometimes during the on period. Giving a definite 16 hours rowing a day. We tried it out immediately and it worked well. Both more tired, I think, but feeling as if we were putting our maximum possible efforts into rowing. But once again there was a terrible position. I went over my figures time and again but there were no mistakes. John refused to believe them which made me furious, as there was an especially good intersection of D.L.

Monday, 20th June [31]
By the time I'd finished my calculations we had done 16 hours rowing with a slight S breeze. Yet our position, the best intersection I've had, gave us about 10 miles as a run. We are a bit dismayed, but disbelieving and if there is no ship to confirm them or any alteration in 24 hours time we will go N, I have decided.

Tuesday, 21st June [32]
Another featureless day, in which we were proved to have

run slightly further. So a reference for the NxENE course. John saw the satellite, the only extraordinary event of the day.

Wednesday, 22nd June [33]
Less progress, which now measures a total of 65m over 5 days in spite of partially favourable winds and hard rowing. We don't understand. No ships to ask now. All the ones we see pass us at night. I decided to row N but the wind was coming from N10°E so we packed in. John fished, without success, with the net and line, harpoon, and every sort of bait. I caught a big one in the net but he got away. We saw a strange manta ray and a turtle.

Thursday, 23rd June [34]
Feeling that to be somewhere else than where we are now would improve our chances of moving, we decided to row South E with a helpful wind. We should do 30 miles every day by rowing 12 miles by the wind and 12 to 20 by the current, providing the wind is with us and the current exists. The mystery of the last few days will remain. That there is no current is proved by today's sight, which shows us to be in the same place as yesterday. The big sea anchor has held us in place against the adverse wind. A ship passed E-W to the N of us this morning first thing, the first for 2 or 3 days. The cigarettes ended yesterday, and we were both so hungry today that we had a cooked curry at midday. I spent the morning renewing the shock cord in part of the tonneau and in making straps of shock cord to keep the oars quiet during rest periods. I opened one or two boxes of cine film, to find, to my dismay that it doesn't give the film speed! So will have to wait to ask a shipboard expert, or guess.

In the afternoon we decided to pump the dinghy up. I had been taking pictures of John rowing and cooking, and we rowed off in the dinghy to photograph *Puffin* being rowed. The dinghy felt horrid, every tiny wavelet lapping under its rubber sheet bottom could be felt, and I was glad to get back to the security of *Puffin*, and to the motion I was used to. The bottom was covered with barnacles, or whatever it is that has a triangular shell with a stalk attaching itself to the hull. We got the wire brush on to them. Another night of idleness, both sleeping until 11.00 a.m.

Friday, 24th June [35]
When we found a favourable wind from a little S of W, I started rowing, and very soon a terrific rain squall came up, gusting to Force 7 or so, and followed by a series of squalls. Even the barmometer, so often threatened with the '3 hour journey', was moved to fall to just below 30. We have not seen sign of shipping for 2 days, and have not to our knowledge been reported for 18 days, which must worry some people at home, including Ma. Later at midnight a ship passed ¼ mile astern on a 160° course while I was snoozing in the dodger between courses. Eventually unable to row because no light to steer by, so packed in.

Saturday, 25th June [36]
Woke to find an unrowable North/NNE wind of about Force 5. Sea anchor out very efficiently, and we lay quarter or stern on, something to do with the increased topside exposed to wind pressures. John competed with a small shark for the school of grey fish which goes wherever we go, with more patience and cunning than before, leaving the net over the side for long periods for the victims to get to like and to play in.

'Nice bit of cod, Madam?' he shouted. 'I'll just see what we've got in today.' But the net plunged again and again without success, except for a tiddler which went back. The small ones were always available, but the big ones, ½ lb each, lay slyly under the keel; sending the small chaps out to see what risks there were.

Gradually the seas got higher, until they began to surpass those of our last storm. Gusting to Force 10. We both tucked in together for the night, as well as all day, with the big sea anchor out over the stern. About every 20th sea broke over us from the stern, with the terrific pressure forcing a fountain of water through the back of the hatch every time. Soon we were pretty wet below.

Sunday, 26th June [37]

John got out to get breakfast the next morning and as I spoke to him through the letter box we were caught half sideways on by a sea which tore down the tonneau hooked up to the dodger. He disappeared from view in a cascade of water exploding across the tonneau. Now every wave that hit us was like a sledge-hammer smashing against the round stern, and echoing in the cabin like bass discords in a guitar chamber. No sights, although the sun was out, because of the variable height of us in relation to the horizon. This battering went on till about midnight Sunday night, with colossal waves rolling beneath us. The odd thing is that in the cabin there is no sensation of the waves being big or small. And the ones that hit hardest are the ones preceded until a second before impact by serene silence: in that one second we could hear foam and breakage beginning to occur, and just feel the boat steepening under the crest of the wave.

Monday, 27th June [38]

We awoke to a sunning calm, and today was drying-out day. Sleeping bags festooned on mast and staff, towels, jerseys, boots, trousers, everything inside out in the sun. We fished while we waited for the wind to come round from NNE to our favourable sector, trying harpooning and netting. The blue fish were in abundance, making swift passes at certain sorts of lure, and I caught a tiddler as bait for bigger stuff, all without success. I have decided to make a spear gun—that should do it.

We saw one ship early, miles away, and another late at night over the horizon. Rowing started with a change to SW in the evening, clear sky and moon risen high but the weather broke again by morning.

Tuesday, 28th June [39]
Seas increasingly severe and hitting us more and more, heavy rain as well. The barometer descended to 29.8 for the occasion, swiftly recovering to 30.3, presumably for a harder blow. Already we are damp again in the cabin, and there will be more drying out sessions when it is over. Oddly the last few days' storms took us NE *into* the wind about 70 miles. The water, incredibly warm for several days, is back to bloody cold today. John looked down a valley between waves this a.m. and saw a freighter 200 yds away on reciprocal course to our own, and almost at limit of visibility. It could never have seen us! We lit the lamp all night, and it rained solidly, gradually abating to a misty, dank and typically Atlantic morning.

'This is just how I imagined it would be, all grey and misty and overcast,' said John.

Wednesday, 29th June [40]
The water too cold to leave one's hand in. No fish. I made a pretty lousy curry last night, porridge and tea this morning. I did my rowing stint and as I came below it seemed to be ready for another blow. Keeping our stuff dry is a major problem. The cabin walls are covered in condensation. The ventilators leak slightly even when closed, and the hatch lets in gallons when it is hit hard enough from sides or back. Some of the rough nights we sleep in our oranges but last night they were wet inside as well. Even rain drips through the hatch covers on to the bunks and sleeping bags. The worst performance is when one man is asleep and the other says 'Unrowable' and has to come in too. He enters dripping after a terrific struggle with tonneau, dodger, hurricane lamp, life line etc., and has to get the lid down immediately to stop a whole sea coming into the cabin. To get boots and oranges off and stowed without soaking everything in sight is impossible. The crashing of waves against the topsides and stern has been fantastic these last few days, yet the boat never has a creak in her,

and when we emerge finally to start our routine again she is all shipshape, though wet.

Yesterday morning 9 inches of water all over the cockpit floor had to be pumped out. We started rowing early in the morning and I managed to sight 3 times and get a fix giving us 90 miles of eastings. As night fell everything became completely calm and windless. John woke me at midnight with a tale of awful eerie sounds. I poked my head up and it happened again, a ghastly low long sigh bubbling in the airhole of a whale lying nearby, shrouded in mist only a few hundred yards away. We trumpeted into the water and knocked the rowlocks against each other under water and were not interfered with. But it is a most unearthly noise to be alone at sea with.

Thursday, 30th June [41]

Visibility down to 50 yards, yet the sun shining through obliquely very early; porpoises jumping and splashing just out of sight, came strafing under the boat in a motionless glassy sea, and looked plump and fine. My first latitude gave us about 10 miles on yesterday, and bears out our present view that wind is *the* vital factor. Yesterday John tried to waterproof the hatch cover with canvas and leather. We are beginning to take pictures, and have already snapped 80 shots. My boots: the linings came out about a fortnight ago. A few days ago I was pulling them on when the back came off in my hand. Today they are down to the size of bedroom slippers since more came away. A fantastically poor performance. Bought in say April early, used 3 or 4 times, including some walking, then packed and not used till voyage. Since then to date worn possibly 40 times at most, always sitting down, and with scarcely any movement. Food. The corner of a menu from an Italian liner floated past today and we picked it up. Later as I was starting my spell of rowing I noticed that the wind was from E of South and although light, was making an uncomfortable and unrowable sea and into wind. Out went the big anchor.

Friday, 1st July [42]

Today was featureless, being misty and cloudy till after midday and still with the contrary wind. There is no point of the rose to which we can row, with the wind as it is, as inevitably we should finish up more West than when we started. At least the old anchor gives us the benefit of the current that is beneath the surface, and we did 42 miles to the NE with its help. I cleaned out most of the boat and found a lot of indescribable slimy filth behind various bulkheads. Powdered this and that blows onto the floor, is wetted and carried into a cranny to fester.

Saturday, 2nd July [43]

After a ghastly night below we found the wind still from about E145°S, and wasted a day making about 30 miles due E. I am getting worried about a number of things. We have not got enough—food, water, paraffin, batteries, yet have seen no ship since 28th June, or 4 days, and we have not been reported or spoken to anyone since 9.6.66 Yet we are now in the centre of the shipping lanes, if our 1965 charts are anything to go by. The boat is much lighter than she should be, and *feels* as if she is badly balanced fore of aft, though I think the sea anchor contributes to a lot of the hammering under the stern.

Sunday, 3rd July [44]

For the 3rd day we are enshrouded in a close mist and fog, with visibility varying from 300 to 600 yds. Today is the first day of no sights due to poor horizon, though. If I have not been seeing the horizon properly for 2 or 3 days, that would mean the chart position is more S than our actual position and would explain the absence of any activity. Today, if possible, more featureless than yesterday. I stripped the footwell store of water bags and cleaned it, letting water and 2 little fish in through the 'Harrier' hole. One fish jumped into the dirty water bucket with paraffin in it and raced round at terrific speed with its head out of the water. The slime and filth was appalling. I learned to splice

David Johnstone (LEFT) and John Hoare

Puffin's mould

Puffin hatched: the mould has been removed

On the launching trolley. The hull grab-rails are visible on its left-hand side

Puffin afloat alongside *Myth of Mallam*

LEFT *Puffin* is still a bare shell apart from her grab-rails. The black rectangle is the entrance to the tiny cabin; the handle enables the hatch cover to be swung up and over for easier access

RIGHT Tying up at Norfolk, Virginia. *Puffin* now has blocks with various rowlock positions; ventilators; rudder; mast tube; and fairleads. The tube will take the radar reflector mast

Johnstone enjoys American confectionery

Aboard s.s. *United States*. The domed cabin ventilators on the deck are screwed shut. The canopy ('dodger') is folded flat

At Norfolk, Hoare hands down oars to Johnstone

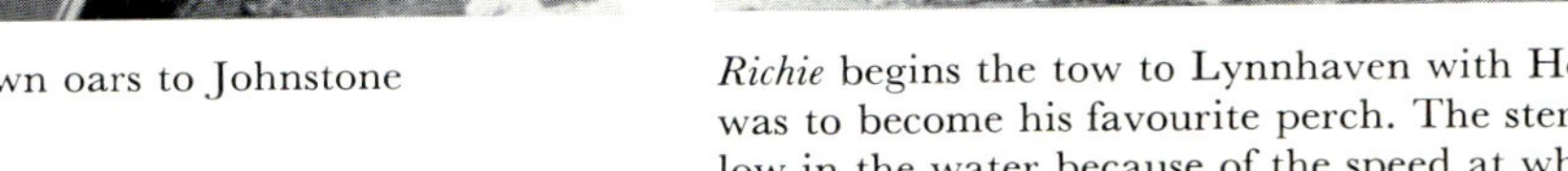

Richie begins the tow to Lynnhaven with Hoare on what was to become his favourite perch. The stern of the boat is low in the water because of the speed at which she is being towed

With Virginia Beach in the background, the journey has begun. Note the radar reflector on the foremast and the red ensign on the flagstaff aft. Although fully loaded, *Puffin* has only inches of her hull in the water

The last time Johnstone and Hoare were seen—photograph taken from U.S.C.G. *Duane*

Day 83—another picture from *Duane*. Johnstone and Hoare are obviously in good spirits. Note the stowage of the spare oars. The large black bag probably contains the inflatable dinghy

H.M.C.S. *Chaudière*

The wreck

Puffin's wreck aboard *Chaudière*, covered with gooseneck barnacles which consist of several overlapping shells attached to the boat by a long rubbery 'neck'. The barnacle has feather-like 'feet' which wash plankton into its 'mouth'

The chromium snap-shackle on the right was attached to the life-line

The snapped rope on the right-hand cleat was probably attached to the sea anchor. The oarsman's footholes can be seen centre bottom

Drawings on the inside of the tiny cabin survived immersion. They appear to be drawn in indelible lipstick, possibly while *Puffin* was at Norfolk. 'Shazam', the magic password of comic hero Captain Marvel, gives him the power of Superman, including the ability to fly

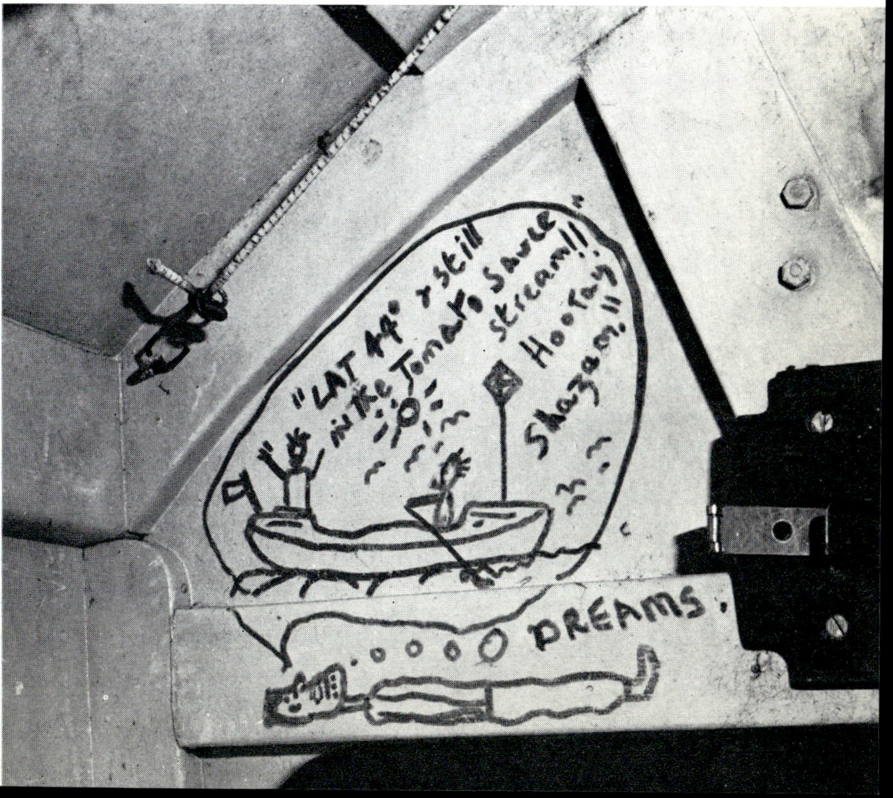

(8) had the flares the Greek ship was
up on us, going 100 yds across our bow
Two officers staring down from bridge.
A cruiser came & had a look, & when we
took turns to row against 20 mph wind
& ingoing tide a rubber necking aircraft
drove John barmy. Too strong wind to row
in, always blowing us shorewards. By late
evening racing into cape Henry with both
Trick to get 2182 forecast. Sea anchors out &
doing the no one
dangerous yachts-
man's Trick, of
drifting onto a
lee shore. Kept
careful watch
& at one time
mistook an un-
marked buoy for the charted
buoy, thereby placing ourselves
on the cape itself. In spite
of predicament a sort of
contentedness reigned in
the face of a real danger.
Eventually all the

Page 8 of Johnstone's Journal. The drawing shows the effect of the rotary currents at the entrance to Chesapeake Bay

(82) the same as those for '65 & '63 we are between the lanes for/from "C" to the channel at Bishop's Rock & the Irish sea at Fastnet, thus we can choose and close gently with one or other at will, or be blown there or carried there on a current, at the same time as making our eastings good. A good tactical position, but one which a strong wind from almost anywhere except 245°, or any strong set, would negate. [I have made a number of corrections to our course (in the light of changing conditions & all the evidence) in the last 24 hours, & feel they have been wise in spite of John's criticism. Without them we would surely be miles out of earshot of the lanes instead of almost certainly between 2 lanes, even tho' our final fix gave our position as one which we had no intention of wanting to reach]; I opened the bilge & found that the Water is getting out of our seawater ballast bags on account of their rotted by paraffin. So in the event of a gale we are going to have a hairy time unless we flood & seal the bilge!

Page 82 of the Journal. Immersion in the sea caused the writing to ghost itself on to the back of each previous page

Page 148—the penultimate page of the Journal. Johnstone's handwriting remains perfectly firm and efficient, smaller perhaps because he was running out of paper a simple splice from the Almanac. The 'Homer' was tried, but no stations raised. Food again occupies our mind, particularly now that we are bored with inactivity. How about some rich fat gammon slices braised with mushrooms, leeks, carrots and onions in a light white sage and parsley sauce with white wine, served with gnocchi al formagio. Syllabub to follow. My actual lunch was 4 biscuits—hard tack, with peculiar butter, processed cheese and honey from a tube. We tried Bill Kaduson's brandy but it was unthinkably frightful.

J : 'What a desperate place this is.'

D : 'Not top of the holiday list, is it?'

A glance at the canvas waterproof chart showed that we are smack in the middle of a bulge surrounded by a blue dotted line saying, 'Fog may be expected one day in five, especially in July'.

Monday, 4th July [45]

As I got out of the cabin I saw a freighter passing our stern. The sun was shining and a horizon was available for sights. A good start. The freighter raced on but I had seen her two funnels side by side and now as she was well past I saw them merge into one. 'Hey John, there's a ship and she's coming back.'

'Where's your wallet, I'll get that out ready.'

She came past at full speed again, slipping her bow well down slowly with the swell, and revealing a thin strip of deck as she rolled.

'Do you need anything?' shouted a khaki-clad man on the bridge, and waved.

I waved back, yelling, 'We could do with some food,' while John then shouted, 'What is our position?'

He lunged on, turned and lunged back at full speed.

'The sod, he's not stopping and it's the fourth of July, too,' I said. He raced away into the gathering mist. We looked after him, thinking he was stopping, then seeing his bow wave had not lessened. He was the first human being and his voice the first human voice other than our own, that we had seen or heard since 9th June. We took a bearing of his course as he went, and he seemed to be on about 226° True. I put the protractor on the chart near our last known position and it coincided with the westward track from the route to the north of Scotland, coming to meet point 'C'. This put us too far N if he was in fact on course.

'What the hell did he slow down and ask what we needed if he wasn't going to stop?' said John. I took 4 longitude sights and averaged them, and got a longitude of about 49° 30W, and then over came the cloud and mist, and that was the end for the day. I fished without success, and even rowed in wind for 2 hours to dispel boredom. Checking the sextant later I found one of the mirrors was loose, and now giving an Index Error of about 9.5′, which is a hell of a lot. Soon after John came out, and took the oars for a spell, there was definitely an engine. We were in a grey cupolared arena about the size of Wembley Stadium, with a bright blotch where the sun should have been. We were all activity. I got flares out, John got the fog horn out and blew several warnings. On came the noise of the engines from the sea. And suddenly we realised it was a plane, the second today—I heard a big high jet earlier.

'I'll bet he's the Coast Guard looking for us. That freighter radioed that we were asking for food.' But the truth of that was not revealed, since the plane, with propellers and not a jet, flew slowly away without seeing us through the fog. An hour later it was back, or another with a similar noise. I saw this one, and I think it was a Neptune, certainly it had a huge tail. It flew about 70°–250°, 3 or 4 miles away at about 2,000 ft. and it would have had a difficult task to find us in the misty conditions. I hope they aren't on a 'rescue' for us, thinking us to be out of grub altogether! An odd thing we saw at the same time was a colourless white rainbow, a huge thick arch of white mist quite nearby and opposite to the sun. Almost a sort of poetic symbol to row through.

Tuesday, 5th July [46]
I was almost in despair of ever making progress this morning. Lying to Percy, the wind to the E of S by about a point, and briskening quickly, the sea and sky grey and bleak. No rowing! I sat outside after breakfast in my oranges. I had burnt a saucepan with the milk and had to sandpaper it clean.

John opened the hatch an inch to say, 'The ole glass is falling.'

'How much?'

'Oh, only three quarters of an inch, although you know this glass. It drops one tiny segment and the heavens crash round our ears.'

But by 12 G.M.T. there was an element of W in the wind, just about a point. I pulled in Percy and started to row, the wind westing splendidly right round to WNW in an hour.

At one o'clock I was shocked to see, right over the stern, what looked like a lighthouse. I got out my glasses, and the rockets and flares, and could just make out a pillar with dark rings round it like a lighthouse, and a thinner sort of mast next to it. After a minute I shouted to John to come up and give his opinion but almost as he put the binoculars to his eyes I had the solution, and a most unlikely one too. It was a vast ocean going Bermudan sloop, hull-down and carrying an enormous striped spinnaker which we eventually saw to be red white and blue. It was running before the prevailing WNW Force 4 or so, about a mile away. A fine thing to see in mid ocean. The day cleared to a blue sky all over, and I got 3 sights with averages of several for each. They put us about the same place as we were 2 days ago—plus say 8 miles or so—but at least old Percy has held us in place.

A tern (with a black head and black eyes, grey/white wings and a white trailing edge, and black trailing edge to the tip underneath) tried to land on the after deck and ensign staff, but hadn't got the nerve. Kept approaching to within 2 feet of it, then flying off to fish and returning. In the end flew away.

Wednesday, 6th July [47]

Overnight a calm and this morning another sailing boat on the horizon bearing 180°. He came and went throughout the day, finally reaching off NE on the southerly which developed at midday. We rowed on NE True, disappointing having hoped for something from the West, and my sights gave us a small day's run, only 25 miles to the S.W.

The big event of the day was the advent of the *Kirsten* of Greenwich. She turned up in the West, and altered course when about ½ mile away to come over and inspect us. About 35 or 40 ft., a Bermudan ketch or yawl, I didn't notice which, she hove to, to leeward.

'Are you all right? Water? Food, anything you would like?' said a young man with a Scandinavian accent and a camera, standing in the pulpit.

'No thanks, we're O.K. for everything,' we lied. We thought they were probably in a race, being the third in 2 days, and they confirmed it.

'We are in a race to Copenhagen,' said a man with an American accent. One of them said our position was 42°N and 52°W. I queried the longitude and he said, 'Well maybe 51.' (42° 10′N/49° 15′W) They promised to report us on landfall.

As they came past, the skipper with short grey hair, sunglasses, bronzed and a Scandinavian accent said, 'Good luck boys' and they all joined in, 'Good luck'. So did we and told them of the other two craft. They sailed quickly off NE, hoisting a dark-blue spinnaker as they went. I thought of the camaraderie of a voyage like theirs, watches to be kept, beers in the saloon in the evening, lobster salads from the deep freeze; it was depressing and I began to feel lonely and sad not to be attached to such a group of people, with their comradeship. And I wondered if I will always do things the hard way! I turned round several times to see them and it took an hour for the head of the spinnaker to set beyond the horizon. Later a heavy throbbing told us a ship was nearby, and a freighter went past to the South on her way apparently to the Mediterranean. Then a Lockheed Hercules flew towards Spain on 100° True.

The *Kirsten* was a blessing. They were the first people we have spoken to since the Russians on 9.6.66 I found myself nervous again speaking to other people. One tends to retire to one's little existence on the boat and accept it as all—and intrusion of other people again is an event to be met.

Thursday, 7th July [48]

Mist and fog again! But this time with a rowable wind, so we are skimming NE True. The mist blew across the cockpit enough to dampen everything it touched immediately, but later the sun shone through palely. I think we are now being taken SE by the current, and that the result of our next fix will be an E or SE run. We are south of the Liner Track with 14 days food (more if one counts the biscuits, ham and egg, etc.) and plenty of water but paraffin for 10 days at the most. A deck throbbing just before dusk and foghorns, with the mist thicker than ever. He passed from SW to NE. A huge school of dolphins cavorted by as we put old Percy out to feed.

Friday, 8th July [49]

More fog and more mist, but the wind gave in 2 points and we rowed briefly. Today's sight gave about 60 miles N for the two days, or 48 hours since last sight. The most depressing area of all, and according to the chart we are in the middle with 200 miles to go to get out. But we can't get out because the winds are always against rowing E, which is where we could escape to. Meanwhile we eat and our stores go down, and no ship will either see us or stop in fog. So we can't row at night because can't see compass, and flag sticks to staff. Aircraft continue to pass o'head, and ships fog-horn distantly. We miss desperately the true horizon to scan—it is part of life we like; we miss the sun, and we hate the damp fog blowing everywhere, wetting hair and forming globs of water on each hair of jerseys, and fogging the windward spectacle lens (3 days since I bust my clear glasses, so now big sunglasses all day—still nothing to see anyway) and nothing can be air dried. John got a strange recurrence of the air pains/wind pains he got in Farnham.

Saturday, 9th July [50]

My nerves are not very far below the surface at the moment. There was a ridiculous and short shouting match which left me very weak and shaky, and I am sad and depressed more than ever, and very unhappy, and I only want to be with my friends and family again, somewhere where the social and physical environment shows a fragment of sympathy and understanding for the normal frailties.

John said yesterday, 'It's like being in jail, this. Eat what you're given, confinement, regular exercise hours, sleep in a cell.' With the difference that there is nowhere we can *walk* and only two of us, and nothing to see or read or do except think. I have been thinking of the future. Buy a house in Italy and do it up as a holiday pad. And for the first time in my life, 2 things: I have almost got a plan, and a woman would fit into it very well!

More fog and mist, heightened sea and wind from S x SSW, which is little help. I did the breakfast, as usual porridge (hot for John, cold for me) and tea. But—about ten goes to light the stove, got it going; it went out, wouldn't restart without meths, so had to be cooled, wouldn't restart anyway, a box of matches. Later it started, then ran out of fuel. I filled it and started again. The meths had run out! The stove started but kept blowing out again, in spite of rigging canopy up to dodger. So took the whole thing into cabin, where heat and fumes were appalling and stove went out again, for no reason. Porridge awful due to bad pack of milk. So the rest of the day can't be worse!

Sunday, 10th July [51]
Last night pitch black so no rowing. This morning the wind had come round to a much more favourable W, later moving to NW before backing to South again, though very light. We got in some good distance. I did breakfast inside successfully. No fog so good sights gave us far too far North, and we have crossed the West bound lane for the 3rd time during the night. We had to get the hooter and hoot off an approaching vessel. Otherwise little progress. In the fog, the damp, we can just see a wave darkly loitering about 200 yds. off. The sun makes a pale light centre in the clouds, and droplets blow across the boat all day. The boat is so light she is difficult to trim, and the off duty man in the cabin is used as moveable ballast. Conversations. 'I wonder if there's some idiot at the newspaper office pushing flags into a map—"I think they are here today!"'

'Not them. They've forgotten us until we get to be one of their stories.'

The white flares. Reed's Almanac says, White hand flares may be used to attract attention by vessel not in immediate danger of shipwreck.

I said to John, 'The last time we saw anyone we *could* have signalled was that boat on the 3rd. Otherwise they've all been enshrouded in fog or it's been night. We've got to use the white flares now if they come anywhere near enough to see, in a useable seaway.' He agreed. We have had long discussions about the T.A., *The Bridge on the River Kwai,* A.I.D., the Army, me joining the T.A., my house in the Mediterranean.

Monday, 11th July [52]
The weather became calm as night fell and John rowed for 6 hours out of 7, the most anyone has yet done. But first thing this morning came disappointment, and this afternoon dismay. The fog came down and the wind sprang up blowing SSE, though only lightly. I rowed into it for an exhausting $1\frac{1}{2}$ hours. But this afternoon we found that, having rowed a True 100° for hours, we had come 45 miles

S, and a little West (for the 1st. time). Ships' foghorns blew to the WNW and N and SE, and aircraft flew over the clouds, but no one saw us except possibly a strange services (Portuguese or Canadian or UK) Viscount or Vanguard, with a sort of landing parachute tail pod like a Buccaneer. It flew 275° or so at 1,000 ft, with one engine stopped, and, when just in earshot but out of sight, flew up and down as if searching for something. I could hear it turning and circling for ¾ of an hour.

Last night, while we had dinner, the biggest fin we have ever seen broke the surface 2 or 300 yds. away. We estimated it as standing (the bit we could see) at least 3′ 6″ high above the water. Also a big 'cruiser' fish lunged in and out of a school of small fish, herrings or sprats, 100 yds. away, breaking surface several times. The little fish sprang into the air in shoals, and a gull which was, luckily for it, nearby, flew up and down catching them as they jumped. As dark fell a vast school of porpoises went breathily past on a several 100 yd. front and later a whale breathed.

Today the fog proved itself capable of greater speed than ever. Usually between the time I have decided to make a sight and have reached for the sextant the sun has gone behind a cloud. Today the visibility reduced to 200 yds. from a full horizon in 3 minutes, and opened up again nearly as quickly.

This evening we are rowing 65°, which from our fix today is a parallel course to shipping lanes N and S of us, (provided of course that the July *'66* shipping routes are the same as those for '65 and '63.) We are between the lanes to and from 'C' to the channel at Bishop's Rock and the Irish Sea at Fastnet. Thus we can choose and close gently with one or other at will, or be blown there or carried there on a current, at the same time as making our eastings good. A good tactical position, but one which a strong wind from almost anywhere except 245°, or any strong set, would negate.

I have made a number of corrections to our course (in

the light of changing conditions and all the evidence) in the past 24 hours, and feel they have been wise in spite of John's criticism. Without them we would surely be miles out of earshot of the lanes instead of almost certainly between 2 lanes, even though our final fix gave our position as one which we had no intention of wanting to reach.

I opened the bilge and found that the water is getting out of our sea-water ballast bags on account of their ordeal by paraffin. So in the event of a gale we are going to have a hairy time unless we flood and seal the bilge!

So much for the Coast Guards fishing kit, which John has used repeatedly without a fish of any sort being caught except in the net, or hit with the harpoon. The hooks have had all the lures on them in all the various combinations, deep and shallow, with and without cheese, butter and curry (all 3 of which were popular as nibblers but not as catchers), with dead little fish and live (hooked through the back and swimming with the line). The last he tried today. The poor little chap was out for perhaps ½ hour trying to lure someone to eat him. Then he was hauled in, unhooked and he swam away eagerly and quickly once off his ghastly lead. The entire kit is a failure, or else the fish are the wrong sort for all the various attractions in it.

Tuesday, 12th July [53]

Part of last night was unrowable due to the beam sea, and all day we have struggled in a beam wind and sea. But 2 things about the sights. My fix of the day before yesterday was utterly wrong and today we have progressed 45m due E. The wrong sight was due to measuring 43 degrees *up* from the lat. line of another square—the 38 or some such lat.—when plotting, and then measuring *down* from the line above to lift the fix off and up to its proper square, placing it there by measuring down again from the line above. The 5 degree gaps are not all the same size. They get bigger, as I knew very well, as the lat. goes North. The oddest thing about today's position is that we are on a point in space coincident with 3 shipping lanes (as far as we know, though possibly this July is different from others in respect of lane positions) and there hasn't been a foghorn all day in spite of day long mist and fog. It cleared just long enough to get a Meridian passage for lat. and one other sight earlier. John caught a little fish about 5 inches long. He killed it by tapping its head on the deck; it lay dismally on the tonneau, looking rather tiny and forlorn while the stove was prepared.

'Very tasty, but I only had a forkful, he had more giblets in him than a sprat or a herring.' There were attempts to catch more, but no success. 'They understand the tricks now and they won't go near anything,' said John, pulling in a line with cheese on it, an inducement to the fish to surface so that the net can be brought into play. The little fish's head on a hook was no temptation.

If you look under the boat as it drifts sideways during rest periods, the fish are under it facing down wind, swimming slowly and confidently with us. The bottom is covered with down and barnacles all over, but I'm not going down to clean them off until we get out the dinghy again. This afternoon our second biggest fin appeared, 20 ft. off the stbd. $\frac{1}{4}$. Two foot of it sticking out of the water and a huge greyish-brown back underneath, the fin triangular. It did not come up to breathe, so may have been a really vast shark. I banged M'sieur and the pump handle together under water, but there was no reappearance.

Wednesday, 13th July [54]

We have now started to pull in our belts. Till now the food for the day has started with porridge, hot for John with powdered milk and a full packet of sugar, followed by tea made of 2 of Archie's little premixed packs of tea, milk and sugar in one cup, and cold for me with tea to follow. This is between 9 or 10 GMT, about 2 hours after dawn, and is prepared by me. Then during our next watch we have the chocolate—plain milk, fruit and nut milk or nut milk—and the fruit—raisins, sultanas or apricots. During the following watch it is a packet of cheese each, with four biscuits with butter and jam (raspberry, strawberry, apricot or blackcurrant, with some honey). Finally John has been preparing an elaborate dinner that takes up to 1½ hours to prepare, consume and clear away. Horlicks, hot, curried-flavour meat, (pork'n beef, steak'n kidney, plain beef, beef and veg, and ½ and ½ with a curry bar of meat). Sometimes with rice or raisins in it, sometimes separately and sometimes with spuds, mashed and dehydrated, with butter and cheese in them, and with peas and beans or corn occasionally (as with all the food, there is most of what we like least—corn). This is often too much for me to finish—filling, tasty, and it sends away all thoughts of food at home until the next evening. This main course is followed by apple, banana (not so popular) strawberries or raspberries (both very good but not so often encountered).

Now last night for the first time, cut down to meat and spuds only, simply prepared to save paraffin—this is the point of the austerity—and, frightful catastrophe, no hot breakfast this morning, just hot coffee. Yesterday's position was wrong. A mis-addition of 1 degree in the GHA, and I put us miles ahead. So today we are back, and depressed with that thought. Still rowing in a beam sea and wind, with scarcely any of the latter at all. All we need is a month's merciful westerly at Force 5 or 6 and we are home. But today fog again and mist, blowing across us thicker than a fine English drizzle, clinging to everything we take outside the cosy little cabin.

Just before rowing this evening John had his first big fishing triumph. He leaned over and saw the big grey fish—big, but only 10 inches in the flesh, though biggest of the shoal.

'I'll get you, you bastard,' he muttered, and I heard other snips of conversation going on. 'We'll start with method number one, that should get him.' A small lump of Oxo and beef-and-pork bar dropped over the side, and he came straight out hungrily to get a crumb. The next piece had a hook in it, and the big fellow was hooked. 'Hey, Dave, I've got him, I've got the big one. The leader of the whole lot, look at him. Fantastic.' The fish got a boot behind the ear which killed him eventually, and he then posed for pictures.

We have made a plan for getting to the shipping lanes within 24 hours. Row due N now until dark. Then row NE5°E parallel to the lanes until just before morning, then listen and row to the fog horn, ready for the 1400–1500 clearing of the fog tomorrow evening. And in the evening foghorns to the north, 2 aircraft, deep ships' engines told us of a shipping lane there ahead.

Thursday, 14th July [55]

But on arrival in the lanes (presumably) this morning there was a stronger South wind, a heavy choppy and unrowable sea, a wet little sun and fog and mist, but no ships' foghorns at all, nor engines. Then at about our local midday came 2 foghorns NNW, and we rowed after them. Also one sight and possibly another. Kit that has let us down; my penknife—the scissor spring broke. My white jersey, white batman top, John's blue batman top—shrunk. The stove—lid bust off. The compass and masthead lights—don't work. My gum boots—rotten. Knife and spoon set—corroded, prong gone, corner of spoon bitten off. Fuel for lighters—won't. Flints—dissolve in the fuel. Orange Helly Hanson and batman white trousers—stink. Screwdriver—blade snapped while in use. Radio—useless in slightest provocation, teaspoonful splashed on it. Harrier—won't work or propeller gets barnacles. Rudder—corroded. Meths tin—leaks. Matches—won't light.

Birds we see: smaller all charcoal grey. Gulls pair of small black with mostly white underneath (both of these in transit, faster flyers and medium flapping speed). Heavy white and grey with marauding appearance—long ocean-going wings always active. Frequent, humped back compared with others. Our usual ocean gulls with white or battleship grey underneaths. The delicate dancers still with us—2 sorts, the one with curlew flight, gullish wings, sudden stroke, erratic direction, untidy smaller but identical colours steady, flies weakly.

Saturday, 16th July [57]

Just after dawn a ferocious wind came up at about W. I rowed in it beginning at ½ hour after dawn and went the fastest the boat has ever travelled. But very difficult to keep on course. It seemed an answer to our prayers but lasted only ¾ of an hour. Late last night we had decided to stop looking for ships, to provide food and just blow along with the wind until the wind changed, i.e. go North, and then E when we were permitted to by the wind. So last night we rowed NNE, and then drifted N. This morning's wind seemed almost like the Fates saying, 'It'll be all right in the end, boys, we'll see you get the grub.' Until the ferocity died down and the direction changed to NW then N, and finally, when I had put Percy out, to E, and then ESE. I had an hour doing odd jobs and an hour's sleep when up it all blew again, this time from WSW True again. But no sights for the 2nd day running so God knows where we are. And still no ships. John got up to row, but within 2 hours we were back on to ENE Magnetic, wavering to WNW. Perhaps he spoke too soon when he said as he got up, 'Here we are at last—the famous shove—that's what Conrad calls it when you blow all the way home on one wind.' Later in the evening it was round to SE for the second 360° turn in one day. So out went Percy at night.

Sunday, 17th July [58]

This morning there has been a change only to North. But as I got out of the hatch there was a ray of hope. On the northern horizon a band of sky stretched from almost E to W. For an hour it lingered and then, like a vast lid the clouds arched up to reveal the blue eye of the real day to be. First a layer of dull grey primer, then white mares' tails undercoat withdrew to leave us with our first really sunny day for ages. The wind blew from the N for an hour, then entered into the spirit and backed to NW and we were off again, festooned with clothing drying in the wind and sun —even gloves, for the N winds have been cold these last 2 days. And so it lasted to the evening, by which time a fix of several sights told us we were 40 miles to the N after the 2 previous days of effort and drifting.

Oddly enough I had dealings with 3 sharks today. The first was a real baby, on a slow cruise round the boat only 3 or 4 inches down. He was about 4 ft. long, and on his second circuit I got his head in the net. I imagine that the expert on sharks would say, 'Make a plan for a shark before you go near it,' and of course I had no idea what to do then. John brandished a knife, and before any action could be taken the fish had somehow turned round and was snapping at John leaning over the side. He was soon on his way unscathed.

The second was bigger and on his second tour I brought the end of an oar blade down on the nape of his neck—if he has such a thing. It had all my weight and the full endways weight of the oar, and must have been a stunning blow. He doubled up and was off in a flash, and the oar's copper tip had a shining section where his abrasive skin had sandpapered off the verdigris. The 3rd, or was it the same one come back for more, was on his first approaches. I had our axe in my hand, and brought the corner of the blade down with a sickeningly heavy accurate blow longways into his skull. This definitely made him roll unsteadily, but he picked himself up and was away to recober in the depths.

We rowed all night, the sky and the horizon so clear that we could see the stars the moment they rose, which must be rare. It led to a few 'ships' being sighted, that turned out to be stars. All during my spells I thought of us pulling all the weed and barnacles along under us with so much of our effort wasted on them, like pulling a forest with us.

Monday, 18th July [59]

We were worse off than a porcupine doing back stroke, and in the morning we pumped up the dinghy and started work. It was a fantastic sight, with not a square inch of hull visible below the water line. Knives and the wire brush took 2 hours to clean things up, and even then there were lots we couldn't reach. John capsized the rubber dinghy, and was grinning at me and back on board *Puffin* almost without touching the water in recollections of recent sharks and fins we have seen. It made a big difference to the effort needed to row, I discovered in my next spell. Then we both made harpoon guns, elastic powered, out of the dinghy oars, and caught absolutely nothing with them. They were prompted by the discovery that from the dinghy one could see at least one one-pounder and several other good big fish we hadn't known were with us. They came out cheekily to the dinghy but wouldn't reappear once we were back on *Puffin*, in spite of tasty bits of barnacle as bait.

The weather remains favourable and now, this evening, calm.

Last night John suddenly said, as we were chatting after dinner during our 'digestive ½ hour', 'Pass my old hat and gloves.' I asked what he wanted them for and he said, 'Oh just getting things together in case it's cold tonite.' But a couple of minutes later came the truth. 'How about a snout, Dave!' He passed me a 'Lucky' he had lit. I had guessed there were some fags still on board, but when none were offered I thought I must have misjudged him. We are going to have one after each dinner for 10 days.

It is difficult not to laugh at our strange predicament. This evening after dinner (mares' tails, rings round the sun and all portending well in the morning) we fished with the harpoon guns. The only time I got a shot at 'fatty', the biggest of the shoal under the boat, the harpoon missed by millimetres and dashed on down to the bottom. We just can't catch fish reliably, we have food for about 10 days more, yet we laugh at it all and say it will be all right in the end. It is impossible to believe we are going to get into trouble out here, yet the signs are all there. We have had no sign of ships again (apart from a highly dubious noise this evening) and have really no notion of where they are to be found. My suggestion would be southwards, but we have apparently crossed over where I thought they were without seeing or hearing *one*. I am amazed at our lack of apprehension, and am only sorry we cannot be reported to relieve anxiety (if any) at home. I think we may be hungry before July is out, very hungry and not laughing much at the sensation at all. Our lack of luck is stunning—hard to credit the absence of lucky breaks which come our way. Last thing of the day, as the sun was setting in fabulous colours, I caught a fish in the net. And during my 2 to 5 watch a ship at last. We heard him first, then saw him at 240°. He disappeared bearing less than SW. Our ears are tremendously sensitive to little sounds, and often we hear ships and see nothing, even at night. But it is astonishing that he always comes at night, and never during the day, during the fog when we can only hear them and worry that they will hit us, and never during the clear spells which sometimes occur, like today. The skies and sunsets have been beautiful, and one wants to photograph them all.

Tuesday, 19th July [60]

An adverse wind all day but we rowed all the same for much of it. John caught 3 fish in ½ an hour, using bits of mine as bait, and on a line of only 6 ft., much shorter than usual. One had one of our washing-up dinner peas in his crop or whatever he has, which was a saddening discovery. A huge school of dolphin/porpoises combined (unless one sort were baby whales) swam past just before sunset, cavorting, jumping, reversing across and through each other like the bands on Queen's Parade, mists of spray blowing from the big ones each time they rose.

Wednesday, 20th July [61]

We have now been at sea for 60 days! Last night 3 ships were seen. John saw two at once to the S, and another to the North at an hour before dinner. So we are in the middle if we are ever going to be. We decided to penetrate further to the South on 105° True, converging with the shipping lane, and in the afternoon we backed to 90° True. Fog for an hour in the morning, but a clear horizon and a quiet sea all day brought no ships at all! Until late in the evening during dinner when there was fog on 2 sides and a clear horizon on 2—I rowed into the fog and stopped just before dinner and we remained on the edge. All day a very light SE and SSE wind has been no help though not much hindrance. 3 hours on, 3 off, pulling hard without the help of a dodger-full of westerlies to press us on. An inspection of the food lockers has now classified the vital statistics of our larder. No more jam—today was the first without. Tomorrow's chocolate and dried apricots are the last 'goodies' and after tomorrow there is only one more dinner to open. Then on to ham and eggs, beef and pork bar and steak and kidney for about a week, and after that just biscuits and Enerzades, tea, coffee and glucose. The paraffin will last maybe another 4 days. So it all looks a bit dodgy, but bar blowing the big distress whistle there is nothing to do but wait for 'our' ship. We have worked out that 220 tins of 1 lb. will only just do!! We are absolutely complacent about the position, and the interesting time will be when we decide the whistle must be blown—I hope we are still in the shipping lane then.

After dinner visibility 60 yds. and no sky, so bed. John played the mouth organ sitting outside in the fog. We heard 5 aeroplanes fly over, so must be in the thick of things. The day is clear, our dismal sight tells us we are in the dead centre of the W bound lane from Fastnet and Scotland and the E bound for the Channel.

Thursday, 21st July [62]

At 44°N 47′ 35W, we are actually rowing *along* the effluent from a ship, (the bubbles from one of those pipes which are always splashing liquid from ship's sides). We have picked up an old light bulb and an American cardboard milk pack with milk in it. (It tasted abominable!) *Yet* we do not see any ships at all, in spite of having heard one very close in dense fog early this morning just after dawn. We are still rowing into our easterly wind—it is now dead E—so nothing goes right. In 48 hours we rowed for 26, at probably not a jot less than 1½ m.p.h. making 39 miles at least, in a direction variously 65° or 105° True. *Yet* we have during these 26 rowing hours managed to go due South—actually S2° or 3°W—about 20 miles in all. We can't row on dark nights because we mayn't light the lamp as otherwise there will be nothing to cook with sooner than there otherwise wouldn't be. Two or 3 aeroplanes flew over, and a ship's foghorn blew strongly to the West, just before we started dinner. We heard the noise of engines thumping. 'He's just in good time before dark if he's quick,' I said. But we heard no more of him. A vast ring round the sun, with mares' tails, told a promise of weather to come, which will probably mean being blown off the shipping lanes, even if one stops we can't go too close in high seas, although the mast is now ready to come out.

Friday, 22nd July [63]
It is difficult to know where to start thinking objectively about the treatment we are getting from the powers which govern the apportionment of chance and luck, for today's efforts have surpassed all others in their proportion of adversity. We woke for the umpteenth morning to a wind from the SSE–E sector, into which we have been rowing these last few days. Whatever may happen with other craft, whatever may be other people's experience, *Puffin* cannot be rowed into a bow sea or a head wind—and cannot be rowed with any speed at all beyond ¾ knot, I estimate. The moment the oar leaves the water the wind or a wave stops the boat, and it has to be restarted almost with each stroke. This is bad for the morale, because of that feeling of working so hard to get nowhere—the sort of thing one would do to stop going over a weir on the river, or to beat a tide at Cowes for ½ an hour, but not day after day after day in the open sea especially when one is in a belt where westerlies are the rule, SW, W, NW, and easterlies the very minor exception.

Furthermore, when one rests one is blown right back westwards. Last night for example the wind gusted lightly causing an unrowable sea in which every stroke was a 'beginning from scratch', and every wave a 'buttock-splitter'. The result of a great deal of hard work in the last 24 hours is, therefore, according to the fix, a *westerly* run of about 5 or 10 miles. Where are the westerlies? Looking back through the log, we have had nothing better than SSW for weeks except for one day of W and one of SW. And where is the 0.8 knot current marked on the chart? Not around 44°N 47°W at this date, where it should be! But our worst disaster was the occurrence of the only contingency I have forgotten to consider these last few searching days, and which made it therefore all the more stunning and depressing. Our ship arrived, came within 1½ miles of us, presumably failed to see us and departed without stopping. At 12.30 I heard the bumble of engines and stood on the thwart to inspect the horizon. In the distant mist I could just see a freighter SW of us and probably on our actual horizon. I woke John and we decided this was it.

I lit a flare (white) and held it above my head. All its 22,000 candle power blazed away, and after ½ a minute it went out. I dropped the hot end into the sea with a hiss and a plop and we watched and listened to the freighter. It steamed on, crammed to the crow's nest with tinned food and paraffin, without altering course or missing a beat. It also got closer, and five minutes later we decided to light a second flare, when it was still approaching and can't have been more than two miles away. John lit this one, holding it high. No sign of any sort from the ship. I got out the fog-horn and blew 'L' or '·—··' several times, meaning 'You should stop, I have something important to communicate'. We both blew 'L' dozens of times. Finally we decided on a third flare, as the ship was still nearly abreast of us. Bits of burning stuff fell into my hair from it as I held it up and waved it. Its smoke raced down wind in a column that no one could miss who was keeping any sort of a watch. We blew 'L' at the receding ship until it could only be heard as a bumble of engines.

Our disappointment—after 7 weeks of not speaking to a ship except the yacht *Kirsten* and 4 weeks of looking for a vessel from which we could buy supplies—was very deep, especially as his failure to notice us was so unexpected. We had been certain that if we could see him and lit a flare we would be all right. Depressions set in and in a second we were arguing violently about how far away he had been. Tempers flared, the binoculars flew the length of the boat at speed, a clenched fist glanced off a stubbly cheek, swearing and insults rang across to the now vacant horizon. We settled down sullenly to sleep and row, immersed in our separate depressions—at the ship and at our angry senseless outbursts.

Within the hour apologies were made and life was resumed on board. Until 16.45 when John said, 'Can you hear engines?' I got up and listened and soon confirmed the throb of heaving diesels. I scanned the horizon with tremendous care, and finally saw a white ship's bridge bearing due E. We did our hair, pulled on pullovers and best batting suits, counted our stock of white flares, now down to 9, and dismounted the mast. While he was still on the approach we lit the first flare confidently, and blew 'L' repeatedly. They weren't looking, they steamed on, soon we were abeam. We lit our second flare. Away drifted clouds of smoke. They steamed on. John got out his convex shaving mirror and tried flashing. I remembered an idea I had had one night while rowing and got out the sextant. Sighting along the first and second mirrors, I held the sextant at an angle in the plane of the sun and the ship and flashed the arm to and fro, confirming the flash as it appeared on the small mirror uprights. Away he went, and we were quickly resigned this time. Less dismay, but no less astonishment at our poor luck.

We changed course to 165° to intersect both ships' courses at right angles. If there was to be a third time lucky, we wanted to be able to shout straight into the Captain's porthole. Strangely, between the first and second ships we got down and had a sigarette and discussed the position. A feature of the two episodes with the freighters was that they were up-wind of us, and would probably have been unable to hear a note of the fog-horn. The wake and dribblings of the first ship blew down wind to us.

Yesterday I had caught a little fish, and after today's vicissitudes he came in handy for bait. But his mates ate him all without succumbing to the hook themselves, in only 20 minutes. I picked up an empty jetsam tin, useful for meths. Yesterday I repaired Percy. One of his bits of wood had come out and I replaced it with part of one of the dinghy paddles. Today we ran out of milk to have with the cold oatmeal. If we stay where we are we're bound to get a ship in the next 2 or 3 days. That's certain. 'I'll bet when one does come it grabs Percy in its propellers and starts winding us up into the mincer—or it'll be so close we'll be lighting flares to tell it to get out of our way!' Our rowing position is surrounded with all that is necessary for the conduct of the boat, except for perishables and spoilables which we keep wrapped in plastic bags in the cabin. To the right on the forward thwart are our 'goodies' tins, now containing our day to day vitamin pills, sun lotion, tooth brushes and toothpaste, knives, skin stuff for blisters and bottom spots, and other odds and ends; between these are 3-in-one oil (for the rowlocks and all the various threads on board), leather oil to stop the bottom leathers from spoiling, squeaking and sticking, the little meths squirter for the stove and the old lighter fuel squirter. Then there is the spanner which tightens the rowlock underneath nuts; and plastic envelopes, one for storing line, and odd bits for tying and making fast various things, another for the toilet paper book (soon to be Trevelyan, I fear) and a third for my soap.

Further for'ard, next to the buoyancy bags which lie behind the oarsman, and under and around the oars, are the waterproof torch, the foghorn, the flares (except for one packet we keep in the cabin, in case we are in there when they are needed—in this connection we always put the horn and the torch just outside the cabin whenever we both spend the night below). On the left (that is, left as you sit on the thwart facing aft) are the plastic boxes for hooks, nuts, screws, washers, etc., and the one for the fishing tackle. Also our two cups, mine blue, John's yellow (I was sick in the blue one on the first night, it being the only receptacle handy, which immediately established its ownership—I was also sick into one of my gum boots incidentally).

Other stores such as the radio for 2181 are on the side and take up space, but we use odd corners for washing which awaits attention, and stuff which must be dried out after storms. On the starboard side, the plywood pocket we installed in the army docks in Norfolk contain old plastic bags, just in case, for packing films in when they are taken etc., and the day and night flares. John's convex rear-view shaving mirror (originally bought for seeing behind when big waves or ships were approaching—until it was realised that the waves would approach from astern, and that ears and eyes were perked for ships all day and night anyway) and the tail-ends of water bags which had odd stuff floating in them : the port pocket was for food until that all was eaten. It now has the Enerzades which we can't eat, the fishing net and the 4½ gallons of water I collected the night before last.

25% of July has now been East winds—as opposed to the charted percentage of 1.6. It is this failure of the weather which is keeping us now within 130 miles of where we were 17 days ago!! (Together with our desire to go near the shipping lanes, which has certainly been a most contributory factor).

Saturday, 23rd July [64]

Nine weeks at sea—and now the 7th consecutive morning of East wind. Rowing into the easterlies is far tougher on the hands than other winds—I wake up after a 3 hour sleep and my first finger middle joint bends as if there is a spring in it, going just half way with reluctance and then snapping down against the palm; once there it returns to ½ way against the spring, then suddenly gets over top-dead centre and springs open. The rest are getting creaky occasionally too, and John sometimes complains of the same symptoms.

We rowed against E all day in brilliant sun, the wind not strong but setting up an awkward 'stopper' sea. Once more my sights say we have gone into reverse. The disadvantage of this is manifold—by going backwards W or WNW we (1) go backwards (2) go away from the shipping lane, which dips South on a 245° bearing (3) delay our food replenishment (4) risk a South wind getting up and blowing us North away from all chance of replenishment. Today our biscuits were without butter for the first time and our porridge once more without milk. Four aeroplanes went due west overhead but there was no sign of ships at all. Rowed 8 hours, but not, I suspect, with a great deal of effect owing to contrary weather. I rowed my night-time spell until 3.00 in a briskening breeze, managing to remember 48 of the elements before time. But Percy had to be put out on account of the sea then.

While John was preparing dinner I made a special sight for the sextant to turn it into a temporary heliograph. Its operation will be uncomfortable and almost impossible under certain conditions but that can't be helped—we are eating ourselves towards hunger and may be saved by it.

Sunday, 24th July [65]

Our 8th day of East winds, brilliant sunshine, 6 westbound aeroplanes but no ships, either in sound or sight. Mr Big has gone, to be relieved by a mackerel-like fish even bigger than him, but no less wily; in fact the new Mr Big may be eating the shoal. He won't touch any bait at all, or even show any interest in such things as bits of beef'n pork or oatmeal bar. We have decided to row N90°E True for 24 hours and then to turn SE if there are still no signs of shipping (we did this tonight in the end). Today there isn't even any flotsam or jetsam. John caught 10 fish, losing two hooks in the process. The hooks could still be seen sticking out of the mouths of the fish, in the clear still water, swimming unconcernedly with the shoal as though nothing was wrong. Perhaps they really don't feel pain at all. They even swam up to subsequent hooks and tried without success to nibble bait. Hooks are now desperately short, 2 3-prongers and that's about all of the size to get these fish under the boat. Mr Big refused to bite. 'Where's ole Hookie?' said John to the ones with their own hooks.

The *Sailing Dictionary* started unaccustomed work today. This evening, having had 4 fish each, which were excellent, and having found that tomorrow's cigarette was our last (I am smoking mine now) we took a sunset. The answers were a major setback—hence the cigarette—49° 25 or 50°W my and John's watches respectively. This means 40 miles SW or so to the ships, and back days and days on our previous hard won miles. John said, 'There's about enough for 7 more days of meals—today's almost the last of the proper dinners with sweets; and the paraffin will last a few days more, say 4, and then we'll be chewing the meat bars. After that there's always the biscuit and the 'Rosylee' and coffee to have cold.'

D: 'Hope we don't end up as craven skillingtons croaking up to a ship's skipper for a bite or two to eat.'

J: 'No, we'll be all right, there's plenty of time yet.'

D: 'There's one thing I suppose I rely on a lot, and that is that after things like this are over I am always finding myself grinning and saying—how the Hell did we ever go through a terrible time like that. It's always all right in the end for me, somehow or other. And somehow the bad bits usually seem to have been all for the best in the end.'

I retired feeling very unhappy and couldn't sleep straight away. I had an afterthought and asked John to pass me the torch. After a look at the chart I told him, 'By the way—you may see the ships from Glasgow going past across the bow from one side to another: I think we could be just about on that line. They'll be pretty far away and going E to W.'

Monday, 25th July [66]

John called me at 2.00 a.m. with his usual, 'Right mate, time's up,' and I called 'Anything happened?' as usual.

'Nothing—but it's nice rowing if that's any consolation.'

I stood up in the hatch—and straight away saw a ship's light almost behind him. He hadn't seen them, and they'd probably only just appeared that moment. We inspected them with the naked eye and with binoculars.

'What do you think—can you see a green light?' I said.

'I thought I could but now I'm not so certain,' he said. (If we can't see a nav light then his bridge can't see us). He got closer. 'Well, shall we have a go?'

'We could flash "L" and if he sees us we could go on from there.'

John flashed a slow beginner's 'L' with the torch several times. After a minute there was a reply—dash dot.

We laughed nervously as we got out Reeds to interpret it. It meant 'No'. There was another signal—dot dot. 'I'm directing my course to starboard'. This was it.

I lighted lamp and tied it to mast. Started to row towards him, John saying, 'Left oar, a bit more left oar,' and soon he was nearby and almost stopped. John said as she approached, 'She's only a little one,' and her engines in fact sounded quiet and rather like a fishing boat. She can't have been more'n 5,000–7,000 tons.

As she came up, the curb of an orange moon disappeared behind her and below the horizon. We flashed more 'L's as we approached, and finally we were just off his starboard bow.

We took down our mast. John hallooed loudly, but there was no reply. He shouted, 'Do you speak English?' and a voice from the bridge said, 'Yes. Is there anything you need?'

J: 'Yes. Could you verify our position please?'

'Position? Yes.' By this time we were twenty yards off, and the ship's loading lights had been switched on.

'Whatever can they think, a rowing boat turning up in the middle of the night in mid-ocean like this,' I said.

The bridge shouted, 'Is there anything else?'

'Yes,' I yelled, 'Can you let us have some food?'

'What do you need?'

'Everything.'

There was a pause.

'Would you like to come aboard?' A ladder was already hanging down the side to water level.

'We'd like to but we mustn't—it would be breaking our rules,' said John.

A line came down to us and I tied it to the sampson post.

'We're the rowing boat *Puffin* from Norfolk, Virginia. We've been 65 days getting here and we're a bit short of food. Can you let us have some?'

Crew members gathered along the ship's side and more officers stared down from the bridge, some grinning, some serious.

'What's that flag?' said someone.

John straightened our old ensign, and explained proudly, 'That was six inches longer when we left. We've had three storms which took the end off it.'

I garrulously talked up to the crew about our school of fish and how we'd had 10 for tea that evening. A bucket was lowered, and in it were two cups and spoons, sugar, milk and a pot of hot coffee. Someone threw down 4 packs of Pall Malls and some matches, and the bucket came down again with 4 beers in it. 'I can't believe it's all happening at last,' I said to John.

'Oh, I knew it'd be all right—we've worked for all this, haven't we?' he said. The bridge shouted down our position, 44° 20′N and 47° 55′W—only a few minutes off my last fix, and it was confirmed in writing in the bucket a few minutes later. Then the food began to come down, 2 loaves, apples and oranges, tinned milk, 2 packets of tea, fish balls, fish cakes, brisling, mackerel in tomato sauce, fish slices, Korn biscuits, a box of Carr's assorted English tea creams and filling biscuits, marmalade, margarine, Winston and Camel cigarettes (1,200) and packets of matches, 6 galls of paraffin, and 4 galls of water. We sent up a wallet, but at first they refused to take it, finally taking only $75.

We asked, 'What nationality are you?'

'Norwegian, the *Bengazi*, bound for Montreal.'

'How's the World Cup going?'

'England v Portugal. Germany v Russia.'

We said, 'Goodbye and thanks, and good luck.'

'Good luck—maybe you'll need it more than us.'

We asked them to report us and I rowed away as they waved. 'As my mother would say, "Good things come in small parcels" and "It always comes to those that wait",' said John as we watched them tank quietly away. We stowed the oars, lit cigarettes, bit into an apple each and reflected on our change of fortune. We stowed most things there and then, writing the contents of tins with paper labels on the lids in red pen. Fish and more fish. 'If the boat sinks we should be able to swim after all this lot,' said John. He settled down to sleep. It was 2½ hours since he'd woken me for my watch. I smoked and looked up at the stars. A bird fluttered round the mast, so I put out the lantern. As I rowed off, due East, into light airs, I marked a star. It had swung over my head to the ENE in ten minutes—a huge bright satellite beckoning us homewards. Soon a yellow dawn broke on our good luck. The day :

9 planes all W'bound, and an E wind that later became unrowable.

We decided to give it 12 hours and then go N. Bread and marge and marmalade and mackerel in tomato sauce, neat tea, cigarettes, and we sat chatting with a renewed confidence. I thought, 'It's been like having no money, and then going to see Nicholas and getting a £50 cheque—enough to be going on with, though not quite enough to finish with.' We would still need more food to see us home. The school of fish was still with us, I had thought that they might transfer to the *Bengazi* with all the weeds she must have.

But this morning both the 'hookies' were there and Mr Big and the rest, faithfully remaining with us. 'If I catch "Hookie" I'll just get our hook back out of his mouth and put him back—it wouldn't be right to eat him now,' said John. In the evening I was very sick over the side—nervous excitement from the meeting, too much mackerel and tomato sauce and bread, and too many cigarettes all contributing. A pity no one could tell us about the cine film—not even the flash bulb photographer.

Tuesday, 26th July [67]

All today just sitting and talking, with Percy still out and a Force 4 from 10°N of E–ENE. When we decided to row North in 12 hours if there was no weather change, the weather man must have been listening—for this slight change means there is no direction we *can* row without going backwards. We sat about eating biscuits, brislings, bread, marge and marmalade and talking about our jobs. A big new thought—if we can't make UK before it gets too cold, go South to Portugal, making the decision in good time easily.

Wednesday, 27th July [68]

We are in our 11th day of wind in the band 105°–75° True, with immensely hot sun and calm and placid sea. Eating brislings on toast for lunch, decided it would soon be rowable, and prepared to take in Percy, when a tanker came straight for us, circled after our signals—arm—and stopped. The *Silverbeach*, westbound. I was certain that she could ensure our independence from shipping lanes for the rest of the voyage, but she had little food to spare. They kindly sent down biscuits, bread, butter, cheese (fresh), apples, oranges, beans, corned beef, luncheon meat, orange juice, beer and cigarettes. We asked about Ridgway, but although they had heard of him, they had no news. They lowered a ladder but did not ask us aboard.

Also confirmed our position as 44° 07N 47° 39W, much more E than my calculations. Then I had a G.M.T. time check and discovered my watch was 1.49 faster than I had thought—but forgot to take into account the 2 minutes addition. The Chinese crew had a woman with them, the first we had seen. They refused payment, and promised to report us. We rowed off and stowed the gear, still only OK for 4 weeks. They also gave us a chart of the North Atlantic, asked 'Are you taking your own sights?', and seemed surprised. 'Have you seen those fish?' they pointed. Our shoal had strayed into the open.

'Oh, those are our fish,' I shouted possessively.

As we rowed away another ship, a grain vessel, passed on the horizon! Three large blue and lime green predators came to inspect our shoal in the evening. For once the danger from above was forgotten as they cruised cruelly round. The shoal, with Mr Big and the 2 Hookies as its hub, came up alongside away from them, a black circulating agitated school of about 30 I dived the net among them, missing them all. 'Poor things, I think we ought to have an amnesty on them while these others are here,' said John.

Thursday, 28th July [69]

We rowed 17 hours from seeing the *Silverbeach* to dinner this evening in placid water and a ghost of an air from E. A fishing boat on its way home from the Grand Banks passed a mile away without seeing us. The sky clouded, and we have hopes of a change. For days the useless barometer rose and rose, to a final height of more'n 30.6 ins. Now the past 3 days have seen a fall to 30.2.

The mystery of the dancing birds was partially solved when I came across about 9 of them sitting on the water. I rowed across and they rose, flitting straight into the air and circling *Puffin*. I now believe them to be all of one sort, and not 2 as previously. I think they use 2 types of flying gait, the cantankerous ternlike flight with sudden gull-winged down-beats and slower up-beats with tip feathers pointed, and then, with the tip feathers spread, a rather untidy blackbirdlike flight, much slower speed but faster, shorter wing beats. This enables them to hover as well. But what do they eat? I suppose people think the ocean is dull, and that every mile looks the same. But this is never true. The only boring views are the ones when the clouds and sky remain unchanged for days, and when we were in the fog. Then, I felt that however long and far we rowed, and whatever progress we made, we would still seem to be in the same place. But given a changing sky, and even if one is remaining almost in one spot due to hard seas, or if Percy is out, one seems to be racing ahead. A change from clear to cloudy seems like a new place to be, not the old one in fact changed. An event—say whales jumping—can alter the effect; one feels one has rowed away from the place even if one is still at it for head-sea or wind reasons.

After the *Silverbeach* had stopped and gone on, I felt we were in a new place with the realisation that it was the shipping lane—it took on a new atmosphere. Previously I had looked to the SE horizon where I thought the ships would appear; now I looked to the NE or SW for them, and we seemed to have been moved South to a new patch of sea just by the appearance of one vessel.

Boredom or the risk thereof, was thereby relieved by 'being' somewhere else. And of course—a change of weather always alters one's view. It is always impossible to believe that it is actually the same and identical glassy smooth sea which becomes rough—when it is rough it is (must be) a different location, where there are rough seas and high winds. I have noticed that over the last few weeks I have stopped thinking about food and the restaurants 'I will go to'—during that period I must have chopped tens of pounds of onions and mushrooms in my mind for various delicious stews and pots. And having made my mind up about the foreign holiday houses, the painting, and learning a musical instrument, I now find it slightly challenged by the idea of a life in N.Z. or Australia—Brisbane or

Perth. I quite got to look forward to all our meals of Archie's grub, and now am not so well on the 'unbalanced' diet we have had since the *Bengazi.* Toothache obtrudes, and I am a bit preoccupied with the idea of John taking a couple out under a couple of Methadene tablets.

(I actually saw a dancing bird do a flight-transition of style, proving the point above.)

Friday, 29th July [70]

Never saw the sea so glassy. As I prepared to get breakfast a vast black dense fog cloud loomed, giving us 50 yds visibility in O wind. But 3 hours later our 13 day vigil was over as a W wind formed during a rain storm. Slow at first and developing as the day went on. We rowed for 14 hours this afternoon. Splendid to experience the easy pull which the wind gives us, with dodger up again.

I was asleep when John leaned heavily to our tender side (the one with me on it). I sat up and he leaned back in board, grinning, with the net full of fish, 5 in all including one of the hookies.

'Those big blue shiny fish are around, and all our poor little shoal are huddled up here near the surface. I just had to dig the net in among them,' he explained. He retrieved 'Hookie's' hook and flung him back in. 'It's only right, after a week with that in his head,' he said. 'I don't understand your sense of justice, Dave.' Most important to preserve our own school for our own use.

'Right—get ready for a right old commotion.' Now came the big sport. He prepared a big line and hook, stuck a little live fish through the back and threw it out. 'Sorry mate,' he apologised to the fish, 'it's all for the glory of the country.' A shiny blue torpedo lunged as the tiddler swam off, and John swore as he pulled in a bare line—the clincher knot, improved version as recommended by the Coast Guards, had come undone with the impact. He attached another hook on nylon leader line and out swam another tiny martyr. Another lunge from a long shiny massive predator, and another expletive. The line, 40 lb. line, had broken without a second thought.

'Right, you bastards, we'll have you this time.' Out went the third little fish, attempting to swim properly but giving a sad agonised performance. He was carrying a nylon cord with a vast hook in his back near the tail, and without thought of safety he beat out into the open. In a second John had the line tightening round his hand as the bait was taken. He hauled until a huge blue and yellow head was half way up the side against the stowed starboard oar. 'Get him with the axe, Dave, quick, he's nearly cutting my hand off.' I already had the axe in my hand. I leaned over from the cabin and gave a terrific chop on the exposed gill. There was a fantastic thrashing from the huge forked tail in the water. John hung on and I swung again and again. Blood spattered over us and *Puffin* as I hacked until a big hole gaped and the struggle subsided to spasmodic violent twitches.

We pulled him in and lay him on the tonneau, a four-foot long, 40 lbs. silvery blue, efficient-looking killer. We took out the hook and held up the prize, best side forward, for pictures. By this time the bait was nearly dead, and not putting on a very good act, so a couple more strokes with the net replenished the bucket, and a fourth fish swam off, to be taken straight away. The second predator reached the side intact. I held the cord while John hacked, but after a flurry of terrible blows the fish straightened the hook with a tremendous bout of violent struggles and flopped back into the water to disappear immediately.

Now came the task of cutting up the monster. The sport was over, as the big ones had descended to about fifteen feet, a bit wary of activity anywhere near *Puffin*. John put on the leather rowing gloves and opened the swiss Army penknife saw blade. It took ten minutes to get the head off. 'Those that live by the sword . . . ssswt!' he said as he threw it over the side after inspecting the backwards facing teeth inside. We turned our attention to the body, and were astonished when the bait fish slid out of the truncated stump into a pool of blood and entrails, dead but not marked. He went straight into the dixie with the others for our dinner. John slit the big fish down the belly and pulled out the guts. They were flung overboard and soon sank, to be inspected, like the head, with interest by the school, and concern at a much greater depth by the four surviving predators. We jointly filleted the rest into steaks and fillets, throwing the vast heavy backbone away. The tonneau had to be rinsed in the sea, and then I cut off the heads of our dinner. Two more fish came out whole from the inside of the big one, seven remaining late members of our own school, and eviscerated the tiny corpses. They were very good for dinner, but the big one was tasteless, and after a couple of mouthfuls he refused to go down. We decided to try to dry the rest for an emergency. We were both thrilled with excitement by the whole episode particularly while it was taking place.

Saturday, 30th July [71]

Rowed 16 hours with a W/SW/WSW wind from Force 5 to gusts of 9, at speed! Difficult to keep course, but we really feel progress is being made. When I put Percy out to do breakfast, he went off horizontally at walking speed. The marauders returned for dinner at 6.00 tonight, and I conducted a ten minute battle with them with our sole remaining dinghy paddle. A dozen good blows got home, but they seemed not to notice, passing again and again under the boat, depleting our resident school at every sortie. Looks like the same 4. Four ships last night, one from the W. No sights now since the *Silverbeach*; it will be interesting to record the progress of nearly 50 hours positive rowing at one fix. A turtle passed near us, or one of those strange manta rays we saw earlier.

Sunday, 31st July [72]

It's as if we are being thrown off the Grand Banks by order. Winds dead astern of our best course—55°—65°—75° are hurling us along at a fantastic speed. The only problem is to keep stern on to the sea. Wind is up to Force 8 at times, mostly about 6, mostly cloud with some sun. Rowing with little effort. I calculated our total July progress first 4 weeks—40 miles per *week* average. Today *alone* we may have done nearly double that. I am concerned about weight, but—if we don't fill the bilges and a really naughty one catches us abeam we could go over; it we do fill them, she may not ride astern well to the anchor, and so catch them that way. A perplexing conundrum, with my own opinion in favour of leaving her light, so that as much as possible sticks up into the wind! Not bothering with sights —we know which way we are going (16 hours to dinner time). The glass has dropped consistently but slowly for about 10 days, and now rests at 30.08 inches. Every time we tap its face it loses another 1/100 of an inch from a height of about 30.60.

John had the first big wild session for ages from 6–9 to-night—'Hey, Dave I've just been inside the greenhouse—don't open the lid,' he shouted after one monster crashed over us. Every 3rd or 4th wave seemed to be trying to smash the stern. I was inside the cabin, ventilators screwed down, lid down, front up and all hatched; stuffy as hell but nearly water-tight, and not possible for longer than three hours. The sea is coming from 3 different directions at once, and the scene looks like the Austrian Alps, all small and steep and tumbling, with some real big ones in it occasionally.

Monday, 1st August [73]

Further 17 hours of rowing in winds from True W between Force 6 and 9, mainly 8. A big one caught us beam on this afternoon and swamped the boat. Whales drive by inspecting us and the marauding marlin were back to make certain dinner was still about. I saw 7 of our tiddlers abreast in a wave which passed alongside, swimming their fastest to keep up. We are back in the old routine, orange suits top and bottom for every watch, too hot in the sun but otherwise needed several times in each 3 hour period. It is very tiring indeed, and I leave the thwart gladly to sleep after each of my watches, physically exhausted. The water is as warm as we have ever had it, and a marvellous Mediterranean blue with plenty of Portuguese men o' war and some flotsam, so we are probably in the tail end of the Gulf Stream. I took a rough sight, obtaining a longitude position line from an azimuth of 267°. It was no more than 80 miles on from the *Silverbeach*'s position on Wednesday last week. Since then we have rowed 49 hours in a W wind of considerable force, and must have done 100 miles there alone. Then there is the current to add, say 0.8 mph = 8/10 x 72=56 and the surface speed of the sea in this wind, say a further 0.5 = 36. Total 192 at least. Then there were 2 days of rowing in the total calm, adding a further 1½ miles p.h. for 32 hours. Is an all in figure in the region of 240 miles. So 80 miles on a bad sight is ridiculous and infinitely depressing, especially as we have been joking about Bishop's Rock being just over each other's shoulders. An appalling melancholy overcame me on obtaining the disappointing position line, and a tremendous desire to be reunited with my family and friends, to return to a sympathetic and comfortable environment—without, somehow, the stigma of failure over the expedition. But I soon reconciled myself to the situation, as 35 miles a day means 50 days only and will not hurt us at all.

I did not tell John the precise situation, and he continued to sing as he cooked the first of the Norwegian fish cakes, which were awful rubbery discs. So he did one of Archie's blocks of meat as well, and I accidentally tipped mine over the tonneau cover.

Tuesday, 2nd August [74]

Our gale gradually reduced to nothing by mid-morning, and then the wind sprang up from the SE, swinging to SSW by dusk. It was a day of wind and pouring rain and of fish. A few deft attacks, denoted at first by swirls of water, showed that our school was being further depleted by green and yellow marlin. Then I saw a fin appear nearby, motionless and, like a dolphin's, and thought, you never know what's watching and waiting in the sea. This fin, five minutes later, became the tip of the tail of a monstrous shark, 18 to 20 feet long and at least 2′ 6 to 3 ft. thick. It lazily swam past 6 feet away and about a ft. down, with a vast triangular fin sticking up. The marlin immediately sheltered with us, moving about agitatedly, and John caught it a nasty glancing blow with the corner of a big oar. Dolphin and snub-nosed whales cavorted, sometimes turning on to their back near the surface to show their white bellies and short flippers. Two raced by, probably being pursued, clearing 20 ft. in a leap several times together.

For several hours Percy was out and we got our much needed rest. I did a sight which doesn't bear thinking about, confirming yesterday's suspicions, only worse! (45° 30N 46° 20W).

Wednesday, 3rd August [75]
We rowed until about midday G.M.T, 9 hours altogether, by which time the wind was about NNW and we had full rudder to stbd and rowed with the port oar. But wind strength grew to Force 9–10 and we couldn't pull her round even with these provisions. The barometer rose slightly and we tripped Percy to carry us South through the middle of the shipping lanes on the wind.

Thursday, 4th August [76]
Rowing began again this morning and by dinner we had done 8 hours in a wind from about 315°–350°. Very hard and slow, but shows willing. Passed the westbound (Fastnet?) lane and on to the more southerly W-bound Channel lane now : 2 ships W bound.

Friday, 5th August [77]
A sight showed us to be about 146 miles on since the *Silverbeach* 9 days ago. Not a stunning average, but it included a right angle to the north, so actual distance rowed was about 220. Only 53 miles to the ½ way mark. A S wind

backed to SE and later to SSE, so we rowed only a 25° course for much of the day. But with darkness it eased on to SW then to a spot N of W via a lot of backing and froing to the N during the late night tonight.

I saw a ship (having heard it 45 minutes before it drew abeam of us) but it didn't notice us. Then a trawler went past even nearer, pitching heavily, and late after dark two more trawlers going W on the E bound lane. After midnight we had a good strong wind from W x S and rowed on well.

Saturday, 6th August [78]

A fine afternoon ended a cloudy day, with plenty of west wind. A ship to the N, so that's where we must aim for food, matches, cigs and biros and G.M.T. check. The forepeak smelled so I pumped it out and corked the hole. The water I caught last night (about a gallon) having swilled out the can, was full of the horrid brown grey fluff which is a bit serious. I found one of Archie's dinners in the forepeak so we did our morale a great deal of good by eating it for dinner. Last night I opened a tin of cod balls, and they were like huge ants' eggs, 2 inches long, in sea water and ghastly to eat. I had 4, John a half, and we tried toasting one. But in the end they went overboard, and we ended with a tin of fruit. So now a ship is vital. 16 hours rowing again.

Sunday, 7th August [79]

All night a variable wind between WNW and WSW as we moved up to the shipping lane. But by midday a Force 6 SW (Magnetic) blasted us along at a terrific pace and probably through the lane. The baby marlin turned up for our fish but soon disappeared. A satellite last night. Venus this morning accompanied by another planet. An aircraft eastbound fast and low. Two ships E-bound about 3 miles to the North in the morning. This morning for breakfast I did the Ham'n eggs with a little condensed milk and they were vastly improved.

I reckon we have crossed the half way line by now, and seem all set for a good fast second half. By mid-afternoon we were obviously in for a big blow. In the cabin I could feel *Puffin* corkscrewing and curtseying heavily. I called out through the letter box to John, 'What's it like?'

'Fantastic,' he yelled. 'We've never been so fast.'

But the loss of concentration in replying cost him his course, and it took five minutes to get back, with an expletive at every stroke. Later I came out done up in my orange suit, harness and life-line, and took the oars without losing the course we had been holding, and it was a thrilling row. Soon the wind was Force 9 all the time, gusting to Force 10. It was a terrific problem to hold course. *Puffin* would veer 5° off, and had to be grabbed immediately or the next wave would put her beam on. So spin one oar into reverse, and back furiously while pulling wildly on the other. Gradually she came round. But as the force grew, it became more of a super-human task, until finally she was blowing along by herself so fast, that to back, one had to put both hands on the reverse oar, arms out straight like struts, my shoulders against the foredeck—even then both arms were nearly crumpled, and I was most astonished at the strength of Ayling's oar, which never even felt like snapping off. By the time I gave over to John it was a very big do indeed and I lobbed Percy while I did cheese, potatoes, spam and tea in the cabin.

Her gyrations on the sea anchor were incredible, vast seas breaking over us. John sat outside, feeling unwell for the first time on the voyage with the motion and stuffiness in the cabin while I had rowed.

Every now and then he yelled, 'Look out' and screwed up his face as a huge wave rose from astern and swamped the tonneau. It was our biggest gale to date. The sea was whitened with the foam of waves which had gone on past, among them the grandad of all the seas we had so far seen, a vast steep forty-footer. It was like going up and down in a lift. Lying in the cabin with my head right down and the letter box open, I could frequently see nothing but sea where usually I should see sky and clouds.

After dinner things grew harder still, and I considered it dangerous to bring Percy in and risk a serious broaching. The difficult part was not the size of the main swell, but the constant battering of cross seas swinging at 45° to them, lurching us out of control.

Monday, 8th August [80]

We were back to an oily calm again this morning and rowed 65°. But an E air sprang up, followed by a SSE. A large freighter went past, showing that we may be on a shipping lane. I lit a flare and hooted 'L' and he hooted back on the horn, but I missed the message. He raced on towards America without stopping. I changed Percy over to the other side, and put Halazones in the white water can to clean it out. We were both very happy before dinner, and decided to look inside a Verkade emergency pack. 'Vitaminised food tablets and dextrose squares. Take a small piece and chew well', said the instructions, in, among other languages, Chinese. I enjoyed the tablets and dextrose, but John said, 'If I were given one of these at home I'd spew it up, wouldn't you?' We have 4 good evening meals, 3 tins of milk, Archie's biscuits, 3 Verkade packs, masses of biscuits and the fish tins—two tins of sardines, coffee for a month, tea for 10 days, ham'n eggs for 2 days.

The storm took at least 3 inches off the flag, and the fly is ½ as long as the Jack only. The raiders came for our fish again, and I nearly caught one in the net. It is a slight shock to discover that the camaraderie of the Atlantic is not quite 100%. It occurred to me that perhaps ships had been told, 'Leave them till they send up the red flare.'

Tuesday, 9th August [81]

We pulled Percy in at dawn to row to a westerly, but after 5 fast hours the wind veered to the North unrowably and out went Percy again. We had a pork'n beef dinner with corn and cheese and tea, and as we were finishing and chatting, a ship went by, too far to do anything about. We let it go, and immediately saw another on our W horizon. In came Percy and we rowed towards its possible track (that of the previous ship). But after a couple of hours it got no closer, and in fact didn't vary its position at all. We peered at it in the gloom of dusk and decided it was probably the Ocean Station vessel (D) on whose position we lay. We tied a flare to an oar and waved it, without result, and later saw its lights in the same direction.

I took five sights and got the position as 44° 02N 41° 37W (?), an increase of 130 miles or 35 miles a day since our last fix—not bad with almost one blank day out of 4. Percy retired to the deeps again and we both slept.

Wednesday, 10th August [82]

No change from NNE–N (Magnetic) winds. All day in the cabin. Our last Ham'n eggs breakfast with Verkade tablets and tea. The water situation is now critical, though we won't go thirsty because of the tablets. We have a gallon of actual water left only. The tablets are okay but taste of salt and are a nuisance—okay sitting in a life raft waiting to be rescued but we have plenty to do without having to bother making water as well—especially as any quantity will probably go fluffy. I came out in the afternoon and made a cup of tea and 'designed' a dinner for a dinner party. My coq au vin now has chicken livers in the sauce, or possibly with rice as a stuffing for tomatoes to accompany the dish. A bad sign thinking about food again.

John made tea later too. 'You rotten old bastard ocean,' he said, staring out over the sea with his tea in one hand and a cigarette in the other. 'You can't rely on it can you, except that it'll get you wet sooner or later.' I'd been out for 2 hours without a drop coming over—he got damp inside 5 minutes.

In the evening we decided to open one of the sorts of Norwegian tins we hadn't yet tried, Kjøttaker, and it proved to be passable, though probably only by comparison with the other cod balls and fish cakes. These were also some sort of ball in a brown meat-type sauce and we ate them all. The stove ran out of paraffin, and as it was dusk couldn't be refilled because our little rusty 'ready' can was empty and would have to be refilled from the main heavy and ungainly 5 gallon drum in calmer conditions. This meant we would also pass the night with no lamp lit —something we often did but not often when there was the possibility of shipping. To the West some colossal battleship-grey clouds built up, underhung with charcoal black and supported in sturdy pillars of dense rain, the orange dusk coming through the chinks. They missed us by a mile, taking with them a week's supply of drinking water. I sat outside leaning against the forward coaming and thought about buying a Frazer Nash Le Mans Replica and getting it done up to new, or an XK 120. From the cabin, against the wind, squeaky strains of *Shenandoah, Clementine*, and other well-known old tunes from John's mouth-organ. To our NNE upwind, a vast square grey and black cloud of our own was forming and I prepared to catch rain water. I got into the cabin, pulled down the lid and watched it pass dryly overhead. I once had to poke a hole in the ceiling above my bath to let water down from a burst pipe flood in the flat above. If I had pushed a long broomhandle into this cloud I'm certain it would have provided a useful deluge.

At 2.15 a.m. the next morning I half woke to see John getting out of bed. He lifted the hatch and let it down on to the snubber and sat on the tiny cabin ledge. There was an instant's pause, then he shouted, 'Hey Dave look! Look! Look!'

I sat up alarmed and said sleepily, 'What! What! What!' I stuck my head out of the opening in time to see a ship, or the bridge, aftermast and poop deck, thundering past only 20 yds. behind us at about 20 knots. A small freighter had gone right over Percy's hawser, nearer even to us than to him. I sank back into my berth and felt about shakily for my cigarettes and matches.

'Blimey,' I said, 'and of course the lamp isn't lit . . .'

John had got up almost in his sleep and had immediately been hit by spray from the bow wave. All he had seen was a vast bow of a ship with huge port light red and the portholes and deck lighting. As it passed we could smell the fumes.

'If you'd asked me why I was getting up I couldn't have told you,' he said. We watched the lights race off innocently to the West. My heart was still going at double speed, and before I lay down again I looked twice more to the East in case another unknowing ship should be more accurate. And supposing the wind had been stronger, with Percy nearer the surface, as he usually is. Would the hawser have been cut by the propellers, or broken by the impact of sudden tautening, or would our cabin roof have been plucked off by its cleats?

'We must definitely fill the lamp in the morning,' I said as I went back to sleep.

Thursday, 11th August [83]

In our southwards tour with the NNEly we now seemed to have passed 3 lanes of shipping each with one ship only in it, excepting the Ocean Station vessel. Or had Percy held us back so well in a wind which never exceeded Force 5 that the 3 lanes were one? They had been alternately W-bound, E, and W if they were lanes, which bore no relation to the charted lanes for May, presuming always that the lane for August is more S than that for July and the same as that for May. Presumptions, suppositions and ifs.

The wind remained depressingly in the NNE True, though lighter. For breakfast I made tea and the last 2 packs of bananas, and Verkade biscuits.

'The most depressing food I've ever eaten,' said John as I passed his biscuits into the cabin. 'The best thing for us is to sleep until the wind changes.'

I thought of waking him with coffee later and asked what it was like with tinned milk, and what the dextrose tablets were like in it—he had tried it.

'Pretty terrible, won't dissolve,' he said, and slept.

Our dancing birds still with us in 6's and 10's, making their odd tuneless little chirruping at night only, though John thinks he heard it once during the day. I have seen one more settling, though only for about 3 seconds. But it settled completely, folding its wings right back. A gull-like bird flew over. Blackish grey top and bottom with pigeon grey breast, short beak (shorter than a gull) and a spike of pointed feathers from the middle of its tail. A similar bird some weeks ago but brownish-speckled underneath.

The water is very warm and lots of Gulf weed, which is in some way blown by the wind into long strands composed of bunches of it 100 yds. long. We have decided on a new course of action with the next ship. If they prove to be unhelpful with the food, in providing only 10 days supply, John will go aboard, ask to see the captain, with both our wallets fastened in his pants. He will explain personally how important it is for us to have a good supply and try and enlist a more sympathetic approach. Possibly even go with the steward to make certain milk, sugar, jam, cheese and some fresh stuff come aboard *Puffin*. If they refuse payment, we will offer $50 for the 'Mission to Seamen' collection box, and this *can* be insisted on.

No sooner said than done. I took a sight making us 43° 53N 41° 00W, and came up to tell John to keep an eye out to the S. There was a ship's mast high on the horizon. Gradually it came closer from about 190°–200°. We decided it was Ocean Station vessel (D) and as its approach was so slow, we pulled in Percy and rowed down to it. It was Captain Albert Frost of USCG in CG vessel *WPG 33*. I rowed cautiously up at first until we saw the American flag; then they lowered ladders and fenders and a voice loudspeakered us, 'Would you like to come aboard?'

At first we had decided to say No until the scene was investigated. But once we were alongside John went up the ladder. I stayed in *Puffin* in accordance with Moxon's bet. John later told me that the Captain's opening remark to him was: 'I'm glad you've dropped by—you can teach some of my boys to row.' John was tottering all over the place as if he were drunk. He said to the Captain, 'It's not my condition—it's just that I'm out of my environment. This is the first time I've felt sick in eighty-three days at sea.' The Captain opened all his portholes and John went to the basin and held his head under the tap.

The sides of *W 33* were packed with lads, shouting, 'What's your name?'

'David.'

'Hey, Dave, do you need water?'

'I *thought* those bags were for water!' I passed up the white can and about 20 bags, and soon they were lowered back bursting with fresh water.

'Torch batteries?'

I showed our only spare, and soon 4 more came down.

'Cigarettes? How you for cigarettes?'

'Well, we're a bit low on most things actually.'

Cigarettes, cigars and matches were soon thrown down. An officer wearing a life jacket came aboard *Puffin* and showed me to have been 10 minutes of arc out on my latitude and spot on on my longitude—43° 47 x 41° 01.2—which was super news, in view of the fact that when I quoted my position he said, 'That's probably where we're supposed to be' and the bad sight—taking sea I had had. He took our names and addresses and promised to say we were well and in very good spirits after eighty-two days at sea, and not to mention any food or water they were going to send down, in order not to upset our folk.

'Dave, would you like coffee or tea?' Three times the cup was refilled, and a fourth time when I spilled one. After the last time I threw up the cup and it fell back on to the deck and smashed!

'Hey, Dave, smile please.'

'Take ya sunglasses off, will ya?'

'Look this way, will ya, fella?' Every sort of camera snapped and buzzed alongside as the CGs took pictures of us. The food started coming down—huge 8lb tins of spam,

Hershey chocolate, evaporated milk, asparagus in tins, chicken soup, vegetable soup, fruit of every sort in tins, fresh lettuce, tomatoes, apples, oranges, potatoes, bread, fig Newtons and sweet biscuits, bacon, eggs (they came on last after John got back). It came down in buckets and since the water had filled both side pockets I started in the cabin. Bucket after bucket swooped down the side on its orange nylon line. I rolled back the bunk cushions and stowed it as it came, right down the footwells and in the middle between the berths. Soon the cabin was crammed with goodies, a huge bag of candy standing finally on top of the pile.

By this time the crew had spotted our ½ doz. marlin (which turn out to be called dolphins in the U.S.A.) Excited shouts preceded the appearance of a forest of fishing rods on the foredeck, and soon there was a yell as the first one was hooked and played. An officer asked me about our fishing, and soon produced some fish hooks which will be just what we need for our small school, if it still exists. The swell was considerable and *Puffin* was going up and down 6 or 7 feet, with huge wet rope fenders being moved up and down manually by two sailors. Later two fenders were lowered to us to tie to *Puffin*.

I found myself very nervous at first—that was why I preferred to row up to the side, to give me something to do. But I was soon answering questions about the boat, the weather we had had, whether the cabin kept dry, how long we had been at sea, where we were from, and where we started from. All the CGs were very friendly. After we had been alongside an hour or so, John returned, throwing down more cigarettes before he descended the rope ladder. The captain came with him, and wished us luck on our voyage. We said Thanks and Goodbye, the eggs came down and we cast off, rowing away as quickly as possible.

After a mile we started on some of the stuff. John chewed an apple as he passed out some pom-poms, then opened a packet of fig Newtons which we nearly demolished, then another sort of cream biscuit, while I rested on the oars and read the little ship's newspaper which had come down. It contained mostly U.S.A. news, naturally, but there was a bit about the U.K. Government—a Parliamentary battle over an austerity bill, which came as a contrast to the bounteous American generosity. This little newspaper started a chain of events which brought back a feeling that the rest of the world was real again, reinforced by our dinner and the magazines afterwards. Then we set to on clearing up, stowing the occasional fig Newton as we worked. The locker under the tonneau was first. I emptied it to find it full of squalor and stench, and opened the 'cock to let in water, pumping it out and repeating this several times. We filled it with all the fish balls, topping it up with bags of sea water to hold the tins in place. Then I sorted out the forepeak in the same way, putting our cigs and the fresh stuff and bread and candy in there. And then we had dinner.

John had apparently been working out in his mind what to do, and soon I was sipping chicken noodle soup, followed by ½ doz. rashers of bacon and a couple of eggs with fresh crisp lettuce leaves and 3 slices of bread, followed by more bacon and lettuce and bread, followed by tinned mixed fruit and cream—our big cup full—followed by another half cup. It was an orgy and I bolted it greedily in the irritating swell, feeling a part of the world again, reintroduced to so many old friends at once. And while I ate I thumbed equally greedily through the magazines—such sanity again, girls looking fabulous, half forgotten by us though often talked about, cars, little snippets of news, (in a Goodyear ad. that an American car won Le Mans), guns, goodies and all the advertiseral paraphernalia of civilisation, baseball, *Time Magazine* and *Reader's Digest*, once so familiar. John then began to tell me about his trip aboard with the captain, as we lay gorged, belching contentedly with properly full tummies, and beginning to feel sleepy with excess. It is astonishing how a full tummy can restore all sorts of depressed morales. All day we had had a cup of Archie's tea (a bad word now) 4 dextrose tablets and 3 vitaminised food tablets (worse) and the peculiar dried bananas. And I spared a thought for the fish balls in brown sauce we had thought were so eatable the previous night at dinner.

On board, John found his legs were unsteady in the new motion of *W 33* knocking into things, and rolling from side to side.

An officer took him to the Captain's cabin, got coffee. The Captain asked what he could do for us.

'We could do with 200 lbs. of canned food and some water,' John answered. An executive officer appeared and made notes about suggestions—corned beef and fresh fruit—away then, and went off to start on the collection of stores for us. John and the Captain retired to the bridge because of the heat. The weather man was sent for to answer questions. John said we were worried about summer storms, but the weather man attached no importance to them.

'You've got nothing to worry about for a long time yet,' he said, as if it would be October or so before anything serious happened.

'Anyway he dismissed my fears.'

He got a chart out and showed John where the present low pressure area was, and said we could expect a change of wind in the next 24 hours. There would be no bad weather for 2 or 3 days and that the Gulf Stream would give us about ½ knot, just here. They said also that we mustn't put out Percy if he is going to go below 100 ft. as the Gulf Stream is only that deep here, and beyond is a cold current going the other way; the *W 33* sometimes drifted 1–1½ knots, he said, due to the wind as well. If we lose the warm water, head SE and it will always return. John told the captain about our near miss, and a horrified expression came on his face when he heard about the spray from the bow wave hitting John. He thought it was a great adventure we were taking part in.

'I've seen your boat and I know you must have gone into

all this very carefully,' he said. 'In this scientific age it's nice to see someone willing to have a go and take a chance to do something worthwhile.' He asked questions about how we came to do it. John told him about Samuelson and Harbo and how it all began, and said we were beginning to wonder how those two ever did it. He laughed like hell at that. John asked him about the 2 paratroopers and he said, 'All I've heard about was a message from HQ' which told him that he might see 2 commandoes who were trying to row from Norfolk, Virginia.

'We expected to see you a week ago.' But he had only heard about one rowing boat.

John asked about the World Cup.

'You can take a bow, England won, it's all over,' said the Captain. 'I'll let you have a few mags to keep you up to date with things.' They discussed C. S. Forester's books and the Captain explained about his last unfinished one before he died. The executive officer came back and said the stores were on board.

J: 'The thing is, we must pay for these stores.'

Capt: 'Well, it makes it so difficult with the forms to be filled in. It's not worth the trouble.'

J: 'Nevertheless we feel we ought to pay.' The Captain said they'd plenty of stores on board and he was only too pleased to let us have them.

J: 'Can we make a contribution to the seamen's fund or the mess fund?'

Capt: (unequivocally) 'No. We'd like you to have this with our compliments.'

John saw himself in a proper mirror for the first time. 'I looked like a pirate with my unkempt beard and hair all over the place.'

Capt: 'You can stay as long as you like—spend the night on board, have a shower, or the facilities of the barber's shop, we've got one on board.'

J: 'It's extremely kind of you but we must press on. The object of my coming aboard was to explain what we wanted and to pay for it.' (stores on board).

I felt pleased that we had been offered the comforts and had been able to refuse and go quietly—it showed the right spirit in which we are undertaking the voyage.

J: 'I saw the shower there—it would have been nice to leap under it.'

He mentioned our flare to an officer. He remembered it, 'We were trying to take star sights when the bright light appeared on the horizon. I thought it must be a ship (the tanker) which had just gone past,' he said.

We forgot a G.M.T. check, photo information, cooking oil, and we didn't get sugar, tea, sausages, but who would complain.

Odd how we cursed the ill North wind which blew us into our own salvation. Without meeting such a vessel as the *W 33* we might have had to make a dozen pickups during the rest of the voyage.

Friday, 12th August [84]

We both slept the night, hoping that the surfeit of fresh food would replenish lowered energy reserves. By 8 this morning John was rowing in a S–SSW wind as predicted by *W 33*'s weather man, in a short easy swell with the dodger up. Bacon and eggs, bread and hot chocolate for breakfast, with 5 fig Newtons, tinned fruit cocktail and biscuits for lunch. A dull day grew rainy and the night was almost my most miserable so far. I was soaked several times from astern, as was the cabin once through a ventilator, and I just couldn't see the course properly. I lit the lamp (or we both did, having had jointly to fill it in the dark) and that only just showed the course on the compass. But it also meant complete blackness beyond the tonneau, and I couldn't see which seas were going to come in. They suddenly sloshed over without warning. One's world reduced to the cockpit only. I put the lamp out and rowed by the flag, checking by torch that we were on course.

Saturday, 13th August [85]

By this eve we had rowed for 24 hours and I guessed a distance of 60 or so miles from *W 33*, certainly no more. Several dolphins (U.S. sort) appeared in a school, at one time 16, and featured two scares. In the first, one raced from a 'cruiser' fish of massive weight and dimensions, taking to the air in its terror until the cruiser fish leaped too, catching it right before John's eyes with a frightful mid-air snap of its jaws. In the second, the whole school chased a 10,000 strong school of small fish which took to the air, and ours caught several in the way that our mate had succumbed. The law of the jungle predominates, and we are fully aware of coming under its jurisdiction in our own way. The school of dolphin keeps with us now for protection.

An old Stratocruiser flew over, but otherwise nothing took place. The wind went W and light, strengthening again as night fell. Fried spam, asparagus stalks, potatoes were dinner, followed by fruit again.

Sunday, 14th August [86] *Monday, 15th August* [87] *Tuesday, 16th August* [88]

3 days of full rowing inc. fair winds from NW to SW, with patches of S, SE and N for brief periods. We dug into the goodies, with a consequent rise in energy. Potatoes and tomatoes and lettuce going bad so we are hurrying through these. One sight today (16th) and hope for another.

This afternoon total calm in high pressure prior to another burst of SW/W, we also hope. The second sight gave us a fix of 45° 09N 40° 05W which is about 22.5 miles a day under ideal conditions. Disappointing to say the least. About a dozen gulls swooped back and forth over me this evening rather ominously, and I began to see them in a different light—as the prospective perpetrators of a rather ghastly scene like *The Birds*, with me as their victim. There was no reason for this attention on a calm sunny evening. In pairs from astern, and peeling away on each side, and from the beam fast at masthead height always looking down beadily at me.

When I told John about it he said, 'You should have

caught one of the bastards in the net then we could have had a fresh stew.'

We discussed what day it was today.

'Well, last night we had beans with the spam, and the night before you remember you found the tomatoes and lettuce were going off so we tried to finish them off, and the evening before we had spam and sparrow grass, and that was the 13th, I am sure, because it was our first meal on the new spam and we had two bacon and egg dinners and the *W 33* met us on the 11th.'

We view our position today cheerfully—not that it is a cheerful prospect but we are used to that sort of blow and don't mind. I have worked out that it will be about 60 days from here on.

D: 'Do you realise that's more than we started off expecting to do altogether?'

J: 'Yes, and if we aren't careful we'll miss the Motor Show—that's on about October 20th.'

D: 'Mid-October, it's bloody ridiculous, isn't it?'

Wednesday, 17th August [89]

Late last night the wind came round in the calm spell and started blowing E. By night we were both in our bunks with a Force 3 E–ENE, which lasted all day. I spliced a 'Y' into the sea anchor trip line successfully, so that we can lie astern or tripped. The spam, 1st tin, is nearly finished, and we have discovered that the next tin is corned beef. I have invented the toasted spam sandwich for breakfast. B'fast and dinner are almost the same, with toast instead of spuds and beans, and the apple hot instead of cold, and Archie's tea instead of chocolate. We have nearly finished the magazines, too, and we will soon be back on to the resources of our thoughts for entertainment.

Thursday, 18th August [90]

Another day of sun and E wind, coming slowly round to SE but still Force 3 and with an unrowable sea. We ate out of boredom, adding baked beans on toast twice and spam sandwiches for lunch to our usual diet. I spliced another couple of loops into the sea anchor, and it is now all set to measure for the correct tripping procedure. I also did a couple of practice splices, including one conditioned for joining rope ends together. We filmed our first film today—of me doing a splice, and another of John getting dinner. Two aircraft flew over to the N of us on a W course, maybe inferring that we are near to the southernmost of the shipping lanes.

Friday, 19th August [91]
All day indoors, reading, sleeping, swearing at the weather and playing 'How many States—Counties—Countries', and finally the game of six headings, motor cycles, cars, film stars, etc., and then choose a letter.

Wind from SSE magnetic improving to S magnetic as evening fell. Tomorrow we row, (I hope) but Eustace has fallen really deeply, so one *can* only hope. Not worth rowing in S mag. but worth tripping Percy for. I am melancholy. We both agree it breaks our stride terribly to put out Percy, and John agrees that afterwards (indeed after evening sleep) one feels like a new boy at school going out to face the elements again, with an extra heartbeat of anxiety and I suppose a little fear of the unknown.

Saturday, 20th August [92]
At midnight last night we rowed again in a Force 3/4 SW, which has since westered well, and rolling us home at a good speed. I estimate about 70 or 80 gulls gathered this p.m., wheeling low, strafing, and landing and taking off nearby. The landings are ugly—the bird approaches with feet splayed and settles at speed, slopping forward as its breast hits the water—but the t/o is superb. A dozen or so firm strokes of the feet to windward with wings spread gets it out of the water and airborne, without flapping once. It lets the crest of the wave throw it into the windstream, and immediately wheels down wind to gather speed. On the water the birds are rightly nervous of fish, and every

five seconds one dips its head under to make certain nothing is about to grab it by a foot.

Yesterday a vast 'dolphin' which had been inspecting us swam over to a resting gull. The bird saw it 6 ft. away and was off in a panic. Today's big flock was a small type of ocean gull of which we have seen only a few so far, and recently. Top of wing and back pale brown flecked with outer panels crisply divided and dark brown/black. Under, mostly white, head white (and neck) with v. dark cap and glasses. Dark bar on tip of tail, and then white bar. Also a dark skua-like bird with the tips of two central tail feathers pointed and one inch longer than the rest.

I found an anchor buoy of alloy floating, and we picked it up, also a good bit of wood. The ecology of the ocean is fascinating. Each thing had small one inch to 1½ inch crabs clinging to it. I shook them off, and they scattered across the top of the water to our hull, horror-struck at being cast off. I was towing (laundering) my blue costume, and two are now in that. Also in the costume hundreds of them, colour beige, clinging in groups to every seam. Two nights ago I took down the mast to reduce windage, and slipped in a swell. The mast fell across the deck and when I moved it the radar reflector fell off. I got the truck of the mast hooked under it twice, but it sank slowly away, on its long downward journey, until we could no longer see its silvery glow. (The crabs—they must have as slight a chance as we of finding girl friends on their perilous voyage.)

Sunday, 21st August [93]

A new type of dancing bird came past alone, dancing a great deal for no apparent reason. More the shape of a martin than the others, which are still with us, one day up to 20 of them last week.

An assessment of the food proved us to have, besides Archie's biscuits, a few oranges, other biscuits, Kornis and the awful fish balls, the following (enough for 30 b'fasts, 26 dinners, 28 beverages): 14 milk tins (two were open with rusty holes, and milk all over the cabin bilges) 4 sparrow grass, 2 large beans, 2 pears, 1 peaches, 1 spam (6 lb.), 1 corned beef, 10 soup (3 tom, 3 veg, 4 chicken nood). So not too clever, and we will need as much again. Besides which the amounts set aside for meals may not be enough, and they include the not-very-special Norwegian meat balls.

A ship last night, on our own course, and aircraft heard but not seen. Force 3/4 W and WSW, not really strong enough to be a lot of help. I feel tired and listless, no proper diet (I think I eat in a day what I would normally eat at dinner only at home).

Monday, 22nd August [94]

A year since I thought of the idea.

John rowing in a Force 5 WNW in bright sunlight, swearing every time a wave sprays a sleeping-bag he's drying. Underwear hanging from the dodger, jerseys laid out on the tonneau, dirty black, red and golden towel on hatch cover front. The almost following sea lashing against the stern ¼ of an inch of plywood away. Rudder creaking, oars sending a knocking echo through the boat to the 'Banjo' sound-box of a cabin. I tapped a fag ash away, orange peel heaped in the ash-tray, and reflected on our sight. (Bet 5/- we'd be home in 39 days—unlikely but heartening). 93 days at sea behind us. If there's any money, buy the cottage in N France, invite friends over. Slap, roll, up and down movements all day, and night, every day and night. Tom soup and the mouldy bread, trimmed, for breakfast, corned beef and spud slices, fruit, Archie's tea, for dinner. 5 hours away—rationing, hungry. How many miles from U.K., Azores, Virginia Beach, Newfoundland? One ship in eleven days. Everything damp from humidity and gales and last night's squall (with Percy out and tripped, and rain like never before, getting in everywhere, me soaked and shivering and tired at 4 a.m. until I got into the wet berth on port side, covered with soaked sleeping bag and got 5 hours consecutive sleep.

And thought back to the previous fateful August in the

Bush in 1965, and back further to the August of '64, Nairobi, Seychelles, Open Country, B. Dennison, Taylor Commercial, Culligan; and how it all begins and why it's the right time and the right thing to do, and the jobs I'd tried for and failed to get.

Now wind whining and buffeting in the open cabin front.

Tuesday, 23rd August [95]

Most of the above is for today. Yesterday nothing happened except for a bit of construction with small pieces of canvas and rope and the 2nd dinghy paddle. Hungry and tired and listless, and on a reduced diet. No more chocolate, spuds until today only, the last of my biscuits went last night, the last apple this p.m.

The sight mentioned on Monday sent us unbelieveably backwards—a retribution for what? When I pulled Percy in this a.m. after the squall, a chocolate and yellow spotted fish, fattish, accompanied him. My batman trousers went o/b while drying on the mast; one minute there, the next gone. We searched but found nothing. The stick caterpillar/scorpion/insects in my trousers I boiled in seawater, and they all were killed. I think I have let our axe go o/b.

Wednesday, 24th August [96]

The squalls increased in severity until they reached an incredible climax during my row from 1 a.m.–5 a.m. One squall approached so blackly that I thought at first it was a big wave. Had to stop rowing because of darkness—inability to see the flag—reduced down to the Jack by 6 ins in 48 hours—and we broached and were immediately ferociously swamped by a vast breaker, at about 2 a.m. Water covered the boat to the depth of the thwarts almost, and soaked the cabin by squeezing in everywhere. Wind up to and beyond 9 made course-keeping a colossal feat of strength. Backing til the oars creaked and jumped out of the rowlocks; crabs caught, forcing the handle suddenly into my tummy : sometimes a 2 min. job of incessant maximum output, gaining a point, then losing two on the crest of a wave. I was broached while rowing by an immense breaker which once more swamped us inside and out, hitting me in the face so hard it squeezed down past my hood in pints on to my jumper. For 4 hours I scarcely let go of the oars, but eventually there was too much N in the wind to row a favourable course, and I immersed Percy.

This evening still a boisterous sea but less wind, the bearing 335°. I never saw such enormous waves, with actual liquid canyons between each; the whole surface of the sea track-marked as if by tanks, by the wind in tiny rivulets, foam streaking after a breaker for 200 yds. and more, *Puffin* receiving some tremendous blows without a creak.

I was really beginning to think I had the measure of the squalls after a 3 hour daylight row yesterday evening, and approached the usually rather frightening night gale without a qualm—until the two big boarders, which were so huge and powerful and engulfing as to be really scaring. I prayed for it to ease, under the less undignified guise of a prayer for less of the North and more of the W, though we were doing a fantastic speed when running with the wash in the eve. A phosphorescent wake even without rowing; just the dodger and *Puffin*'s broad stern windage to drive us homeward. But we must by now be 60 miles S of the ships, and well on the way to the Azores! The fury of a stiff gale, much less a storm, has to be experienced to be understood. The way the boat is tossed about, being thrown full weight into the sides of the cockpit by a big roll, a wave dragging an oar through the rowlock—something I couldn't do with my hands—and dropping it into the sea, to be grabbed before it dashes behind into the dark—is all pretty frightening and I don't suppose I will ever get accustomed to 'weather' at sea. I have had to pump out full bilges 3 times in 24 hours.

Thursday, 25th August [97]

Late last night, lying to Percy, John was tacking parts of

the Gentex cover over the hatch lid to avoid seas coming through the cracks, I thought of my idea of motor boating round the world. We rowed in rain and slopping seas all day, damp, tired, but on our way.

Friday, 26th August [98]

During the night, winds our way—WSW, SW, W, WNW back and forth, Force 4–6 or gusting 7. A fish with a number of blue scales fell in the cockpit, garfish, and we had him for breakfast. A good drying day provided the sea doesn't wet things. We have not had a fix for 10 days (one that we like! !) and today the sextant showed signs of wear—the secondary mirror is loose again, and a tiny flange is breaking. Tonight I took a fix from two rather rough sights and the results were the most unbelieveably small we have ever had, at a time when we were expecting something big—looks as though hundreds of miles of progress have just disappeared into thin air. The net gain over the ½ way mark is 5 miles or so. We just can't explain it except for: back eddy of the stream, inaccurate watch, inaccurate sextant or readings. None of these fit to that fantastic extent. Look back over past few days, all speeding SW NW and westerlies. Even John looked grave and worried when usually he stands up to the bad news with a grin. I looked at the first sight unbelieving, and stunned when I had the second for ½ an hour, unable to consider what it meant to us. So the second fix running is backwards, and we are within yelling distance of the USCGC *Duane*.

Saturday, 27th August [99]

A further fix today made an equally incredible result, though further South by 90 miles??? There was a N wind in light gusts all day and we stopped rowing, doing repairs. John changed over the oars, the old ones were losing their leathers, which were rotten and dented, and the rowlocks which had opened enough to allow the oars to jump out. Also the 2nd Gentex cover fixed in place over the dodger as a bad weather cooking cover against the wind. Our position now is that we must get to the ships but aren't sure how. They're North of us, but we can't get there and are going backwards, and we don't know why. A bit of a predicament. After dinner a cigar. As John said, 'Ridiculous—here we are with cigars in our mouths, and hardly any food in the boat.'

Sunday, 28th August [100]

The oars John installed were our 9′ 6″s with sawn off handles and the buttons moved. They had to be changed this a.m. for the 2nd pair of 9′ os.

All day on repairs—foot of soft berth, Gibson Girl etc., in a light gust of Force 1–2 from the N. A good drying day, the boat festooned with almost everything wearable on board out in the sun. The net caught the caterpillars, and they were burned off with a brand of burning cotton wool. A new bird. Black all over except underneath, wings of greyish/white with dark fringes, and diagonal white bars one on each top wing. Short black beak and fast*ish* shallow wing-strokes. John said 'The smallest bird we have seen on the voyage.'

Monday, 29th August [101]

Our 100th day at sea. A splendid 4/5/6 SW/WSW blowing us to the shipping lane 77 miles to the NNE of our position yesterday. Drizzle and rain with bright periods. 3 peach halves for breakfast, soup and Kornis for lunch, Archie's biscuits for tea, and spam and Kornis for dinner. We have now scored one victory over the pundits who said we would be at each other's throats all day. We find more and more to talk about, and the range of subjects is endless. A gull took off near me with a swift run up the wind and up on approaching wave, and continued bicycling with his feet up to 40 feet, shaking off the last drops as he wheeled away.

Tuesday, 30th August [102]

I should have a sight later on which will doubtless prove

something or other. But meanwhile, some of our thinking this a.m.: (1) The voyage is a row-the-Atlantic voyage, not an exercise in carrying food. Therefore by finishing the voyage we achieve our aim, and to pick up food on the way is better than failing to achieve the objective for lack of food. (2) By November the weather may be with us, but cold, damp, hairy in the upper lats. of the course. Therefore divide remainder of voyage into 8 weeks ending end of October, and date them. Failure to make good ¾ distance in 4 more weeks means intruding into Nov. at the end of the voyage for certain. In this case, turn SE to Portugal at about 30°W is better than giving up because of the cold. In the meantime, immediate object is: collect 200 lb. minimum of food, from as many ships as necessary as soon as possible, and to hell with Moxon and poor public relations. This food collecting to free us from the shipping lanes may mean success or failure, and we can go South East without worrying about proximity of ships. So it may be possible in a few days to guarantee success, even going into November on the Portuguese latitudes without danger. What is unthinkable is to give up because of the food or fed-upness in end October still 100s of miles out.

My sights today resulted in a disastrous fix—we had guessed respectively 70 and 60 miles of progress from a very favourable SW, and the fix showed about 15 miles. We have been over every possible factor time and again. Watches—they can't both be that far out, as it would mean 4 minutes error. Sextant—although it is in poor health, its error can be checked at 0°. My calculations—I have checked my P.L.s and am using the same method I have successfully used for 10 weeks or so, and there is no question of a mistake. The compass—I constantly check its reading with the sun's azimuth, both at midday and at the time of my sights; we have rechecked many times that we are *not* in error in saying 'Compass to chart—deduct W variations' and vice versa, and we are therefore not rowing the wrong course, we have been at it too long, and know the sun's stars' and moon's positions too well, to row a reciprocal course. Meanwhile we lash along in ½ a gale and get nowhere. One solution possibility occurred to John—there is a mid-Atlantic undersea mountain range. Supposing deep currents are hitting it and sweeping up to the surface in places, swirling W again at 2 knots. It (or some other current) would account for a lot, and I now consider it likely in view of the fact that there's a 56 and 19 and 20 fathom patches ahead of us.

Last night our meanest dinner—corned beef and hard tack, biscuits and sugarless coffee. And while we were having it we were very nearly capsized: our closest pass for days. A colossal wave broke behind us, abeam, throwing us on to our stbd. side 80° or so. Without a drop coming aboard it threw us 20 ft. in this position, the foam pressing and ruffling against the bottom. We recovered as the wave spent itself.

'That was very peculiar,' I said to John—realising immediately that I had been very frightened, sitting to port and staring *ahead* at the sea foaming below us.

He peered out of the cabin. 'What happened? It felt as if we were in a plane barrel-rolling.'

My heart didn't stop banging for an hour.

Wednesday, 31st August [103]

5 hours of Percy as it blew with too much North. Otherwise rowing fast on 65° and 45° True. 3 peach halves ¼lb. corned beef, four Kornis and a packet of hard tack. Coffee twice, and that's all for today. John just put the oars down, unable to go on.

'I'm completely whacked,' he said. 'I couldn't go on; the oars were just going up and down.' No sights as too rough but maybe a sunset. The cabin and everything in it is damp again, and the 2 sleeping bags actually wet. So we live in our oranges day and night with occasional breaks to dry out if the sea looks kindly. John tried dextrose in the coffee, with no significant difference.

'I wonder if we ought to force a packet of Enerzades

down us each day,' he said. 'I can remember saying ages ago it'll be a rum day when we have to eat those.'

A 12ft. shark this evening, which stayed until dusk. A ghoulish thing to have with us, slowly swimming under the stern, it showed a scimitar fin and a pale grey top and white underneath.

Thursday, 1st September [104]

More easy rowing on 30° and 50° True with following winds of about Force 4. Tired and hungry! The hunger brings on awful depressions. 'I'll never see them at home again. We'll never be able to stop a ship in these seas, and we'll be sick with hunger before there's a calm.'

A ship passed W-bound late tonight, first observed SSW and disappearing shortly afterwards. I was asleep in the footwell, and suddenly felt inspired to get up and have a look, for no reason. I stood and found myself staring straight at the lights in the direction I first looked. Our first since *Duane*. Eventually lack of wind and inoperational lamp sent me below to sleep.

Friday, 2nd September [105]

Combined sight yesterday and today gives 24 miles of progress to E x S in 2 days, making an average in ideal conditions since *Duane* of 5.2 m. per day. (21d; 110 miles). A further usual conference about all possible causes of lack of speed produced nothing, except that there is something very odd about this part of the sea. If our speed goes on like this the U.K. is out of reach without any doubt. But we both are trusting in the bad spell to end suddenly and to find ourselves flying along any day; then the food will be the only factor. But where are the ships? Suppose the lanes have come S again to the May lanes in September, while we struggle N. looking for them? A bit of a naughty thought.

Today at midday the wind rose again well from SW Mag and we are holding a True course of almost N x E. An oar went o/b and it took us 11 minutes, *after* getting out a replacement, to row back 30 yds. *at the outside* to get it, with both pulling an oar apiece. It makes nonsense of the suggestion that we aren't making progress *over the water,* but it still doesn't disprove the possibility of an adverse eddy. My main and only course at dinner was fat corned beef with 3 hard tack biscuits powdered over it.

Saturday, 3rd September [106]

07.05 this morning we saw our first huge liner in a torrential rain storm an hour before dawn, thudding along at tremendous speed. And during the afternoon 3 planes flew overhead. Birds. A very small bird rather like a dancing bird in style and behaviour. Fawn and grey/blue, white head, black eye, white bar across stump of tail, dark tail, short dark down-pointing beak. Laconic casual flight with slow beat but fastish stroke, no attempt to progress, frequently 4 ft. from me. Inspected the sea, 5 ft. up, occasionally dropping in a sudden clumsy tangle of wings to gather something from the sea, sometimes changing its mind half way down. Pestered by dancing bird for an hour. The Grocer gull again. Flecked brown upper wing with dark outer panels, black/brown cap covers eye, white bar at base of tail, tail dark. Fast swooping accurate flyer, medium/large. I was throwing away the coffee dregs and let go of my cup. Luckily it floated and was retrieved.

Attention to flag staff and flag, and to our poor old 'Little Wizard' rusty lamp whose wick is now only 3 ins. long. Cleaned out under side pocket stbd. and dinghy. Water in 2 of the 3 Verkade packs and the day and night flares. No rowing because of NNW wind Force 2.

In the High Court of Justice
The Principal Probate Registry
In the Estate of David Wannan Johnstone deceased

I GEORGE MATTHEW RATTRAY of 4, Carne Hill Bracknell, Berkshire make Oath and say as follows :

1. I am an Experimental Officer in the Marine Division of the Meteorological Office Headquarters Annexe Eastern Road Bracknell in the County of Berks.

2. There is now produced and shown to me a list of purported extracts from the log of the rowing vessel *Puffin* covering the period 11th August to 3rd September 1966. From the particulars therein given it is possible to arrive at the likelihood that *Puffin* was somewhere in the general area around Latitude 43–50° North : Longitude 37–38° West on the 3rd or 4th September 1966.

3. There is now produced and shown to me a list of observations from ships within the area covered by Hurricane FAITH hereinafter referred to on the 4th September 1966. The Ocean Weather Ship at Station 'D' (44° North : 41° West) reported as follows on the 3rd and 4th September 1966.

Date	*GMT*	*Direction*	*Wind*	*Force*	*Waves moving from*	*Height in feet*
1966						
3rd	18		Calm		NWN	6–7
4th	00	ENE		7	NEN	8
	06	SE		8	SEE	14
	12	WNW		11	WNW	over 30
	18	NWW		8	NWW	30

4. Combining the information referred to in the preceding paragraph with that found in the weather charts at the material times the following conclusions may fairly be drawn. At 1200 GMT on September 3rd, Hurricane

FAITH was centred at about Latitude 38° North : Longitude 55° West. It was deepening rapidly and moving very quickly North Eastwards and at noon on September 4th the centre was at Latitude 48° North : Longitude 39° West. Within a radius of approximately 300–400 miles from the centre, the winds attained Force 8–11 or 12, the direction changing cyclonically as the system moved across the area. Ahead of the centre the winds were South easterly–South westerly Force 10–11. These extremely strong winds were quickly replaced in the rear of the hurricane by others of generally similar strength, blowing from between West and North West approximately. The storm passed across the general area where *Puffin* is presumed to have been and must have caused very high, confused and often steep seas, with breaking at the crests. The changes in wind direction had caused interaction between various wave trains, moving from a number of different directions, giving rise to an extremely dangerous situation in which a boat the size of *Puffin* would almost inevitably be overwhelmed.

SWORN by the above named GEORGE MATTHEW RATTRAY at Bracknell in the County of Berks. this 12th day of December 1966. } G. M. RATTRAY

Before me
R. Cecil J. Bird
A Commissioner for Oaths.

3

On September 3, after a three-month voyage, Ridgway and Blyth, spotted off the Galway coast of West Ireland, were met and towed the last short lap to Aran, to be accorded a hero's welcome. The paratrooper's first question was about the other two men: he was told there was no news. He disclosed that he and Blyth had seriously considered giving up their attempt several days earlier, after some eighty-five days at sea; the approximate date of that decision was 26th August, four days after which Johnstone, on *Puffin*'s one hundred and second day at sea, recorded in his Journal plans to carry on into November if necessary, heading South towards Portugal, rather than give up. '*What is unthinkable is to give up because of the food or fed-upness in end October . . .*' his mind having by then already accepted a further two months of struggle aboard the tiny craft.

English Rose III was put on triumphant display in Johnstone's home town, Farnham, and Ridgway's and Blyth's magnificent achievement received deserved acclaim.

PART THREE

Commentary

1: Days 1 to 107

Out of the substantial material available from analysis of the Journal, comment will be limited to the suitability and performance of *Puffin*, her equipment and crew. *Puffin*'s suitability breaks down into her seaworthiness and ease of rowing. The equipment is easily considered. As to the crew, the criteria will be their technical, psychological and physical fitness, initially and as the voyage progressed.

Of *Puffin*'s seaworthiness there can be no doubt; she survived no less than fourteen gales of varying degrees of strength, including two hurricanes, the second of which presumably capsized her but failed to sink or even appreciably damage her. She was designed to be rowed with internal and external buoyancy bags fitted, the latter seven feet long and strapped to her sides, to prevent her capsizing and an aftdeck saddlebag to make her self-righting. That they were never fitted to the boat is clear from the photographs taken at her departure and, much later, by *Duane*. They would have helped prevent her capsizing. She was also designed to sail with a ton of stores stowed in net lockers along the boat's sides and with seawater ballast methodically placed in her bilges. It is known from Johnstone's notes that the net lockers were scrapped, and it is almost certain that *Puffin* was inadequately ballasted, which would seriously affect her stability and, allied to the absence of the external buoyancy bags, allow her to capsize in hurricane conditions and not right herself. For example, on day 29 the decision is recorded that the water bags should be replenished with seawater as the boat's cargo was too light in weight. Days 43 and 51 contain references to the boat being much lighter than she should be and feeling badly balanced, so light that she was difficult to trim, the off-duty man in the cabin being used as movable ballast. The next day, with the seawater ballast bags leaking, Johnstone realised that in the event of a gale they were going to have 'a hairy time' unless the bilges were flooded and sealed to give the boat weight. Again, on day 72:

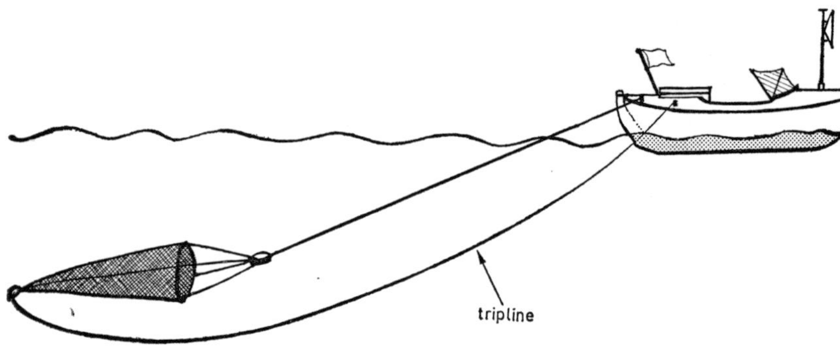

FIG 7 *Puffin* lying to a sea anchor

> *I am concerned about weight, but—if we don't fill the bilges and a really naughty one catches us abeam we could go over; if we do fill them she may not ride astern well to the anchor, and so catch them that way. A perplexing conundrum, with my own opinion in favour of leaving her light, so that as much as possible sticks up into the wind!*

At the same time there was no easy answer to the conundrum, as by trimming the boat so that she was heavier at the stern, the pull of the sea anchor necessarily trailed from the stern in bad weather caused heavy pounding. Johnstone's decision was probably the wrong one, if only because pounding, whilst it might be uncomfortable, would be much less likely than insufficient ballasting to lead to a capsize.

As to the rigidity and basic strength of *Puffin*, after she had already encountered six gales:

40. *The boat never has a creak in her.*

Her internal buoyancy bags were punctured very early on, but this would not deleteriously affect the boat, already too buoyant; nor would it affect her capsizability. A factor which certainly handicapped the oarsmen was the boat's tendency to accumulate marine growth, which creates additional drag. Theoretically, this should not exist outside coastal waters, but *Puffin*'s bottom was not treated with conventional copper anti-fouling paint, relying instead on white top coating. After nearly five weeks at sea (day 34) the boat's bottom was scraped, but by day 53 it was again covered with down and barnacles.

Notwithstanding this, on day 57 *Puffin* went faster than she had ever up to then achieved. Yet the next day:

58. *All during my spells I thought of us pulling all the weed and barnacles along under us with so much of our effort wasted on them, like pulling a forest with us. We were worse off than a porcupine doing back-stroke.*

The following day a second cleaning operation took place at sea:

59. *Not a square inch of hull visible below the waterline. Knives and the wire brush took 2 hours to clean things up, and even then there were lots we couldn't reach.*

It made a big difference to the effort needed to row.

It was nearly ninety days later that *Chaudière* hauled the wreck aboard, and at that time *Puffin* was solidly covered with weed and barnacles, inside as well as out. She might have fared better had her hull been treated conventionally. At all events, it can now be concluded that a slow-moving vessel accumulates considerable marine growth in mid-ocean.

Puffin's performance is another matter, the Journal recording complaint after complaint about the difficulty of keeping her on course, notwithstanding the use of her trimming rudder, and the impossibility of rowing her at all in adverse winds. Correspondingly, favourable winds sometimes, though by no means always, sped her on her way.

In the early stages of the voyage the men also experienced difficulty in keeping the oars in the water; it would take them some time to settle down to the motion of the boat in a seaway, and to estimate both wave effect and also the boat's attitude in relation to the seas they encountered. Probably after three weeks or so they would have become ocean-orientated and begin to deal with the rowing situation to a large extent automatically: they would have become experienced.

They realised at the outset that they were in fact at the mercy of the wind the whole time, and with the wind against them their progress, notwithstanding any benefit from the current, was slow and heart-breaking. But in addition they found *Puffin* extremely 'tender', although at this stage of the voyage fully laden. To some extent that was the consequence of abandoning the net-locker system and the consequent reduction of the boat's metacentric height. For three days, between days 22 and 24, the men were unable to row at all. They did not know that by then they had survived Hurricane ALMA. Rowing hard, their progress during their fourth week at sea continued to disappoint them: daily milages of five and a half, ten and thirteen, despite partially favourable winds, when they reasonably expected to make good thirty. The wind continued to head them, not only impeding progress but helping to push them back westwards. Their difficulties are summarised by the following entry:

63. Puffin *cannot easily be rowed into a bow sea or a head wind—and cannot be rowed with any speed at all beyond ¾ kt, I estimate. The moment the oar leaves the water the wind or a wave stops the boat, and it has to be restarted almost with each stroke . . .*

When one rests one is blown right back westwards. The result of a great deal of hard work in the last 24 hours is, therefore, according to the fix, a westerly *run of about 5 or 10 miles.*

To a considerable extent, loss of way can be attributed to inadequate ballasting.

By day 72, with winds dead astern of their best course (between 55° and 75°) hurling them along at great speed, their only problem was to keep stern on to the sea. With the boat pointing correctly, rowing was easy and they achieved a rate of two and a half to three knots with little effort.

At day 73 there appears a calculation based on a number of assumptions from which Johnstone concludes that, against a distance of 240 miles, which by all accounts they ought to have made good in the previous three days, their navigation showed that they had covered only one-third of that distance. The calculation is set out in tabulated form in Appendix 2 (page 233).

Realising almost from the outset that their best chance was to row frantically whenever the wind was favourable, they rowed in storms of up to Force 10, though course-keeping presented a terrific problem, the waves and the wind tending the whole time to put her sideways on to the seas, in which position *Puffin* became prone to capsize. Even then, under what Johnstone describes as 'ideal conditions', their daily average on days 86 to 88 was as little as twenty-two and a half miles. Then at days 102 and 105 :

102. *We had guessed respectively 70 and 60 miles of progress from a very favourable SW, and the fix showed about 15 miles.*

105. *24 miles of progress to E x S in 2 days, making an average in ideal conditions since* Duane *of 5.2 m. per day.*

It is clear that *Puffin* was impossible for one man to row except in favourable winds, and that even when winds were from the small sector which was favourable to her the boat was extremely difficult to keep on course, tending to veer off and present her beam to the wind. It would have been preferable for the men to row in tandem for say three-hour spells, taking turns at three hours' rest alternately. She was extremely 'tender', according to Johnstone, rolling alarmingly as much as 90° in either direction. Difficulty in course-keeping and excessive tenderness were probably both contributed to by inaccurate trim, or balancing of the boat, as well as ballasting, a difficult matter in a small boat on a long voyage where large quantities of stores which contribute to the ballast are steadily reduced eventually to nil. The dodger, whilst a considerable help when filled with a following wind would be a severe handicap to rowing and course-holding in any other winds. Appendix 6 shows what a small percentage of favourable winds was experienced, and to how small a sector of the compass they were confined. Moreover the dodger, while providing protection from the weather, increased the 'topsides' or wind-hit surfaces of the boat and contributed largely to the effect experienced by *Puffin* of trying to present her beam to the wind. Fig. 8 illustrates.

The degree of roll mentioned by Johnstone is probably exaggerated, the normal assessment of a 45° roll being 90°, because at 45° sides and bottom are virtually indistinguishable. Probably *Puffin* would start to swamp before 70°, even in still water. In open sea waves, when rolling she would probably take in water over the gunwales at 30° and, if she continued to roll, would capsize; had the external buoyancy bags been fitted, that on the side of the direction of the roll would, of course, help prevent the boat going over. *Puffin*'s shape may contribute to her tenderness.

Apart from the area of the bows, where the hull flares in the direction of the deck, the hull is so shaped that there is nothing to stop her rolling from one side to the other, especially if the metacentric height is reduced by abandoning the net-locker storage system.

The section shown on the working drawing (Fig. 3 at

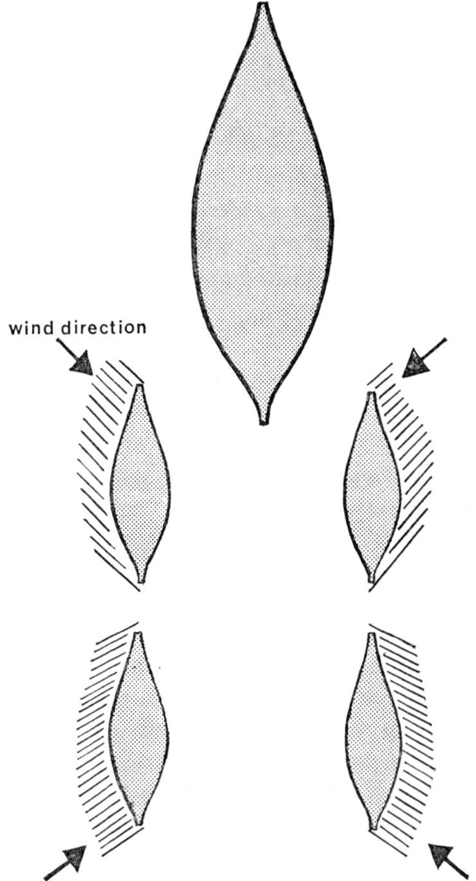

FIG 8 Wind from any quarter tends to cause *Puffin* to present her beam to it. The hull shape shown is at her water line

page 4) illustrates how little of the boat is below the water-line, and what a great area is exposed to wind effect. It also shows the shape of the boat, not unlike an egg lying on its side. From the position proposed for the external buoyancy bags shown in 'Section in Fore Cockpit Well' it is possible that they were abandoned because they would get in the way of the oars. From the record he made while at Norfolk it is clear that Johnstone was very alive to the importance of the boat's balance, and that he took pains to ensure that she was properly trimmed. But the effect of a large beam wave on a boat of *Puffin*'s size can be seen from the comparative drawing, Fig. 9.

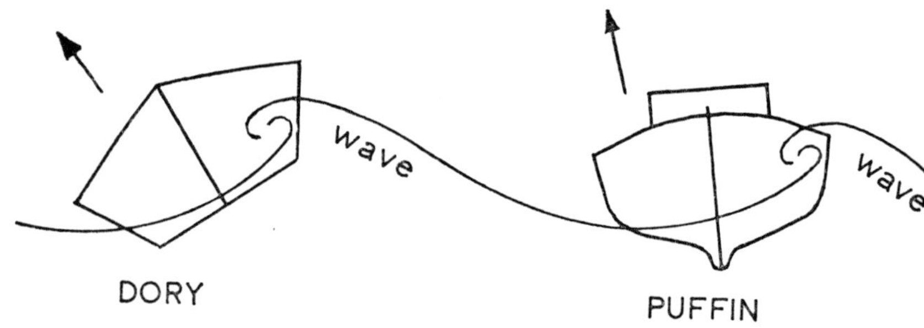

FIG 9 *Puffin* and the Yorkshire Dory beset by a beam wave. *Puffin* resists the wave and ships water. The Dory yields to the wave and stays dry

Puffin's erratic progress, while attributable in small measure to the weed grown on her hull, stems largely from the adverse winds and adverse currents she experienced. The general direction of the Gulf Stream drift notwithstanding, strong adverse easterly winds would set the boat back westward towards America unless the oarsmen rowed strenuously round the clock, which might enable them to stand still. Continuing backwards progress would not be surprising even after such winds had ceased to head them, for had a strong easterly been blowing for two or three days the upper surfaces of the sea would continue to move in a westerly direction for some time. But adverse winds affected progress not only by the effect on the sea's upper surface but also by the effect on *Puffin*'s hull itself, as seen from Fig. 8.

Puffin's behaviour in the Chesapeake Bay gives some indication of current effect; it took approximately ten days to escape the rotary tides that swilled them about in such demoralising fashion. At that stage the situation was almost clownish, and many men would have given in there and then. In retrospect, by that time having learned a little about *Puffin*'s performance in an open seaway, Johnstone would have been wise to have done so.

Enough is published about the Gulf Stream itself for all practical purposes, that is sufficient for powered or sail-driven vessels. It is known that its position shifts with the seasons and that winds not only influence its direction and velocity but also its position. But for accurate navigation at sea, even in a large powered vessel, account must be taken of the effect of two or more currents setting neither in the same nor opposite directions. For example, the Gulf Stream, setting roughly east-north easterly, might encounter a wind-driven current from the north-west, creating between them a resultant current of considerable velocity setting somewhat south of east. Both the velocity and direction of such a resultant current would depend on the strength of its component elements, the Gulf Stream

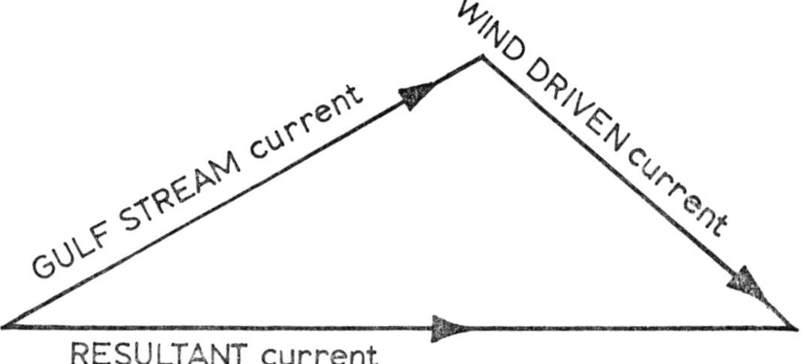

FIG 10 A resultant current

current and the north-westerly wind creating the wind-driven current.

Fig. 10 is scaled roughly to show that where the Gulf Stream flowing at 0·8 knot is encountered by a current created by a wind of 50 m.p.h., the resultant current will attain a velocity in excess of one knot. Small wonder that Johnstone was perplexed at the curious nature of *Puffin*'s progress.

62. *In 48 hours we rowed for 26, at probably not a jot less than 1½ m.p.h. making 39 miles at least . . . Yet we have during those 26 rowing hours managed to go due South . . . about 20 miles in all.*
63. *Where is the 0·8 knot current marked on the chart?*

But the most important piece of information lacking to him is that it is by no means uncommon in the Gulf Stream to encounter strong head currents of as much as six knots when, although knowing himself to be in the Gulf Stream because of the water's colour and warmth, he would be unaware that all the rowing in the world would not prevent his boat going backwards at a rate of up to a hundred miles a day. Such a phenomenon is likely to be followed by following (that is favourable) currents, and then beam currents, which would make dead-reckoning navigation impossible.

Again, the effect of a six-knot head current encountering a gale-force wind from the boat's stern would baffle the crew; they would expect their boat to fly eastwards towards home, yet it would in fact move backwards to the west, because the wind-driven current would attain a velocity of only two knots. Or, with the wind still favourable but the current coming from the beam, their boat might be set to the north or south by many miles in a day, ending them up in an incomprehensible position. Experiments carried out by the U.S. Naval Oceanographic Office have included placing six transmitting buoys in the Gulf Stream in a single location; after several days the buoys were widely separated, and after thirty days were drifting in totally different directions, hundreds of miles apart.

It is also little known that the major currents of the Gulf Stream are confined to the narrow bank of its North Wall, and are not to be found throughout the width of the stream. In the area of its North Wall the currents in fact flow parallel to isotherms depicting sea temperature, the direction of flow being such that warm water is always on the right, and the current's strength is proportionate to the temperature gradient: in areas where the isotherms are closely packed, currents may reach a velocity of as much as six knots. As the current not infrequently sets to the west, that is towards America, it directly contradicts what is shown in the charts and atlases, where all the currents are inaccurately presented as moving eastward. Johnstone's perplexedness is hardly surprising. It is a pity that among the experts he encountered not one gave him that information; or he forgot it. Both he and Hoare suspected the truth, however:

34. *We should do 30 miles every day . . . 12 to 20 by the current, providing the current exists . . . That there is no current is proved by today's sight, which shows us to be in the same place as yesterday.*

102. *One solution possibility occurred to John—there is a mid-Atlantic undersea mountain range. Supposing deep currents are hitting it and sweeping up to the surface in places, swirling W again at 2 knots. It (or some other current) would account for a lot, and I now consider it likely . . .*

And after their encounter with U.S.C.G. *Duane* on day 83 they had learnt of contrary currents running below the surface.

We mustn't put out Percy if he is going to go below 100 ft. as the Gulf Stream is only that deep here, and beyond is a cold current going the other way; the W 33 *sometimes drifted 1–1½kts . . . due to the wind as well.*

It is even more of a pity that Johnstone had not learnt in advance the more elementary fact that tidal or other currents, including the Gulf Stream, would only affect *Puffin* in windless conditions, and that wind from whatever direction sets up its own current along the top foot or so of the sea's surface. As *Puffin* was designed to float in little more than one foot of water, even when correctly ballasted, the wind-driven currents would not merely affect but virtually create her performance. He should perhaps have realised it by the experience gained by day 11, when he recorded that they were at the mercy of the wind the whole time. Instead of relying on the Gulf Stream, he could to all practical intents and purposes have disregarded it. Had he known that, he would surely have been less demoralised at *Puffin*'s erratic progress, and made his dispositions accordingly.

The list of equipment taken by the oarsmen (Appendix 4) is comprehensive, and their preparations in that field were obviously thorough. Although mishaps befell minor items of gear, the electronic and other navigation equipment continued throughout to function adequately. Relying on wristwatches rather than the more appropriate chronometer, without regular time checks they would be unlikely to have the dead accurate time necessary for celestial navigation. It therefore speaks the more highly of their watches as well as Johnstone's navigational skill that his position finding should have been as accurate as it was, proven by the two occasions when sextant fixes were confirmed by passing ships (*Bengazi* on day 66 and *Duane* on day 83). It is a pity that the Journal did not include daily entries of the ship's position, which would have enabled more accurate plotting of *Puffin*'s track.

Provisioning also was thorough. Estimating a sixty-day crossing, by day 17 they had already realised their underassessment, emphasised undoubtedly by the eleven-day 'tour of Chesapeake Bay', and accepted *Orient City*'s offer of supplies. Thirty days later, and by now aware of the slowness of their progress, they prevaricated to the yacht *Kirsten* that they were not short of food or water, and within a further four days (day 51) the decision had been taken to use white signal flares to attract the attention of the next passing ship. From then on their voyage was conditioned by the need to stay in the shipping lanes, so that they could replenish food supplies as necessary. The profundity of their miscalculation is understandable, the consequences severe. A vessel making a sea passage should be independent of outside assistance except in case of a grave emergency. *Puffin*'s dependence on other vessels meant that her primary objective ceased to be to row the Atlantic, and became instead to stay in the shipping lanes.

Put in a more neutral way, *Puffin* could only row the Atlantic if she stayed within reach of vessels which would re-victual her at periodic intervals, corresponding with the quantity of food the tiny vessel could carry. The necessary abandonment of that self-sufficiency meant that the success of the voyage became dependent upon the measure of luck enjoyed in making contact with ships at the requisite intervals; an impossible basis for a sea voyage but one which, in their determination to achieve the crossing, neither Johnstone nor Hoare seems to have acknowledged. Had they with prescience allowed for a 150-day passage, the time it would on the best showing have taken *Puffin* to achieve the crossing, the necessary amount of food could not have been stowed in the space available aboard; and it would in any event have weighed the best part of two tons, so that the oarsmen would have had the exhausting task of propelling a total of nearly three tons dead-weight through the water in the initial stages of their voyage : a depressingly tiring start. And except in adventure stories, fishing from small boats at sea has rarely provided a supplementary diet of significant proportions, so that as a matter of practice a boat must be fully provisioned before leaving harbour.

The attempt to row the Atlantic, an adventure of high

hazard, was not undertaken rashly. Although Johnstone's decision was impetuous, the nine-month interval between conception and the commencement of execution provided ample opportunity for its abandonment, with neither shame nor dishonour, particularly when after nearly four months all efforts to obtain money to build a boat had failed. In the face of that adversity and a total ignorance of the art of ocean rowing, Johnstone showed the same determination as emerged when he was actually at sea; the first requisite of success for such an adventure was part of his natural endowment.

The attempt to row the Atlantic provided the very challenge he had been looking for; something he did not know he could do, not having done it before. He was able, therefore, to employ the purposive singlemindedness which led to his overcoming the many difficulties encountered in getting the adventure off the ground. Books have been written about why men undertake this sort of mission, but little account taken of man's natural spirit of adventure, a questing instinct which both Johnstone and Hoare possessed in large measure.

At the same time, suffering from a nagging sense of failure exemplified by his inability to stick at the many jobs he had undertaken over the years, Johnstone had been undergoing a period of critical self-analysis and had arrived at a stage where he was determined to prove to himself and the world that he could undertake and conclude a task demanding prodigious physical, technical and psychological toughness; in other words, a supreme test, one which would demonstrate positively and finally his physical, psychological and spiritual adequacy to himself: and, in relation to the world at large, superiority.

His approach was balanced; scientifically he equipped boat and crew to the highest standards, and by degrees screwed himself down to an awareness of what he was undertaking: decreasingly a fame-and-glory idea, as his aliveness to the realities of the ocean crossing grew, and with it his acceptance of the unique quality of the role into which he had now cast himself. He was no longer able to pretend that he was like other men; that battle had been fought and lost. On the way over to Cowes for *Puffin*'s single outing he had envied all the people going there for such normal reasons, admitting that he did not feel a part of them or of any section of society. The Atlantic attempt was therefore an escape from reality, from an insufficient self which had been conclusively proved unable to form adequate human relationships and had thus prevented him from acquiring a sense of responsibility towards other people.

The seeming paradox apparent from his concern that others should not be involved, nor their lives endangered, is explicable in terms of independence of purpose. This was his attempt, his show, and nobody ought to be involved in it or interfere with it apart from Hoare. If they reached a point where they needed outside help then they had failed, and were ready to face all the consequences of failure. By the time he had crossed the Atlantic in the *United States* he had recognised that his battle would henceforth no longer be against other men, their lethargy or energies or conventions, nor with the quirks of his own non-conformity, but with the implacable ocean itself.

Physically he and Hoare were entirely fit for the voyage; else they would have been unlikely to survive 106 days in the Atlantic in a tiny boat, ceaselessly buffeted and thrown about by heaving gales and storms, soaked to the skin by torrential deluges or simply the dank condensation of sea fog, frequently lying cold and wet in bunks into which the ocean cascaded pitilessly. By no means an athlete, though very strong, Johnstone had toughened up by undertaking strenuous manual labour. Hoare, on the other hand, was a tough, fit, rugby footballer, formerly a paratrooper and boxer, who enjoyed rowing in the North Sea for exercise. As the voyage progressed there were few signs of physical let-down, apart from the last few days, when, on short commons, the men were weakened through fatigue and hunger, and the first day out when they were seasick; something common to half the people who ever go to sea. Indeed the worst symptoms experienced by the men was nervous tension, usually when encountering other vessels.

27. *For several days very bad tummy nerves, and a tranquilliser sorted it out finally yesterday.*
47. *I found myself nervous again speaking to other people.*
49. *John got a strange recurrence of the air pains/wind pains he got in Farnham.*
66. *Very sick . . . nervous excitement from the meeting.*
83. *I found myself very nervous at first . . . we cast off, rowing away as quickly as possible.*

Unlike Ridgway and Blyth, their hands did not seem to suffer from their rowing, doubtless because they wore leather gloves which they kept oiled. Only a single detriment is recorded :

64. *Rowing into the easterlies is far tougher on the hands than other winds—I wake up after a 3 hour sleep and my first finger middle joint bends as if there is a spring in it. . . . The rest are getting creaky.*

So far as energy is concerned, it seems that so long as their calorific intake was sufficient they generally felt strong and fit. Yet at a time when they had recently replenished their supplies and were presumably eating well, three days of continuous gale took its toll :

73. *I leave the thwart gladly to sleep after each of my watches, physically exhausted.*

The effect of sufficient or insufficient food is exemplified by the contrast between day 83, after they have been revictualled by U.S.C.G. *Duane*, and the last days of the Journal, when their supplies are running out.

83. *It is astonishing how a full tummy can restore all sorts of depressed morales.*
86. *We dug into the goodies, with a consequent rise in energy.*
93. *I feel tired and listless, no proper diet (I think I eat in a day what I would normally eat at dinner only at home).*
94. *Hungry.*
    Soaked and shivering and tired.
95. *Hungry and tired and listless, and on a reduced diet.*
103. *John just put the oars down, unable to go on! 'I'm completely whacked . . . I couldn't go on.'*
104. *Tired and hungry.*
105. *My main and only course at dinner was fat corned beef with 3 hard tack biscuits powdered over it.*

By the time they were hit by Hurricane FAITH their resistance must have been so lowered that they would be unable to take whatever protective action might have saved them from disaster.

How did they come to be in mid-ocean at the time when the hurricane season had started, a time by when, according to their plans, they should long since have been home and dry? What navigational expertise did they possess? Hoare was admittedly ignorant of the art, but Johnstone had sailed in his father's boat throughout boyhood, then owned his own sailing vessel. He had also sailed off the East African coast. Throughout he shows familiarity with the sea, its language and terms (see Appendices 1 and 2); he confidently handles the Consol gear and radio direction finder; takes the electronic log to bits and puts it together successfully (although frequently not working, it registered 1,432 miles when the wreck was recovered); understands the use and handling of the sea anchors and steering oar; obtains an accurate latitude sighting by sunset on day 12, confirmed by the submarine *Cutlass*, and recognises the weather symptoms which form an important part of seamanship.

19. *The signs were all there.*

He makes mechanical adjustments to the trimming rudder and keeps a D.R. (dead reckoning) position allowing for the effect of the Gulf Stream, wind, and surface wind-driven current.

Later in the voyage he splices sections of rope into the sea-anchor tripline, a chore unfamiliar to many sailors as well as landlubbers. There were few occasions when he did not know where he was; what he did not understand was why he was there. Yet he made the cardinal error of failing to satisfy himself that the information he was given about local currents, let alone the Gulf Stream, was correct in detail. Certainly up to a point the charts corroborate the information he received, but as an experienced sailor he should have investigated more deeply, especially as he placed such a great measure of reliance on the constant east-north-easterly set of the Gulf Stream. In the end, remarkably he and Hoare seem to have worked out the answer for themselves, when at day 102 the Journal postulates the theory of a west-setting current of two knots.

Most remarkable of all, however, is the way in which, haphazardly and in full knowledge of his ignorance of sextant navigation, he took with him a sextant and sufficient books to enable him to master and practise that important art during the course of the voyage. He had had some lessons on *American Charger* between New York and Norfolk, but it was not until day 23 that he attempted to master the art of celestial navigation.

23. *Five days ago . . . after mastering, albeit rather roughly, the sextant and the Reeds', I decided to go in for something a bit more abstruse in the way of navigation.*

Today I got . . . out . . . Little Ships Astronavigation. . . . *I spent three hours reading it . . . and then . . . started to put it into practice.*

Again, he recognised the strange variety of the Gulf Stream current:

42. *At least the old anchor gives us the benefit of the current that is beneath the surface and we did 42 miles to the NE with its help.*
48. *I think we are now being taken SE by the current.*
64. *Once more my sights say we have gone into reverse.*
95. *The sight mentioned [on day 94] sent us unbelievably backwards.*

There are only two points at which his sextant navigation can be satisfactorily checked: his fix at day 62 estimated at 44° 00′N 47° 35′W was confirmed three days later (after continuous adverse winds which would prevent any progress) and by *Bengazi*, which gave their position as 44° 20′ N 47° 55′W; and on day 83 an estimate of 43° 53′N 41° 00′W was ratified by *Duane* as 43° 47′N 41° 01′W. It can therefore be concluded that he had adequately mastered the art of navigation by sextant, the only serious omission in his navigational preparations for the voyage, and one of which he was aware.

However, the men's attitude towards the chore of rowing seems haphazard at times. From the outset they found it irksome, and preferred to rely on wind and current to help them home. Indeed, but for the extraordinary percentage of adverse winds and the physical impossibility of carrying enough provisions for a one hundred and fifty day journey they would very likely have achieved the crossing in that time with a minimum of rowing. Additionally, frequently short of paraffin, they preferred to save it for cooking rather than for the lamp which provided the chief means of illuminating the compass at night, with the result that more often than not they undertook no night rowing.

Their approach is perhaps exemplified by the entries on days 15 and 16, by when the Gulf Stream has become an escalator on which they will ride effortlessly home.

15. *When we are swinging along—100 miles a day—why bother to add one's puny 15 or 20 miles? The temptation is to do nothing because we are whipping along.*
16. *Why don't we leave ourselves to the current?*

When they found the sea 'unrowable' they retired to the cabin, whereas even their 'puny' few miles a day would have made a considerable difference to their progress and to the avoidance of the demoralisation which resulted from its lack. Clearly there must have been days when the weather was such that rowing was impossible, for example :

91. *All day indoors . . . swearing at the weather.*

But on days 99, when there was a north wind in light gusts all day, and 106, when the wind from north-north-west was as light as Force 2, they were perhaps not justified in abandoning the chore. Had they realised that rowing even in adverse winds would at least have made a small contribution towards reducing their backwards direction they would presumably have kept going instead of relying on the sea anchors to hold them stationary until the winds improved. As it was, by a point half-way through the voyage they seemed at last to appreciate the necessity for more effort, and from then on persevered, despite difficult seas and headwinds, and wherever possible rowing at night.

53. *. . . all day we have struggled in a beam wind and sea . . . today we have progressed 45m. due E.*

Similar entries can be found on many of the Journal's pages from that time on, with records of a seventeen-hour stretch on days 69 and 73, twenty-four hours on day 85, and full days of rowing on days 86, 87, 88 and 97.

Perhaps the men's attitude is summed up by the following entries :

15. *There is a strange angle to this effort of rowing which we both seem to notice. When things are very discouraging it is hard to find the energy—say when it is important to row against a wind in the first week of the voyage: and when we are swinging along—100 miles a day—why bother to add on one's puny 15 or 20 miles? We both hate rowing but not to a serious extent. It is bearable as the day's penance of boredom. . . . The temptation is to do nothing because we are whipping along.*

Several factors governing their mental responses to the physical challenge are revealed. Favourable wind or current, or the discovery of favourable progress with or without them, a full stomach : each was sufficient encouragement to continue the boring penance. Conversely, it took little to discourage them. It is the more remarkable that at no time was there the slightest suggestion of giving up, apart from the awful seasickness and depression of the first few days out when the offshore currents were rotating *Puffin* so relentlessly. The slow progress due to adverse winds and currents which led to the necessity to seek provisions from passing vessels, and thus diverted their efforts from the prime task of crossing the ocean, contributed substantially to the same demoralisation which led to haphazard rowing. And in turn the desultoriness of the rowing contributed to the same lack of progress. It was a vicious circle.

Yet morale generally was as frequently high as it was low, and the Journal's pages are tinged with glints of bright humour :

18. *D: 'If a shark came swerving up and took my hand and this thermometer just then, it would have been very tricky.'*
J: 'You could have taken his temperature!'

On day 21 the tempestuous seas were described as front-row forwards and the Houses of Parliament. And Hoare kept up the men's spirits conventionally with tunes on his mouth-organ. It took nearly four weeks at sea before the following apprehension was recorded; perhaps it is surprising that it did not appear a fortnight or three weeks earlier :

27. *The full enormity of the task . . . beginning to dawn on us, and there is a certain depression in the air.*

Two things are getting us down; the continuous round-the-clock activity . . . means no sleep for more'n 4 hours, and the movement is boisterous, giving no peace while doing anything.

I would love to go for a walk or even be able to stand up for a couple of minutes.

This is the one and only complaint in the Journal at the effect of the oarsmen's chosen way of life, and from that time on they accepted the sea's mauling and their own incredible discomfort; morale was low only when they were worried about *Puffin*'s behaviour, their lack of progress, and consequent food shortages.

After lying to *Kirsten* that they were not short of anything (day 47) Johnstone's depression accelerated noticeably until the time when nearly three weeks later, and desperately short of supplies, they managed to attract *Bengazi.*

50. *My nerves are not very far below the surface at the moment. There was a ridiculous short shouting match which left me very weak and shaky and I am sad and depressed more than ever, and very unhappy, and I only want to be with my friends and family again.*

51. [*The newspapers*] *have forgotten us until we get to be one of their stories.*

We've got to use the white flares now if [*ships*] *come anywhere near enough to see.*

54. *Today we are back, and depressed with that thought.*
57. *No sights for the 2nd day running so God knows where we are. And still no ships.*
59. *We have had no sign of ships again, . . . and have really no notion of where they are to be found.*

In fact, Johnstone's navigation was again excellent, and *Puffin* was actually in the shipping lanes, for two days later they spotted three ships, and several more on the subsequent days before they were sighted by *Bengazi* on day 66. The effect of their failure to stop ships during those intervening days is understandable.

63. *. . . our worst disaster was the occurrence of the only contingency I have forgotten to consider these last few searching days, and which makes it therefore all the more stunning and depressing. Our ship arrived, came within 1½ miles of us, presumably failed to see us and departed without stopping.*

Our disappointment . . . was very deep. . . . Depressions set in and in a second we were arguing violently . . .

There followed a terrible fight, but within an hour the men had apologised to each other, and there was no other dissension throughout the long voyage. Yet at the same time as these gloomy episodes were occurring the men's mood seemed to swing into alternate optimism, and when on day 44 Johnstone describes their patch of sea as desperate Hoare agrees with, 'Not top of the holiday list, is it?' And the decision is taken to scrape the boat's bottom in mid-ocean on day 58 because 'we were worse off than a porcupine doing back stroke'. Their despair cannot at that stage have been very profound.

59. *It is difficult not to laugh at our strange predicament . . . we have food for about 10 days more, yet*

we laugh at it all and say it will be all right in the end. It is impossible to believe we are going to get into trouble out here, yet the signs are all there . . . I am amazed at our lack of apprehension . . . I think we may be hungry before July is out, very hungry and not laughing much at the sensation at all. Our lack of luck is stunning. . . .

61. *It all looks a bit dodgy, but . . . there is nothing to do but wait for 'our' ship. . . . We are absolutely complacent about the position . . . John played the mouth-organ sitting outside in the fog.*

After twice failing to stop ships, one of which certainly sighted them :

63. *If there was to be a third time lucky, we wanted to be able to shout straight into the captain's porthole.*
    If we stay where we are we are bound to get a ship in the next 2 or 3 days. That's certain. 'I'll bet when one does come it grabs Percy in its propellers and starts winding us up into the mincer. . . .'

65. *The 'Sailing Dictionary' started unaccustomed work today.*
    D: 'Hope we don't end up as craven skillingtons croaking up to a ship's skipper for a bite or two to eat.'
    J: 'No, we'll be all right, there's plenty of time yet.'
    D: 'It's always all right in the end for me, somehow or other.'

Yet after that sustained display of confidence :

I retired feeling very unhappy.

Bengazi's arrival saved them. In sixty-five days at sea they had learnt how difficult *Puffin* was to handle, and having experienced an absurdly large percentage of adverse winds and inexplicable current effects they knew that their progress had been pathetically small. They had suffered acute depression and longed for the comfort of home. At times they had not even known where they were. They were down to seven days' supply of food and were almost out of paraffin. Yet there was absolutely no thought of giving in. They would not even go aboard *Bengazi* because it would be breaking their rules. What rules? (Both Ridgway and Blyth feasted aboard a passing vessel.) Apart from re-provisioning the only luxury they allowed themselves was garrulity, when by all sane notions they should have surrendered. Instead :

> *We said 'Goodbye and thanks, and good luck.'*

Filling their bellies they sat chatting with renewed confidence, alone in their tiny world, while a huge bright satellite beckoned them homewards before a yellow dawn broke on their good luck. That day the wind again became unrowable, and on day 67 there was no direction they could row without going backwards. But by now they had become attuned not only to discomfort but to the prospect of a very long voyage.

> *A big new thought—if we can't make U.K. before it gets too cold, go South to Portugal, making the decision in good time easily.*

Silverbeach, on day 68, added a little to their stores, giving them an estimated total of four weeks' supplies and two days later they thrilled to the excitement of big game fishing.

> *'Sorry mate' [John] apologised to the fish. 'It's all for the glory of the country.'*

They had averaged only forty miles a week throughout July and, hopeful that on day 72 alone they had achieved double that distance, Johnstone became acutely miserable again when he discovered that in fact their progress since *Silverbeach* after four consecutive days of favourable westerlies totalled no more than eighty miles.

> 73. *80 miles on a bad sight is ridiculous and infinitely depressing. . . . An appalling melancholy overcame me . . . and a tremendous desire to be reunited with my family and friends, to return to a sympathetic and comfortable environment—without, somehow, the stigma of failure over the expedition.*

Had the men then decided to give in there would have been no shame, no stigma, no failure except in the limited sense of non-completion of their mission. They had already overcome the ludicrous horror of the Chesapeake Bay tour, and had since undergone every experience available to men at sea save shipwreck itself. Their minds were, however, directed, seemingly effortlessly, towards the prospect of arriving in Portugal in the winter, still months ahead. The temptation to describe this attitude as mere pride must be rejected; it is in fact the manifestation of a rare single-minded determination, the all-essential bridge across the yawning gap between the conception of an idea and its execution.

> *But I soon reconciled myself to the situation, as 35 miles a day means 50 days only and will not hurt us at all.*

It is difficult to understand why, short of supreme optimism, Johnstone should have thought they would average thirty-five miles a day when their average up to that time was more like twenty. Presumably he thought their appalling luck could not but improve. But he knew also that they would still have to continue looking for ships to provision them, and he must by now have realised how difficult and time-consuming a task that was. If his thinking was not entirely realistic, it was positive. It was also manly, for he concealed their true lack of progress from Hoare, and in so doing must also have concealed his own thinking and despondency.

> *I did not tell John the precise situation, and he continued to sing. . . .*

Next day, however, his fears were justified :

> 74. *I did a sight which doesn't bear thinking about, confirming yesterday's suspicions only worse!*

But he continued to accept alone the responsibility for their situation, as a skipper should, and three days later his buoyancy had returned, although he had acknowledged that it was vital once again to stop a ship for food.

> 77. *Only 53 miles to the ½ way mark.*
> 79. *I reckon we have crossed the half way line now, and seem all set for a good fast second half.*

And even when a day later a large freighter ignored their signals his only comment seems more optimistic than otherwise.

> *It is a slight shock to discover that the camaraderie of the Atlantic is not quite 100%. It occurred to me that perhaps ships had been told, 'Leave them till they send up the red flare.'*

By day 82, with the water situation now critical as well, Hoare was happily rendering *Shenandoah* on his mouth-organ. Johnstone however was beginning to lose confidence. Their failure to secure help from ships which had obviously spotted them, something utterly contrary to the unwritten rules of all seamen, had now made him suspicious. He expected, and was entitled to expect, the assistance liberally given by one vessel to any other whether at sea or in harbour, and obviously could not understand why they had been refused it. It is possible that the answering signal of the freighter on day 80 had been imagined, but doubtless he remembered also the strange occurrence on days 27 and 45 when their signals had been ignored. Now near desperation, the men became determined to secure help.

> 83. *We have decided on a new course of action with the next ship. If they prove to be unhelpful with the food, in providing only 10 days' supply, John will go aboard, ask to see the captain, with both our wallets fastened in his pants. He will explain personally how important it is for us to have a good supply and try and enlist a more sympathetic approach. Possibly even go with the steward to make certain milk, sugar, jam, cheese and some fresh stuff comes aboard* Puffin.

A similarly paranoiac tendency appears again when at last *Duane* stops, to treat them royally.

> *I rowed cautiously up at first until we saw the American flag. . . . At first we had decided to say No* [*to going aboard*] *until the scene was investigated.*

Further entries demonstrate the extent to which Johnstone and Hoare had by this time opted out of the everyday world, the effect, doubtless, of living alone for so long in their microcosm and to some extent the effect of hunger. The drogue had long since become Percy, and was put out to feed; the barometer was by now Eustace.

Again it is impossible to explain the absence of any thought of surrender when their fortunes had for a second time reached a nadir, except in terms of an *idée fixe*. Their sole object in remaining alive was to complete the Atlantic crossing, no matter how long it took, no matter what further tribulation lay ahead: or die in the attempt. The 'rules' must continue to be adhered to, so Johnstone stayed in *Puffin* while Hoare boarded *Duane* solely to ensure that adequate supplies were obtained. The men's attitude represented singlemindedness of purpose of an utterly heroic quality. Nevertheless they wanted approbation, and with quiet satisfaction Johnstone recorded the little congratulatory speech which *Duane*'s skipper made, praising their adventurous spirit. Refusing the comforts of a bath and a haircut the men pulled away quickly, Johnstone pleased to have demonstrated exactly the right spirit in which they were undertaking their voyage. Within hours the oarsmen were temporarily plummeted into the world of reality by the newspapers and magazines given them by the American vessel.

> *This little newspaper started a chain of events which brought back a feeling that the rest of the world was real again.*
>
> *It was an orgy and I bolted it greedily . . . feeling a part of the world again. . . . And while I ate I thumbed equally greedily through the magazines—such sanity again. . . .*
>
> *It is astonishing how a full tummy can restore all sorts of depressed morales.*

Three days later, during which they had rowed continuously but achieved a disappointing daily average of only twenty-two and a half miles, the optimism of full stomachs still reigned.

> *We view our position today cheerfully—not that it is a cheerful prospect but we are used to that sort of blow and don't mind. I have worked out that it will be about 60 days from here on.*

Hoare was as happy-go-lucky as ever, viewing a total of

five months at sea in a fifteen-foot boat with the equanimity of superb courage.

> *'If we aren't careful we'll miss the Motor Show—that's on about October 20th.'*

But an air of foreboding was present also.

85. *The law of the jungle predominates, and we are fully aware of coming under its jurisdiction in our own way.*
88. *I begin to see [the gulls] in a different light—as the prospective perpetrators of a rather ghastly scene like* The Birds, *with me as their victim . . . always looking down beadily at me.*

Adverse winds for a further three consecutive days, with attendant idleness, accentuated Johnstone's gloom, while at the back of his mind the problem of supplies worried incessantly.

91. *I am melancholy . . . one feels like a new boy at school going out to face the elements again, with an extra heartbeat of anxiety and I suppose a little fear of the unknown.*
93. *An assessment of the food . . . not too clever, and we will need as much again.*

On short rations, tired and hungry, and weakening physically, he thought back to the fateful August day in The Bush a year earlier when it all began, and why it was the right time of his life to embark upon the adventure and why it was the right thing to do, 'and the jobs I'd tried for and failed to get'.

It was the beginning of the end, the beginning of the full acceptance of his self-responsibility and its consequences: the attrition of spirit and body which frequently prefaces death. After a sight which once again had sent *Puffin* unbelievably backwards, a Force 9 gale added its might to the sapping of energy and resistance whereby their will to survive was being undermined, and the men prepared for their fate. Johnstone's reaction was calm and resigned, his being pervaded by a quiet dignity, his sense of humour unabandoned.

96. *I was really beginning to think I had the measure of the squalls . . . and I approached the usually rather frightening night gales without a qualm . . . I prayed for it to ease, under the less undignified guise of a prayer for less of the North and more of the W.*
[It] is all pretty frightening.

On day 97 the men rowed in rain and slopping seas all day, damp and tired, but hopeful that they were on their way home. Next day a fix showed that they had in fact once again run backwards, with hundreds of miles of progress just lost in thin air. At the ocean's assertion of uncontradictable authority, Johnstone was stunned and unbelieving, and 'even John looked grave and worried'. They knew now that their only hope of survival was to get to the ships, not to surrender but to re-provision, but were not only unsure which direction to steer: they knew that despite all their efforts *Puffin* was out of control, taking them relentlessly backwards without their knowing why. 'A bit of a predicament,' Johnstone understated the position.

Part of his new-found peace of mind, the bridling at last of his turbulent, aggressive, restless personality, was the pride he took in the depth of understanding he and Hoare had achieved.

101. *We have now scored one victory over the pundits who said we would be at each other's throats all day. We find more and more to talk about, and the range of subjects is endless.*

Day 102 saw a final effort to rationalise their situation, a final desperate plan to achieve the success which in their hearts the men must now have known could never be attained; it allowed for the voyage to continue into November, making for the warmer water of the Portuguese latitudes. After three months in the tiny *Puffin* they could contemplate a further three with absolute determination.

> *What is unthinkable is to give up because of the food or fed-upness in end October still 100s of miles out.*

But the very next entry records a disastrous fix, a day's run of fifteen miles against an estimate of sixty or seventy; Hoare evolved his theory of a west-setting current. That evening *Puffin* came near to capsizing. 'That was very peculiar,' said Johnstone. Next evening, with the men close to exhaustion, on an insufficient diet and with everything in the cabin soaked, a twelve-foot shark joined station with the boat, staying until dusk.

103. *A ghoulish thing to have with us, slowly swimming under the stern, it showed a scimitar fin and a pale blue grey top and white underneath.*

They continued to row, but hunger and mercilessly rough seas brought on awful depressions.

104. *I'll never see them at home again. We'll never be able to stop a ship in these seas, and we'll be sick with hunger before there's a calm.*

Despite everything, and by now beyond doubt fully aware of their desperate situation, hope was not abandoned, and there occurred a last burst of optimism, the final expression of explosive will-power.

105. *We are both trusting in the bad spell to end sud-*

denly and to find ourselves flying along any day; then the food will be the only factor.

But food was only available from passing vessels, and of those there were none. 'Where are the ships?' Johnstone implored despairingly. Then, in quieter vein again:

Suppose the [shipping] lanes have come S again. . . . A bit of a naughty thought.

They now knew that there was no question of their reaching England.

Next morning a large ocean liner during a torrential rainstorm, and in the afternoon three planes overhead, indicated that they were close to the shipping lanes.

This last day of the log contains no note of demoralisation, no suggestion of transmitting an emergency signal on the Gibson radio. Instead there are peacefully poetic descriptions of birds, and of the crew's attention to their boat. The Journal manifests a quiet resignedness to their fate, a readiness to die but without inconveniencing others, or to live should the fates so ordain. It is unthinkable, had they managed to stop another passing vessel, that they would have entertained any thought of surrender; there was absolutely no question of it at any time. They would have revictualled, re-moralised and continued happily on their way.

Day 107

According to the U.S. Navy Oceanographic Office's publication *North Atlantic Tropical Cyclones 1966*, Hurricane FAITH began as a poorly defined depression over the Ivory Coast of West Africa on 18th August. Under satellite observations, as it moved westward at a forward speed of about eighteen knots the storm developed slowly, reaching tropical storm intensity on 22nd August and hurricane strength on the following day. Generating winds of seventy-five knots FAITH continued westward. Its centre, passing twenty-five miles north of St. Martin in the Leeward Islands on 26th August, reached a position north of the Dominican Republic the following day. The storm then turned to a north-north-westerly course, slowed to a forward speed of about five knots, and intensified rapidly.

For the next three days FAITH held this course, as winds increased to 105 knots. Late on 31st August FAITH turned towards the north-east. On 1st September the storm passed about 205 miles north-west of Bermuda, generating maximum winds of ninety-five knots, with gales extending out to 300 miles in the south-east quadrant. The *Alberto Bennati*, an Italian tanker located some 200 miles west of Bermuda on 1st September (about 370 miles from the storm's centre), was crippled when twenty-five-foot seas generated by FAITH flooded the engine-room, killing one crewman.

Moving eastward, FAITH continued to deepen. On 3rd September the storm turned north-eastward again, with its forward speed increasing to near forty knots the following day. Two men, attempting to cross the Atlantic in a row (ing)-boat, drowned as the hurricane crossed their path. On 6th September FAITH, now extra-tropical, passed over the Faeroe Islands and the following day moved inland near Nordoyan, Norway. Continuing as a deep low-pressure system the storm moved across northern Norway, Sweden and Finland then turned northward over Novaya Zemlya. During the storm's trek across Scandinavia a Norwegian ferryboat, off the Denmark coast, was swamped. One person was killed. By 12th September the storm became a stationary LOW centred over Franz Josef Land, and finally dissipated over the Arctic Ocean on 15th September.

What happened to *Puffin* can only be imagined. The probability is that with one of the men on deck and the other sheltering in the tiny cabin, and therefore unattached to the boat by his life-harness, the mountainous cross-seas and hurricane-strength winds capsized the tiny vessel. Fig. 11 indicates how a large cross-sea would have that effect. With water flooding in as she was tossed violently upside-down among battering waves the height of a five-storey building, the man in the cabin must have forced the hatch downwards to fight his way into the ocean, hoping to cling to the handrails on the upturned hull, and right the boat. The strength of the sea and the wind's violence would afford him no ghost of a chance and he must surely have been immediately swept away; the man on deck would also have been pitched into the raging sea, unable, because of the sheer weight of water, to reach the boat, until his lifeline snapped, and the relentless ocean dispassionately embraced its challengers.

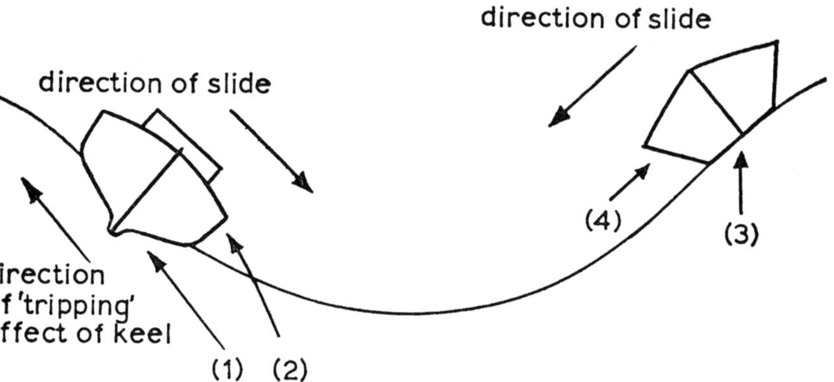

FIG 11 The effect of a large cross-sea in the capsize of *Puffin* and the Yorkshire Dory

(1) *Puffin*'s keel may contribute a braking effect to her slide and set up a force in the opposite direction
(2) There is no surface shape to stop *Puffin* continuing to roll towards the water, or to stop her filling once she has rolled sufficiently far
(3) The Dory skids down the wall of water on its flat bottom
(4) The Dory's sides flare outwards and repel the intrusion of the sea

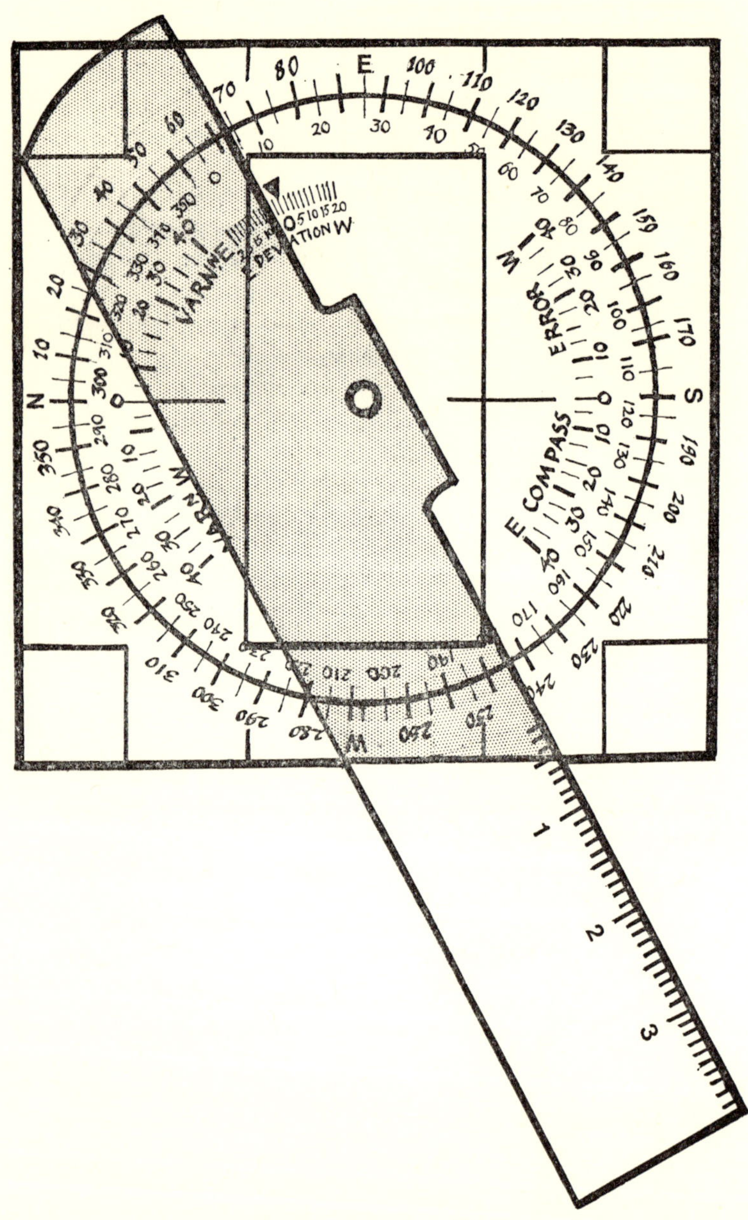

FIG 12 The protractor found in the wreck

FIG 13 The Homer radio receiver, used also in combination with the Heron direction-finder

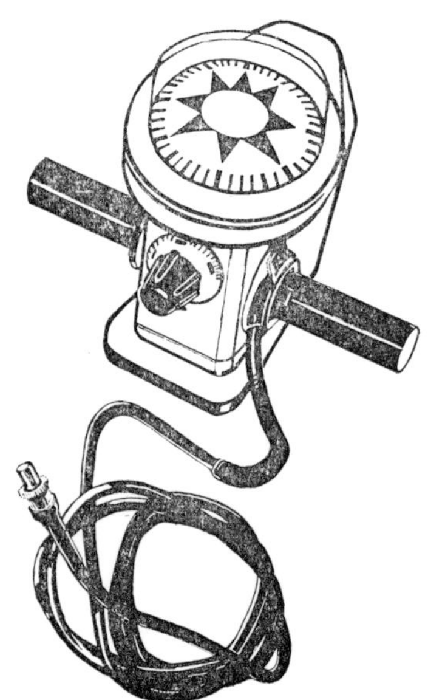

FIG 14 The Heron is hand-held; its handle is at the back in this view. It incorporates its own compass on the top. The black horizontal bars are its direction-finding aerial

FIG 15 The Harrier. The left-hand section is the propeller which is fitted to the underside of the hull. The centre section houses its machinery and includes meters showing distance run and speed. The right-hand section is an

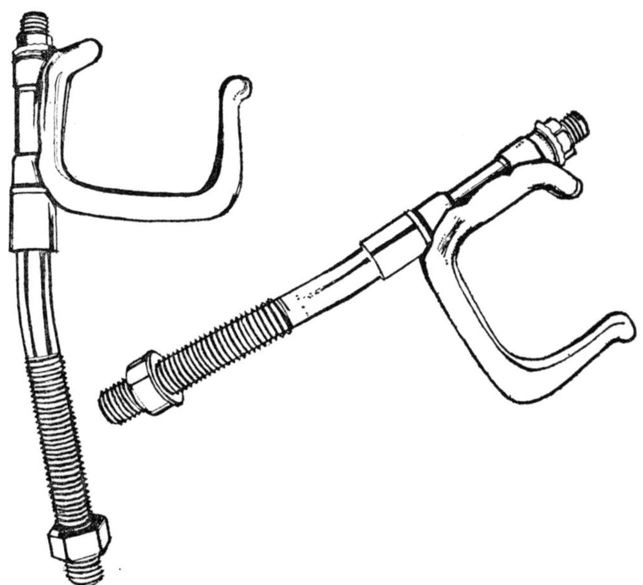

FIG 16 The rowlocks which were specially made for *Puffin*

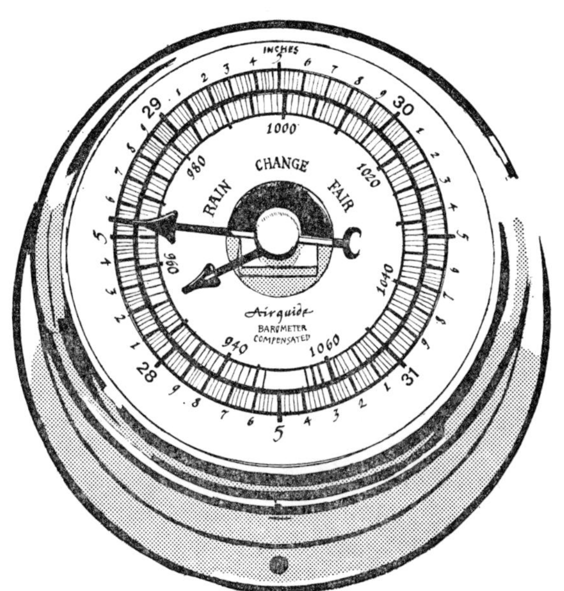

FIG 17 'Eustace', *Puffin*'s barometer

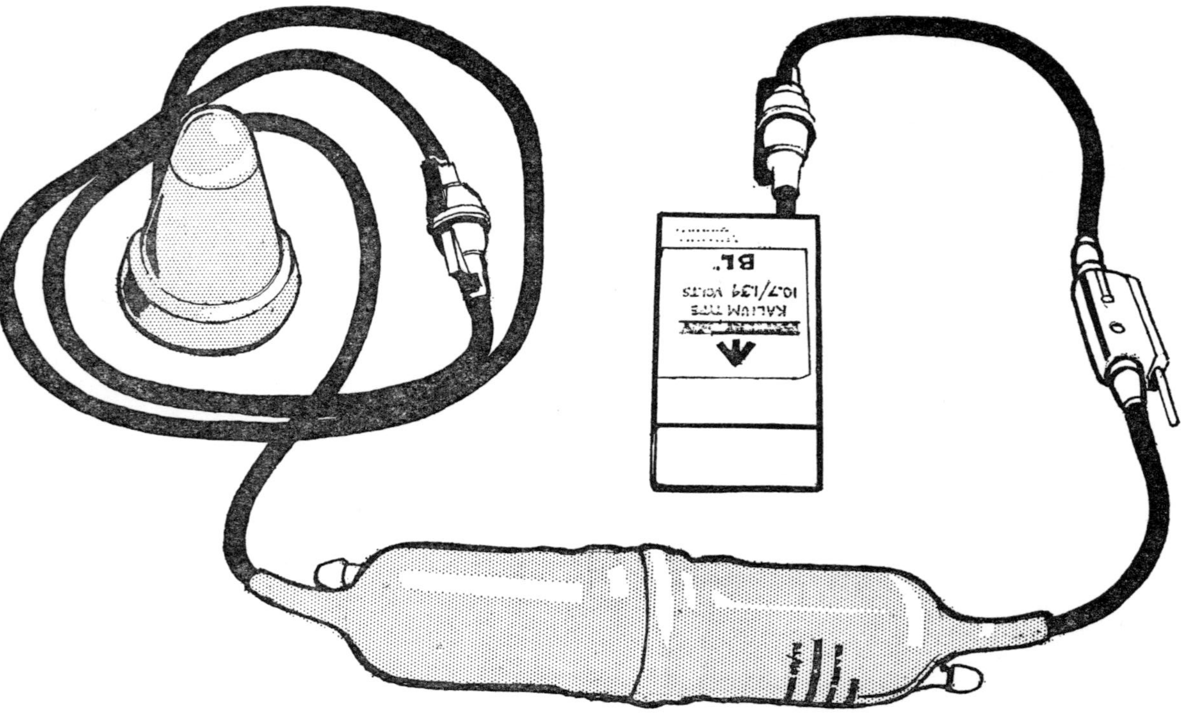

FIG 18 A floating flashing light found in the wreck. The battery (top centre) sinks until it is supported by the buoyant cylinder (bottom centre) which houses the flashing mechanism. The lamp section (left) floats at the end of its lead

2: The Eternal Spirit of Adventure

Our ancestor the hunting ape was an adventurous creature who left a warm, secure den to win food for his family. It is not a far step to envisage a hunter leaving the den for the *sport* of winning food, enjoying the contest not only with his prey but also with the elements, pitting his wits not only against creatures he soon found to afford an insufficient or unworthy challenge, but against the physical difficulties of terrain : mountains, rivers, forests and later ocean and sky : which, conquered, afforded a sense of considerable achievement and, unconquered, remained a continuing challenge. He might also the more easily retain the admiration of his mate, or gain that of a potential mate. In the course of the contest he might suffer physical hardship from which, provided he emerged in one piece, he would derive a satisfaction which we might today describe as masochistic. It might soon have become unsporting to chuck rocks at sitting birds.

The behaviour of small boys indicates that this is a natural and not an artificial propensity : while their mothers take the well-beaten track from A to B, the small boy may understandably choose to hive off from A along a muddy path, over a field or two, slinging the occasional stone at a bird or a rabbit on the way, over the top of rather than round a hill, slither on his backside down a rocky scree, and arrive at B in a state of exalted breathlessness, his trousers holed, his knees torn, and the uppers of his shoes separated from the soles. Some boys are of course more adventurous than others, who might go along with mother, perhaps casting sidelong envious glances at the scampering figure on the skyline. This spirit of adventure is present in most young males to some degree. With the passage of the years and an accompanying load of responsibilities, its expression may become increasingly difficult, but that it continues to be present is manifested less by the exploits of our mountaineers and sailors than by the vicarious satisfaction the less adventurous derive from those exploits. From the snug security of their armchairs they are actually participating in the adventure, in a limited way self-identifying, and thereby expressing their own suppressed adventurous spirit. In general the public acclaims him who has successfully demonstrated a spirit of adventure, a characteristic which incidentally enures only during the period of physical sufficiency; roughly that of sexual capacity. This acclamation points to a frank appreciation of qualities admired among mankind, such as courage, endurance and heroism, which combine in the adventurous spirit. As the demonstration of the adventurous spirit proves an ability to continue to survive, regular reminders become increasingly necessary as our way of life removes us further and further from such natural activities as food-hunting.

It can be argued that the adventurous spirit can be satisfied in ways which bring benefits to all of mankind, such as laboratory or space research. Leaving aside the debatable question of whether the results of such research are indeed beneficial to mankind, certainly some adventurous satisfaction is available from mental and intellectual contest, but it does not equal that of the physical: we give due praise to the achievement of scientists, but it is the solo voyagers we rave about. The particular pride when man can claim however remote a (tribal) kinship with the heroes: 'They're British/European/white/black. So are we; that's the stuff British/Europeans/white men/Negroes are made of': explains the vicarious satisfaction derived from an innately adventurous spirit which has passed the test of continued ability to survive. The particular grouping with which we can, however loosely, associate ourselves, has proved a survival ability by the successful demonstration of the adventurous spirit. And the greater the current need for the demonstration (that is the further 'civilisation' removes us from nature), the more autistic the thinking becomes, until kinship will be claimed with humanity, so long as a suitably distinguished relationship can be made between humans and, say, Martians. The prophet who exemplifies the adventurous spirit is not yet without honour, not even in his own land.

Recognition of man's need to demonstrate his continuing ability to survive may be a goad to adventurers : Someone must from time to time renew the truth. Nobody has done it for some time : I'd better do it. In that particular sense it could be that the adventurous who fulfil their spirit of adventure are natural leaders, at the head of their tribe, mankind's champions who pick up a metaphorical gauntlet thrown down by the mountains and the seas, and more sophisticatedly the seabeds, the earth's intestines and the planets themselves. A scientific or quasi-scientific aim may mitigate the ostensible abandonment of responsibility which frequently accompanies the expression of the adventurous spirit. The underlying purpose is nevertheless the expression of that spirit, and the scientific element no more than a justification for abandonment of responsibility, acceptable to the abandoned. After all, those expeditions are superficially directed at the prolongation of life, whether by military or nutritional means, and the vigorous healthy who would normally expect to survive life's everyday vicissitudes are not generally concerned to reach or extend old age; that is more usually the prerogative of the already aged, becoming progressively unready to face life's ending.

It is true also that man basks in the approbation of his fellows. For some domestic approbation suffices; others desire to be appreciated by a larger public : to hit the headlines and be talked about. They may believe themselves endowed with out-of-the-ordinary qualities meriting wide recognition; or they may merely exemplify the immaturity during which man is insufficient to himself, not yet having learned what he is or how to accept what he has found himself to be. But, interestingly, and conversely, the same larger public is on the look-out for the man with out-of-the-ordinary qualities, to admire, revere or adulate; looking perhaps for the God in every man, the superior human who may be that desirable mystery, the man-God, Superman himself. Some men are genuinely cast for the role, others are frequently thrown into it by an avid, bored society needing to heave itself up to a higher level, vicariously; a society which as quickly discards the idol found wanting or worn out, replacing him with the new model. This too may be part of society's necessary renewal of its knowledge of a continuing ability to survive.

The temporary abandonment of responsibility which accompanies the expression of the adventurous spirit is more easily understood by contemporary society than forgiven. 'Irresponsible' is a pejorative term, connoting a failure to conform with widely accepted tenets of behaviour. It can be argued that responsibility is an obligation not only towards others (spouse, children, parents, friends, clients, colleagues) but also towards the individual : self-responsibility : and that total abjuration of self-responsibility leads to the kind of imbalance associated with saints and martyrs. Probably there is not a great deal wrong with being a saint or a martyr, but the criticism can be levelled that their behaviour indicates a total absence of self-responsibility, which not only leads to a somewhat reckless abandonment of the natural propensities of human life, but frequently betokens the absence of the elementary survival instinct of the normal animal. From that point of view, self-responsibility is a normal and proper human propensity, and the only remaining room for argument is the degree of self-responsibility it is proper to dispose, in relation to responsibility at large. It goes without saying that that must vary from individual to individual, depending on such unrelated facts as mental and physical make-up, and the existence and extent of his human relationships. Obviously a man with a wife and six children, parents, several business partners, and a few hundred work people all depending on him would be more than a little irresponsible if he were to attempt to swim the Atlantic Ocean; whereas an unmarried unemployed orphan, utterly alone in the world, might well be encouraged to embark upon some relatively sane adventure which would win him fame and glory.

There are, of course, those who, lacking the capacity to form adequate human relationships (that is relationships with a person or people sufficient to satisfy certain basic needs) never acquire a sense of responsibility towards other people. They may be the subject for commiseration, but they are spared the agonising appraisal which should preclude the determination of what degree of self-responsibility the individual ought to acknowledge. Everyone runs away from reality from time to time. There are differences of degree, and in the method selected for the escape, but in every case the escape is from an insufficient self. When insufficiency is adequately balanced off by the companionship of 'sufficient' people, escape may become unnecessary. In the case of the individual unable to form adequate relationships : and for some, anybody is sufficient, for others nobody : the need for escape from reality can amount to a supervening force sufficient to overcome, at least temporarily, what may be a natural abnegation of self-responsibility.

In circumstances where responsibility towards others is healthily balanced by self-responsibility, the adventurous spirit may understandably be exploited where a solitary man feels the need to escape from a reality he finds unpleasant, at any rate for the time being. His psychological state is then ripe for the infusion of an entirely natural propensity : the fulfilment of the adventurous spirit, which will if successful lead to the demonstration of leadership towards which he feels himself goaded, perhaps by the very society which will benefit from the successful demonstration by vicarious enjoyment of the knowledge of continued survival on the part of one of the tribe.

Johnstone's preparatory reading, which included such titles as *Physical Fitness, Survival, Shipwreck Survivors, Lifeboat Handbook, Hazards to Men in Ships Lost at Sea, Guide to Preservation of Life at Sea after Shipwreck*, was a clear indication of his realisation of the role into which he had cast himself. It became his function to demonstrate to his fellow men that he was able to survive an exceedingly stern test, the result of which survival would be a revival of confidence by mankind, needful to renew, vicariously, its knowledge of its continuing ability to survive. He and his crew were entitled to risk their lives; they caused trouble to no stranger, grief to their families only. Undoubtedly they had weighed in the balance the measure between their responsibility to their families and to themselves, and unhesitatingly decided to follow their adventurous calling.

3: Conclusions

Puffin's failure to accomplish the Atlantic crossing is due to a combination of circumstances, some forseeable, some not. The immediate cause was obviously her capsizing in conditions where she could not be righted, but had she made anything like reasonable progress she would have been at least 1,000 miles nearer home by the time Hurricane FAITH hit mid-Atlantic: perhaps 1,500 miles had she left Cape Cod as planned. Her poor progress stemmed from a multitude of interlinked causes to which priorities cannot be fastened.

The ten wasted days in the Chesapeake Bay were the outcome of ignorance mixed with undue reliance on insufficiently corroborated advice. The decision to leave from Virginia Beach was the consequence of Johnstone's anxiety to avoid Ridgway's challenge; it did not take enough account of the disadvantages of having to row an extra 500 miles, nor of starting from outside a bay among severe rotary currents, rather than a cape where currents are generally less complex. That in turn led to the early diminution of food supplies necessitating replenishment from passing ships, to achieve which it became a prime objective to seek and stay within the shipping lanes. Almost at the outset *Puffin* had to breach a cardinal rule of the sea: self-sufficiency. Her poor progress continued, aggravating and extending the breach right through to the time when her voyage was abruptly terminated.

Other factors include *Puffin*'s apparent unsuitability for singlehanded rowing and the difficulty of trimming her so that she would not constantly battle to present her beam to the wind; the trimming rudder was inadequate to combat that effect: probably only the combined effort of both men at the oars would have sufficed, when they would have had to put in many more rowing hours than in fact they did. Though due to some extent to the effect of hunger and fatigue, a more persevering attitude towards the chore of rowing was frustrated principally by their belief, based on erroneous chart information and in denial of all the evidence of their own experiences, that they were being swept constantly homewards by the Gulf Stream. There is no indication that they knew of wind-driven surface currents, the only ones of importance to a rowing-boat, or of resultant currents where tide and wind conflict. Such knowledge would have created understanding of what was happening to *Puffin* and reduced the demoralisation manifest whenever incomprehensible positions were read from the sextant fixes. It would not however have influenced the effect of the series of remarkable and uncharacteristic headwinds, which contributed to the poor daily average for the voyage of a mere fifteen miles a day. Unfortunately, not only headwinds but those from most segments of the compass proved adverse to their boat's progress, as she became unrowable unless conditions were dead calm, or the wind was from almost dead astern. A considerable volume of this missing information, particularly the boat's performance in a seaway, would have been available had sea trials been carried out; but Ridgway's challenge led to the abandonments of trials of any kind apart from the single outing in the sheltered waters of the Medina. Sea trials would also have foretold the extent to which marine growth on the unconventionally painted bottom caused drag, contributing, although nominally, to *Puffin*'s slothfulness.

If Johnstone's navigation left little to be desired, the conduct of both men in the teeth of monstrous adversity represents heroism of an outstanding order. With ample opportunity and justification on more than one occasion to surrender honourably, the thought simply never entered their heads. They were determined to carry on to the end, an end which they had calmly contemplated might be tragic; they committed themselves to it from the outset and did not flinch when face to face with its reality. Their precondition that nobody should risk his life to save them was fully met.

Johnstone's and Hoare's attempt was not worthless.

Their courageous behaviour constitutes an epic in the history of man's unending struggle against the sea, brilliantly exemplifying the eternal spirit of human adventure. *Puffin*'s voyage, through the almost miraculous discovery of the Journal, has made a positive contribution to man's knowledge of the oceans, yielding much unfamiliar information in particular about the capricious Gulf Stream.

The future will see new attempts by brave and adventurous men to row across the Atlantic, and by scholars to investigate the behaviour of the earth's waters. For them, Johnstone and Hoare have made things easier.

PART FOUR

APPENDIX I

Nautical terms used in the Journal

AFT towards or at the stern

ASTERN behind the boat

AZIMUTH the bearing of a celestial body in relation to the boat, from which compass error can be ascertained

BALLAST weight placed strategically in the boat to increase stability

BEAM width of the boat

BEAM ON sideways on to the direction from which the sea is running

BEAM SEA a sea coming from one side of the boat and crossing its axis

BERMUDAN a type of sailing rig including a tall triangular sail set from the mast and flying behind it

BILGES the bottom of the boat where water collects

BOW SEA a sea coming from ahead of the boat

BROACHING coming up to the wind then broadsiding into the sea's trough

BULKHEAD partition athwart the boat, dividing it into compartments

BUOYANCY BAG an air-filled bag stowed in the boat, or sometimes attached to its sides

BUTTON a stud preventing the oar slipping from the row-locks

CLEAT a horned attachment to the boat, round which ropes are fastened

COAMINGS the sides of the boat extended upwards vertically to protect the cockpit

COMBER a long foaming wave

DF direction finder: a radio device for finding the boat's direction in relation to a radio beacon whose position is known

DL INTERSECTION direction line intersection: a means of ascertaining the boat's direction by reference to the crossing of two known lines, usually the boat's latitude and its longitude

DR dead reckoning: the boat's position estimated by calculating the approximate distance run, speed and direction from its last known position

EASTINGS amount of distance made good in an easterly direction

EST Eastern Standard Time

FATHOM six feet depth of water

FIX the position of the boat, obtained by use of radio, physical sighting of known objects, or celestial navigation

FORE OF AFT towards, but not quite at, the rear of the boat

FOREPEAK a locker below deck at the front of the boat

G.H.A. Greenwich Hour Angle: the angle at the pole between the Greenwich meridian (0°) and the meridian through an observed celestial body

GIMBELS concentric rings which hold compass or stove horizontal irrespective of the attitude of the boat

G.M.T. Greenwich Mean Time; clock time at the Greenwich meridian

HATCH hinged or sliding deck cover through which access is had to the cabin

HAWSER rope used for towing the sea anchor

HEAD WIND wind coming from dead ahead of the boat, impeding or preventing its progress

HELIOGRAPH a signalling mirror

HOVE TO stationary, facing head into wind

INDEX ERROR a small error occurring in the majority of sextants and allowed for when calculating the boat's position

KETCH boat with two masts, the foremast being taller

KNOT speed of one nautical mile (about 2,000 yards) per hour

LATITUDE SIGHTING measurement north or south of the equator obtained by measuring the angle, at ship's noon, between the observer's eye, the sun and the horizon

LEE SHORE a coast towards which a boat is blown by the wind

LEEWARD towards the sheltered side of the boat

LOCAL NOON the same as ship's noon

LONGITUDE measurement east or west of the Greenwich meridian (0°)

MACKEREL CLOUD scale-like cloud at high altitude, presaging stormy weather

MAGNETIC (COURSE) direction to be steered, taking account of magnetic variation

MAGNETIC VARIATION the difference between a true course and a magnetic course, caused by the magnetic attraction of the north and south poles, and varying according to their proximity

MARES' TAILS whisps of cloud at high altitudes, presaging strong winds

MERIDIAN ALTITUDE the moment when the sun reaches its zenith

MERIDIAN PASSAGE the sun's passage (from east to west) across the observer's meridian (a meridian being an imaginary circle extending from pole to pole)

NOON SIGHT ascertaining the boat's position by measuring, at ship's noon, the angle between the observer's eye, the sun and the horizon

P.L. position line

PORT left-hand side of the boat, facing forward

POSITION LINE an infinite line, representing the boat's bearing in relation to an ascertained object (celestial or ashore) somewhere along which is the boat's actual position

PULPIT a safety rail at the front of the boat

QUARTER half-way between the boat's widest point and its stern

RECIPROCAL (COURSE) the opposite direction to that which is intended to be steered. This is a mistake which can happen when, e.g. through tiredness, the 'N' point on the compass is read as 'S'

ROSE (COMPASS) the perimeter of the compass dial, marked to show the points of the compass

ROWLOCK device through which the oars are levered to provide propulsion

RUNNING sailing with the wind blowing behind the boat

SAMPSON POST projection above deck level of the foremost vertical timber of the boat, used for tying up

SEA ANCHOR canvas drogue for the boat to lie to in bad weather

SEXTANT instrument for measuring angles between the earth's surface and astral bodies such as the sun, moon and stars

SHIP'S NOON the moment at which the sun reaches its zenith at the particular longitude where the boat happens to be

SPINNAKER a balloon-like fore-sail used in light airs

SPLICE a method of interweaving one piece of rope or cable with another or with itself

STARBOARD right-hand side, facing forward

STEERING OAR an oar operated from the boat's rear end to control steering

STERN ON with the boat's rear end facing the wind

SUNSHOT a sextant sighting of the sun

TENDER adjective describing an over-quick reaction of the boat to wind, waves or ballast

THWART plank placed across the boat to provide a seat

TOPSIDE uppermost vertical surfaces of the hull

TRIM horizontal or lateral balance of the boat : to balance it horizontally or laterally by adjusting ballast

TRIPLINE rope used for altering position of sea anchor from roughly horizontal to vertical, thus relieving the pressure of the water and enabling the sea anchor to be pulled in

TRUE (COURSE) direction to be steered related to a chart, ignoring magnetic variation

WEATHER loosely used to mean considerable quantities of wind

WINDAGE effect of wind blowing on the boat's vertical surfaces

YAWL same as a ketch, but with the smaller (after) mast positioned behind the rudder post

APPENDIX 2

Technical and slang terms and otherwise unexplained references in the Journal

DAY

1 N. SETTING TIDE a tide moving in a northerly direction

2 GAZ gas fuel, for the stove

HARRIER the electronic instrument recording speed and distance run

4 WARREN'S SEA ANCHOR Warren Henderson, of the Gentex Company who provided life-jackets, gave the men two small sea anchors

5 WTAR a U.S. weatherbroadcasting ship

CONSOL CHART a chart giving bearings of the boat from consol radio beacons, which transmit patterns of dots and dashes, merging into a continuous signal. The number of dots and dashes counted are referred to the chart, to obtain the boat's bearing

ARCHIE'S CURRY Archie de Jong, of the Horlicks Company, had largely provisioned the expedition

TONNEAU horizontal cover protecting the cockpit, with a vertical 'bib' up the hatchway opening to the cabin

STAIR-ROD RAINWATER very heavy rain

6 SWEDES CRASHED heads on the pillow

2 ON 2 OFF WITH A BREAK OF TEN AT THE 55 MINUTES two hours' rowing, followed by a two-hour break while the other man rowed, stopping every fifty-five minutes for a ten-minute rest

COLIN Colin Mudie, the boat's designer

5 SEC LIGHT a marine beacon flashing every five seconds

FMC Fatstock Marketing Company

7 'ORANGES' waterproof outersuits, coloured orange to show up if the wearer goes overboard

LONG JOHNS long-legged underpants

DODGER water- and windproof hood at the forward end of the boat to provide cover for the oarsman

CONSOL FIX ascertaining the position of the boat from the audible consol transmissions

B & G Brookes & Gatehouse, the company manufacturing the Harrier and other electronic equipment

9 PONY defaecation

10 $2\frac{1}{4}$ KTS speed of two and a quarter sea miles per hour

HOMER radio receiver capable of receiving consol and other radio beacons

HERON a hand-held direction-finding radio incorporating a special compass

11 HANGING ON TO 100° with difficulty maintaining a desired course of 100° (slightly south of east)

12 TWO ON, TWO OFF alternately rowing and resting for two hours

GULF STREAM AXIS the middle line of the breadth of the Gulf Stream. Not in fact the area of the Stream with maximum current effect

13 OPEN COUNTRY one of Johnstone's Home County haunts

14 SQUEAKER the Homer

16 TIME CHECK verifying the accuracy of the clock

ESCALATOR the Gulf Stream current

17 SNOUTS cigarettes

GIB Gibraltar

18 TIME TO ARC a table in the nautical almanac indicating when local (ship's) noon can be expected at the boat's assumed longitude position

STANDARD the ensign flying at the stern mast

JOHN DUDLEY & PAM husband and wife, close friends of Johnstone

GIBSON GIRL emergency radio transmitter

19 SHOCK CORD tough elastic cord

21 RADAR REFLECTOR metal device fixed to the foremast to enable vessels with radar to know that the boat was in their vicinity. Not considered useful at close range, but of some benefit at a range of five miles or greater

FORCE 9 see Appendix III, Beaufort Wind Scale

23 REED'S *Reed's Nautical Almanac*, the standard book carried by every vessel, packed with vital information for the seaman including navigation, meteorology, tide tables, and encyclopaedic nautical intelligence

SOLAR navigation by reference to the known position of the sun

ASTRO ditto by reference to stars

NAV navigation

O/B overboard

29 BOB TAYLOR the reporter assigned to the adventure by the sponsoring national newspaper

37 LETTER-BOX the top section of the hatchway's vertical opening, the bottom being covered by the 'bib' extension from the tonneau cover

NO SIGHTS BECAUSE OF THE VARIABLE HEIGHT OF US IN RELATION TO THE HORIZON to obtain a fix by use of the sextant the boat has to be reasonably steady so that the height of the observer's eye above sea level at the moment of taking the sight can be accurately known. This measurement forms an important element in the formula used for obtaining a sextant fix (see Appendix I)

44 ALMANAC see *Reed's* (day 23)

KADUSON an American public relations officer

46 LYING TO PERCY Percy is the nickname by now given to the sea anchor (see Appendix I)

53 M'SIEUR the lavatory bucket

5° GAPS GET BIGGER AS THE LAT GOES NORTH on a Mercator projection chart the latitude scale increases progressively in the direction of the poles, due to the chart representing a round area as flat. A degree of latitude, shown at the sides of the chart, always scales sixty miles at that latitude (5° scales 300 miles), but the degree scale used must be the one for the particular latitude at which measurement is being taken. For example, 5° at the latitude of the Equator scale 300 miles at that latitude, but very much less at, say, latitude 40°N

65 ROSYLEE rhyming slang for tea

DASH DOT = N possibly the signal was dash-dot-dash-dot which is C, indicating affirmative

DOT DOT in fact this indicates 'I am directing my course to port' (my left-hand)

66 NICHOLAS Thompson, Johnstone's literary agent

69 N.Z. New Zealand

73 The calculation made this day can be set out as follows:

During three days (72 hours) of strong westerly winds:

	Miles covered
1. Assume rowing propulsion through still water of 2 m.p.h. for forty-nine hours of actual rowing time; approximately	100
2. Assume east-setting (i.e. favourable) current of 0·8 m.p.h., giving a further	56
3. Assume that surface speed of the sea caused by strong westerly wind gives an additional speed factor of 0·5 m.p.h.	36
Total	192
During two days of total calm, assume rowing propulsion through still water of 1½ m.p.h. for sixteen hours of actual rowing each day	48
Estimated grand total	240
Actual distance made good	80

79 AYLING the oarmaker who supplied *Puffin*'s oars

80 HALAZONES water purifying tablets

RED FLARE a distress signal

OCEAN STATION VESSEL (D) one of several vessels of different nationalities stationed at various N. Atlantic positions, to radio weather conditions. Vessel (D) is at 44°N 41°W

82 FRAZER NASH, XK120 two particularly fast sports cars

83 MOXON Oliver Moxon, with whom Johnstone had wagered £10 to £1,000 that he would row the Atlantic in 1966

86, 7, 8 SPARROW GRASS asparagus

91 EUSTACE presumably a pet name given to the barometer

92 T/O take-off

96 JACK the Union Jack of the ensign

CRABS CAUGHT dipping the oars too deep in the water

BACKING rowing facing forwards

102 COMPASS TO CHART—DEDUCT W. VARIATIONS see *Magnetic course* in Appendix 1

RECIPROCAL COURSE a course exactly opposite to the one desired, occurring when the north pole of the compass needle is, through error, taken as its south pole. This can happen when the helmsman is tired.

APPENDIX 3

Beaufort Wind Scale

Beaufort number	*Limits of wind speed in knots*	*Descriptive terms*	*Sea criterion*	*Probable height of waves in feet*
0	Less than 1	Calm	Sea like a mirror.	—
1	1–3	Light air	Ripples with the appearance of scales are formed but without foam crests.	¼
2	4–6	Light breeze	Small wavelets, still short but more pronounced. Crests have a glassy appearance. and do not break.	½
3	7–10	Gentle breeze	Large wavelets. Crests begin to break. Foam of glassy appearance. Perhaps scattered white horses.	2
4	11–16	Moderate breeze	Small waves, becoming longer: fairly frequent white horses.	3½
5	17–21	Fresh breeze	Moderate waves, taking a more pronounced long form; many white horses are formed. (Chance of some spray.)	6

Beaufort number	*Limits of wind speed in knots*	*Descriptive terms*	*Sea criterion*	*Probable height of waves in feet*
6	22–27	Strong breeze	Large waves begin to form; the white foam crests are more extensive everywhere. (Probably some spray.)	9½
7	28–33	Near gale	Sea heaps up and white foam from breaking waves begins to be blown in streaks along the direction of the wind.	13½
8	34–40	Gale	Moderately high waves of greater length; edges of crests begin to break into spindrift. The foam is blown in well-marked streaks along the direction of the wind.	18
9	41–47	Severe gale	High waves. Dense streaks of foam along the direction of the wind. Crests of waves begin to topple, tumble and roll over. Spray may affect visibility.	23
10	48–55	Storm	Very high waves with long overhanging crests. The resulting foam in great patches is blown in dense white streaks along the direction of the	29

Beaufort number	*Limits of wind speed in knots*	*Discriptive terms*	*Sea criterion*	*Probable height of waves in feet*
			wind. On the whole the surface of the sea takes a white appearance. The tumbling of the sea becomes heavy and shocklike. Visibility affected.	
11	56–63	Violent storm	Exceptionally high waves. (Small and medium sized ships might be for a time lost to view behind the waves.) The sea is completely covered with long white patches of foam lying along the direction of the wind. Everywhere the edges of the wave crests are blown into froth. Visibility affected.	37
12	64+	Hurricane	The air is filled with foam and spray. Sea completely white with driving spray; visibility very seriously affected.	

APPENDIX 4

Schedule of Equipment mentioned in the Journal

Harrier log and speed recorder; signal flares; 2 small and 1 large sea anchors; consol charts; routeing charts binoculars; safety harnesses; compass; hand-bearing compass; waterproof suits; showerproof suits; batman suits; jerseys; long underwear; consol receiver; radio direction finder; buoyancy bags; Homer radio receiver; Heron direction-finding radio; Gibson emergency radio transmitter; radar reflector; oars; sextant; *Reed's Nautical Almanac;* barometer; hurricane lamp; primus stove; wire brush; inflatable dinghy and pump; bilge pump; sleeping bags; seaboots; passage charts; protractor; foghorn; fishing kit; harpoon; penknife; screwdriver; lavatory bucket; axe; spanner; lubricating oil; leather oil; waterproof torch; nuts, screws and washers; fishing net; leather rowing gloves

APPENDIX 5

H.M.C.S. *Chaudière*
15th October 1966

'*Artefacts from boat* Puffin'

1. 21 cans of soup—brand name KJØTTAKER
2. 1 camera—NIKONAS—serial number—921845
3. 2 batteries—dry cell
4. 1 rubber glove
5. 8 water bags—4 contained fresh water
6. 2 charts
7. Barometer—stopped at reading 28.06 inches
8. 'Reliance' field glasses—serial number—10255
9. Compass—'Brooks and Gatehouse Limited'—good condition
10. 2 cans of film—exposed
11. Mileage indicator—'Brooks and Gatehouse Limited'
12. Piece of rubber—suspected of being a container
13. Bell and Howell 16 mm camera with carrying case, instructional booklet and film magazine
14. 1 pair of sandals
    1 white cotton vest
    1 vest—thermal underwear
    1 plastic poncho—black
    1 set of dividers
    1 pair of rubber gloves
    1 pair of shorts—thermal underwear
15. 1 plastic bag—small
16. Light meter—could not be opened
17. Woollen socks—2 pair
18. 1 heavy turtle neck blue sweater
19. 1 cloth cap
20. 1 wet picture—from a magazine
21. 1 sea anchor
22. 1 radio head set

23. Generator equipment—serial number—9/1065/50
    Ref.—5A/4969—small light, generator, battery, wires
24. Combination radio receiver and D.F. fixing aid
25. Log impeller
26. one broken pair of sun glasses
27. one container—exposed film
28. Small bag—comb
    —bottle of pills
    —tie clip
    —box of matches
    —cigarette lighter
    —coins—U.S.A.
29. One journal consisting of 149 hand-written pages

T. J. Starkey
W. A. Middleton

J. I. MANORE
Commander
H.M.C.S. *Chaudière*

APPENDIX 6

Winds recorded in the Journal

Day	*Force*	*Favourable*	*Neutral*	*Unfavourable*	*Sea conditions*
1				S	
2				N by NE	
4	3			E	
5	0–1				calm/swell
	4–5				rough
6	1	W			
	1			SSE	
7	3–4			S	
				E/ESE	
8	0–1				calm
9	1–2			S	calm
10	4			NE	rough
11				NNW	
				NNE	
12	C				
13	0				
14	4–5			N/NNE	rough
16				SSW	
17	1–2		SW	S	swell
				SE	
18			SW		rolling swell
20	5–6				
21	7–9		SW		*severe gale*
				NE	
23				NE	
24	9			SE	*severe gale*
25	4			S	
26	6		SW		boisterous
28	0				
29	0–1			S	
33				NNE	
35	7				*near gale*

Day	*Force*	*Favourable*	*Neutral*	*Unfavourable*	*Sea conditions*
36	5–10			N/NNE	*storm*
37	8				*gale*
38	0–1				calm
39	8				*gale*
41				SSE	
42				E	
43				SE	
46				S by SSE	
	4			WNW	
47				S	
50				S by SSW	
51	0–1	W		NW	
				S	
52	1			SSE	
53					beam sea
54					beam sea
55	4–5			S	choppy
57		W		NW	
				S	
				E	
				ESE	
				SE	
58				N	
				NW	
59				E	
60				E	
61				E	
62				E	
63				SEE/E	
64				E	
65				E	
66				E	
67	4			E/ENE	
68	0–1			E	calm
69	0 1			E	
70	0–1	W			
71	5–9	W	SW		

Day	*Force*	*Favourable*	*Neutral*	*Unfavourable*	*Sea conditions*
		WSW			*severe gale*
72	6–8	W			*gale*
73	6–9	W			*severe gale*
74				SE/SSW	
75	9–10			NNW	*storm*
76				NNW	
77				S	
				SE	
			SW	SSE	
				WNW	
				N	
78			W by S		
79	6–9/10			WNW	*storm*
		WSW			
			SW		
80	0–1			E/SSE	calm
81		W		N	
82	5			NNE/N	
83				NNE	
84				S/SSW	
85	1–2	W			
86			SW	NW	
87				S	
88				SE	
				N	
89	3			E/ENE	
90				E/SE	
91				SSE/S	
92	3–4	W	SW		
93		W			
94		WSW		WNW	
96	9			N by NW	*severe gale*
				N by NNW	heavy squalls
98		WSW	SW		
	4–6/7	W		WNW	*near gale*
99				N	
100	1–2			N	

Day	*Force*	*Favourable*	*Neutral*	*Unfavourable*	*Sea conditions*
101	4–6	WSW	SW		
102			SW		
103	4–5				rough
104			SW	SSW	
105			SW		
106				NNW	
107					*hurricane*

NOTES

1. The Journal appears to record all winds worthy of note. Where none is recorded it is reasonable to assume that the sea was calm and windless. Where the sea is described as calm, wind Force 0–1 has been assumed; and where it is described as rough, or unrowable, wind Force 4–5 has been assumed.
2. The very high proportion of unfavourable winds (71% of those recorded) and the very small proportion of favourable winds (15½% of those recorded) relates only to a rowing-boat, particularly to *Puffin*. A sailing boat would have been able to make considerable progress in most of the winds recorded (though not in the calms), and of course a powered vessel can comparatively ignore winds from whatever direction.
3. The uninterrupted run of easterly winds from Day 59 to Day 69 is remarkable for the area.
4. The winds experienced on Days 57 and 79 are indicative of tropical revolving storms, which produce currents of abnormal strength, sufficient to set a large ocean-going vessel sixty miles in the wrong direction in a matter of eighteen hours, and affecting the ocean within a radius of one hundred miles from the storm's centre.

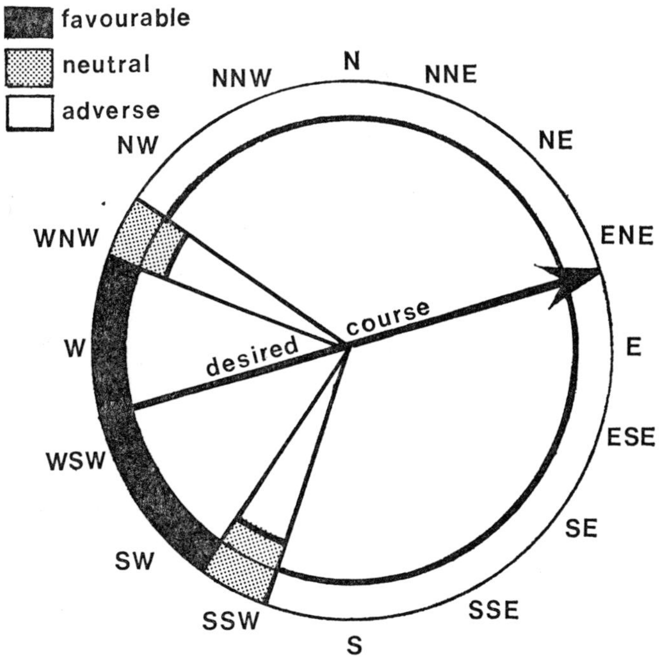

FIG 19 Key to wind effect on *Puffin*

APPENDIX 7

Tests carried out at Littlehampton, Sussex, 24–26th February 1968

Puffin's wreck was transported from Lisbon to England, where it lodged under a tarpaulin in Colin Mudie's garden until collected in November 1967 by the man I had invited to prepare her for sea tests, and who promptly volunteered to be my crew. Bill Harrington, a highly experienced seaman in his fifties, owns the Britannia Boatyard at Littlehampton where I keep my own sloop. Having sailed boats all his life and won many rowing trophies in his younger days, he gave up engineering consultancy several years ago to become a yacht chandler.

Puffin was in 'as fished out' condition, festooned inside and out with marine vegetation, slimy and oil stained, her bilges foul. But the hull and decks were sound except for a hole bashed in her side when lifted aboard *Chaudière*, and the grab rails and cleats were in good order. The considerable work necessary to make her fit for sea included scrubbing her inside and out; making and fitting covers for the bow hatches; making a new hinged cabin hatch cover with side and front flaps, and a stretcher for the bow oarsman; repairing the bilge pump; making a rudder, tonneau cover and a hood; making and fitting a mast and mounting a radar reflector; making new rowlocks to match those found in the wreck; as well as patching the hole in the hull.

Launched into the Arun River she was as bouncy as Johnstone had found her, but a ton of shingle in 28 lb. plastic bags settled her hull in the water down to a point midway between the datum water line and paint line. In accordance with Colin Mudie's advice, ballast was placed in the bilges and also high under the gunwales and in the forepeak, great care being taken to ensure that the boat was trimmed so as to be perfectly balanced in all planes. Arrangements for sea trials included the provision of the diesel motor vessel *Elizabeth*, owned by Doug Osborne, an experienced boatman who is also a coastguard, and whose equipment included two-way radio telephone in case of emergency. *Elizabeth* would tow us either towards the Winter buoy three miles offshore, or out to the Owers Lightship, depending on the direction of the wind, and stand by all day while *Puffin* was put through her paces.

Our equipment, however, included everything we might possibly need in the event of losing our escort, such as if she broke down, or a sudden fog descended and separated us. Food, an inflatable dinghy, radio direction finder, signal flares, Harrier log, torches, safety harnesses, life-jackets, navigation equipment, three sets of nine-foot spoon-blade oars, and Bill's and my combined weight, must have added a further 400 lb. to *Puffin*'s cargo.

The other trials were to be in the harbour itself : the first, to test stability and performance in totally calm conditions; and the second to ascertain *Puffin*'s self-rightability by capsizing her. The sea trials were of course to ascertain stability and performance in a seaway, preferably under rough conditions. In that respect, we could not have been more fortunate, for with an established north-north-east wind at Force 5 it was rough without being unpleasant. While we were out, wind force increased to 6, followed by a warning of an imminent easterly gale, but our good luck held, and we completed our trials and were on our way back to Littlehampton in *Elizabeth*'s wake before the wind started getting up seriously, to make the ride home extremely wet. Towed at five knots, *Puffin*'s bow hatches shipped quantities of water, her bows digging deep enough to alarm Doug Osborne some twenty yards ahead, and also rendering her rudder ineffective.

The exercise produced the following results.

Preliminary note: References throughout to 'two oarsmen' means one oarsman with a pair of oars in the bow position, and a second oarsman with a pair of oars in the aft position.

A. 24th February, Littlehampton Harbour, slack water.

I STATIONARY

1. Fore and aft balance	excellent
2. Tenderness (measured on clinometer)	inclination 4° with one man standing on gunwale inclination 10° with two men standing on gunwale the boat returned to her normal position with a gentle motion

II ROWING

1. Fore and aft balance	excellent
2. Tenderness	no noticeable roll
3. Extent of yaw	nil
4. Speed, one oarsman	$1\frac{1}{2}$–$1\frac{3}{4}$ knots
5. Speed, two oarsmen	$2\frac{1}{2}$ knots
6. Need for use of rudder	appreciable, whether one oarsman or two

Note: The aft rowing position was unsatisfactory, in that the oarsman banged his knuckles against the cabin hatch when sweeping the oar blades back in preparation for the next stroke.

B. 25th February, rowing approximately three miles off Littlehampton. Wind NNE Force 5 gusting 6, later ENE Force 6 gusting 7. Current roughly West-setting 0.7 knots.

GENERAL

1. Fore and aft balance	excellent
2. Tenderness	
(*a*) Head on to wind } (*b*) Stern on to wind }	roll about 5° in either direction
(*c*) Cross wind and beam sea	fairly sharp roll between 15° and 20° in either direction, sufficient to put gunwale down to sea level so that water slopped in over the sides
3. Extent of yaw	nil
4. Speed, one oarsman	approx. 1.8 knot
5. Speed, two oarsmen	not measured
6. Need for use of rudder	essential

TEST 1 *Head on to wind and current, dodger down, rudder lashed, one oarsman.*

It proved impossible for one oarsman to row the boat round head on into the wind, the boat insisting on presenting her beam to the wind, with the ensign at right angles to the boat's longitudinal axis.

With one man rowing and the other operating the rudder, the result remained the same.

During this test, with the boat beam on to the sea, everything below decks became soaked with seawater so that the bilges had to be pumped. Persisting with the exercise, the boat was momentarily rowed round head on to the wind but promptly turned beam on again.

The exercise was not tried with the dodger up, as it was thought that that would only aggravate the effect noted. See also Test 9.

TEST 2 *Two oarsmen rowing into wind and current, dodger down, rudder lashed.*

It proved possible to row the boat round head on to the

wind, but not to hold her there. The boat always fought to lie beam on and could not be prevented from doing so.

TEST 3 *One oarsman rowing beam on to wind and sea, dodger down.*

There was no difficulty in holding course, but rowing was virtually impossible due to inability to put both oars into the water at the same time, because of the waves and the boat's attitude to them. There was no difference with the rudder lashed, or when operated by the second man.

TEST 4 *Two oarsmen ditto.*

There was no difficulty in holding course, but little way was achieved, probably one-quarter of a knot.

TEST 5 *One oarsman rowing downwind, dodger down.*

This proved impossible, the boat refusing to depart from a beam on attitude.

TEST 6 *Ditto, two oarsmen.*

This proved impossible, the boat again refusing to depart from a beam on attitude.

TEST 7 *Ditto, two oarsmen each pulling on one (starboard) oar, and the aft oarsman attempting to operate the steering rudder.*

The boat came downwind easily, but the moment the steering rudder was released the boat swung round beam on.

TEST 8 *One oarsman, downwind, dodger up.*

With the second man on the rudder, a fast comfortable run downwind was achieved. Concentrated use of rudder was always essential. Loss of concentration by the helmsman for a few seconds resulted in the boat turning beam on to the wind. Following waves, six to eight feet, lifted the stern gently to allow *Puffin* to slide smoothly down with a very comfortable motion. The following calculation shows the rowing speed :

Distance made good (per hour) 3·0 sea miles
Wind Force 5 value 0·5 knot
current 0·7 knot
—— 1·2
——
Therefore rowing speed 1·8 knot
——

TEST 9 *One oarsman, rowing into wind, dodger up.*
With the second man on the rudder it proved possible to row round into the wind, but despite full opposite rudder the boat continued round until she lay beam on.

C. *26th February, outside Littlehampton Harbour. Wind NE Force 3.*

TEST 10 *One oarsman, rudder lashed.*
With the ballast disposed to increase the bows up attitude of the boat by 3°, there was a marked improvement in her rowing characteristics, three knots registering on the Harrier on the way out of the harbour, and a comparable improvement in the open seaway. Although *Puffin* still tended to present her beam to the wind, this was capable of correction.

TEST 11 *One oarsman, rudder lashed.*
With ballast reduced to 500 lb., rowing was lighter but the boat was virtually uncontrollable.

D. *26th February, Littlehampton Harbour, slack water.*

With ballast of one ton, as before, and a buoyancy bag fitted on her aft deck and two below her foredeck, *Puffin* was capsized by crane. She immediately righted herself. This test was repeated, with the same result. The buoyancy bags were then removed, the test repeated, and again *Puffin* righted herself, though more slowly. With ballast reduced to 500 lb. and the buoyancy bags removed, *Puffin* remained fully self-righting.

On inspection, her forward hatches, ahead of the cockpit bulkhead, were found filled with water, lowering the boat's nose. By contrast, the cabin remained comparatively dry, and the cockpit was pumped dry in six minutes.

Note: There was no evidence that the forward hatches under the foredeck had been so constructed as to be watertight. There was evidence that the hatch covers were merely easily removable lids for a storage compartment. This would enable the forward hatches to fill with water, as happened during our trials, lowering the bows, reducing buoyancy, impairing performance and reducing self-righting in the event of capsize. (*Puffin*'s wreck was discovered in a bows down attitude).

MERTON NAYDLER
BILL HARRINGTON

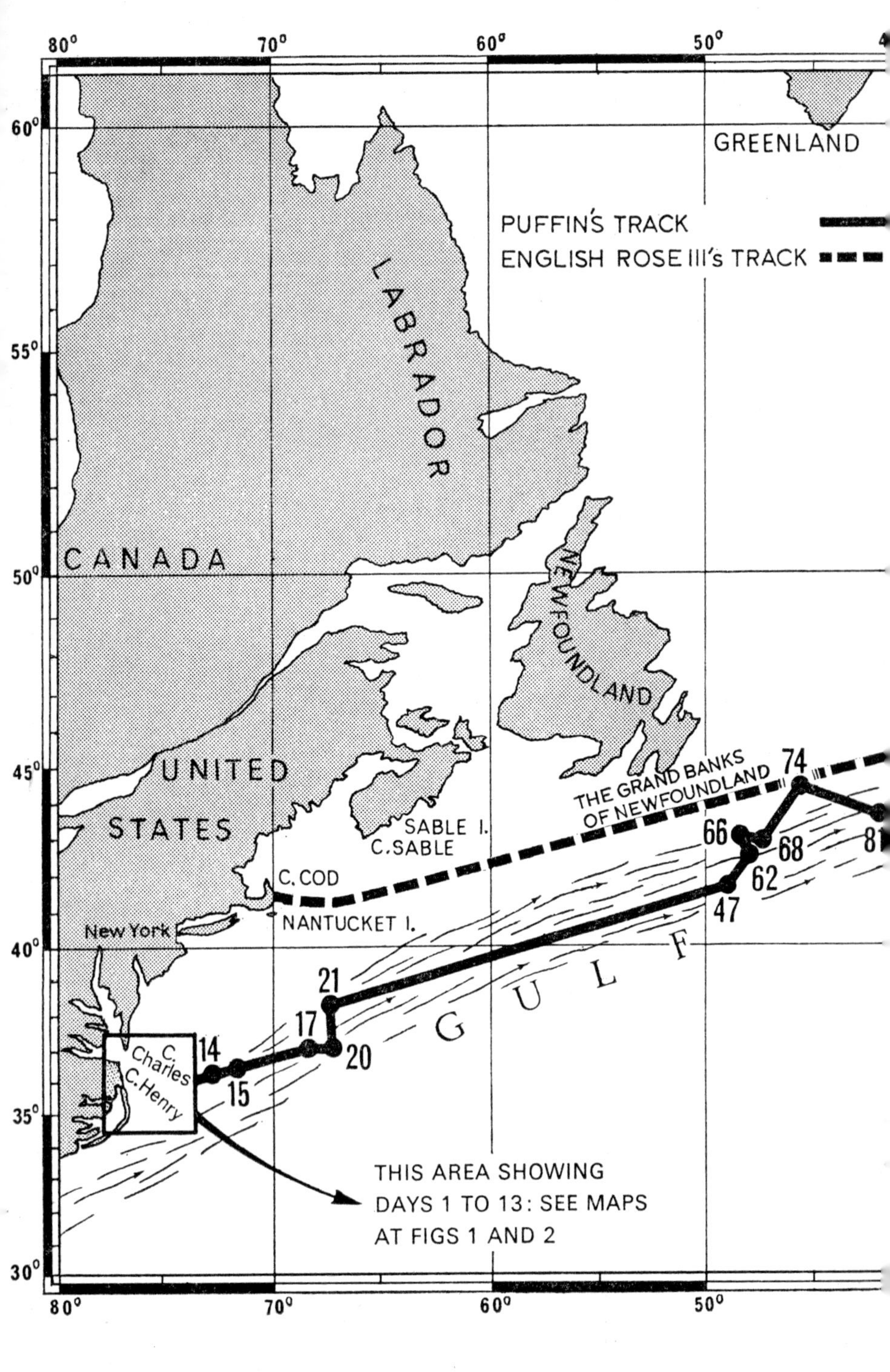

80°
70°
60°
50°
60°
55°
50°
45°
40°
35°
30°
GREENLAND
PUFFIN'S TRACK
ENGLISH ROSE III's TRACK
LABRADOR
CANADA
NEWFOUNDLAND
UNITED
STATES
SABLE I.
C.SABLE
C. COD
NANTUCKET I.
New York
THE GRAND BANKS
OF NEWFOUNDLAND
74
66
68
62
47
81
GULF
21
17
20
14
15
C. Charles
C.Henry
THIS AREA SHOWING
DAYS 1 TO 13: SEE MAPS
AT FIGS 1 AND 2